KU-619-676

RELENTLESS

RELENTLESS

THE INSIDE STORY OF THE
CORK LADIES FOOTBALLERS

MARY WHITE

MERCIER PRESS

MERCIER PRESS
Cork
www.mercierpress.ie

First published in 2015 by Currach Press.
Revised edition first published 2019.

© Mary White, 2019
Foreword © Brian Cody, 2019

ISBN: 978 1 78117 705 1

A CIP record for this title is available from the British Library.

Lyric excerpt from '(Something Inside) So Strong' by Labi Siffre on page 113 written by Labi Siffre, © China Records Ltd; from 'Bold Thady Quill' by The Clancy Brothers on page 127 written by Johnny Tom Gleeson, © Platinum Music Ireland; from 'Caledonia' by Dougie MacLean on page 127 written by Dougie MacLean, © Dunkeld Records; from 'Don't Give Up 'Til It's Over' by The Dubliners on pages 155 and 302 written by Johnny Duhan, with kind permission from the author, © Celtic Collections; from *Any Given Sunday* on page 242 written by Daniel Pyne, John Logan and Oliver Stone, © Warner Bros.

This book is sold subject to the condition that it shall not, by way of trade or otherwise, be lent, resold, hired out or otherwise circulated without the publisher's prior consent in any form of binding or cover other than that in which it is published and without a similar condition including this condition being imposed on the subsequent purchaser.

No part of this publication may be reproduced or transmitted in any form or by any means, electronic or mechanical, including photocopying, recording or any information or retrieval system, without the prior permission of the publisher in writing.

Printed and bound in the EU.

L255,432.

In memory of Bridget O'Brien,
Cork Ladies Team Liaison Officer, 2011–17

CONTENTS

FOREWORD

Brian Cody

It is a privilege for me to be asked to write this foreword and it is fitting that the title of this book is *Relentless* because that is exactly what this group of people have been since 2004 in their pursuit of excellence.

Theirs has been an amazing journey considering that prior to 2004 they had never won a senior Munster or All-Ireland title. Since then, they have won an incredible eleven All-Irelands, five in a row from 2005 to 2009, losing out in 2010, only to regroup and win six in a row between 2011 and 2016.

The great thing about this run, for me, is that so many of these championships were won after titanic battles. Looking back on the scores in the finals, I discovered that five of the finals were won by just one point and another won by two points. This just shows how competitive the championships have been and speaks volumes for the consistency and never-say-die attitude of everyone concerned.

It's very obvious from this book that the fundamentals required for success with any group are truly embedded. This kind of success could not be achieved without an absolutely unbreakable spirit. Certainly, the sense of spirit within the group jumps off the pages.

As in all teams, individuals come and go, but there have been some constants in the Cork ladies set-up since 2004. Remarkably, ten players played in every final from 2005 to

2013, while four of those played every minute of every final – a truly phenomenal achievement by these players.

The other constant, from 2004–2015, was their coach/manager, Eamonn Ryan. Eamonn was appointed in 2004 and was the mastermind behind all their successes up to 2016. The book provides many insights into Eamonn's philosophies and core values. What is particularly interesting is the way he continually developed and evolved as coach, constantly looking for new ideas and challenging himself to become better.

His humility contributed in a major way to a dressing room devoid of ego. We see the uncomplicated style of Eamonn's coaching and how quickly the players bought into his methods. The pursuit of excellence is always at the core of how they train and certainly anybody involved in coaching has much to learn from this book.

In December 2014, this Cork team was voted by the public as the RTÉ Sports Team of the Year. This award was in recognition of their victory in the All-Ireland final against an excellent Dublin team. With sixteen minutes to go in the final, Dublin led by ten points, but thanks to the unbreakable spirit within the Cork players and the inspirational leadership of Eamonn, they fought back to win the game by a point. Relentless indeed!

This award was fitting recognition of what has been achieved by an outstanding team.

On a personal level, I have admired the achievements of the Cork ladies footballers and this particular team for a number of years. I have met Eamonn and some of the players at various functions over the past decade and have always enjoyed their company.

Theirs is a wonderful story.

Finally, I congratulate Mary on bringing this story of excellence in sport to print, and I am sure people everywhere will find it both interesting and inspiring.

THE CHARACTERS

Eamonn Ryan (Coach): The mastermind behind Cork's rise from ruins to glory.

Ephie Fitzgerald (Coach): The man who replaced Eamonn Ryan in 2016. Fitzgerald won a Munster SFC medal with Cork and is a three-time All-Ireland medallist with Nemo Rangers.

The Players: See appendices for the names of the ninety-plus players who played under Eamonn Ryan from 2004–2015.

Frankie Honohan (Selector): The unsung hero and longest-serving member on the management team.

Mary Collins (Manager): The straight-talking instigator who dissolved the club rivalries and brought together the best players in the county for Ryan to mould.

Charlie McLaughlin (Ryan's predecessor): The coach who was unable to bring success at senior level after seven years at the helm, but who transformed underage football in Cork.

Juliet Murphy (Captain, 2004–2007): The first captain under Eamonn Ryan, whose high standards set the tone for Cork's work rate and formed a winning culture.

Captains: Juliet Murphy (2004–2007), Angela Walsh (2008), Mary O'Connor (2009), Rena Buckley (2010 and 2012), Amy O'Shea (2011), Anne-Marie Walsh (2013), Briege Corkery (2014), Ciara O'Sullivan (2015–2018).

Primary Dual Stars: Briege Corkery, Rena Buckley, Mary O'Connor and Angela Walsh.

Eamonn Ryan's Back-Room staff (2004–2015):
Selectors: Ger Twomey, Timmy O'Callaghan, Jim McEvoy, Noel O'Connor, Justin McCarthy, James O'Callaghan, Pat O'Leary and Shane Ronayne.

Statisticians: Tim Murphy and Don Ryan.

Liaison Officers: Eileen O'Brien-Collins and Bridget O'Brien.

Goalkeeping Coach: Kieran Dwyer.

Chauffeur: Cormac O'Connor of O'Connor Coaches.

Other: Brian O'Connell, Michael Cotter, Dr Lucy Fleming, Gráinne Desmond, Eleanor Lucey, Declan O'Sullivan, Denise Walsh, Emma O'Donovan, Sinéad Lynch, Colette Trout, Carol O'Mahony (physios, masseurs, doctors), Peter O'Leary and Pat Lucey (cameraman).

SMALL HEADS AND SMALL ARSES

*'The measure of who we are,
is what we do with what we have.'*
Vince Lombardi

RTÉ Sports Awards, 21 December 2014
Donnybrook, Dublin

In a hotel room in Dublin, Geraldine O'Flynn and Nollaig Cleary each sip on a glass of wine as their captain, Briege Corkery, readies herself for a live television interview later that evening with RTÉ's Darragh Maloney.

Angela Walsh sits on the end of the bed, but the Ladies Gaelic Football Association (LGFA) 2014 Players' Player of the Year nominee isn't drinking. She's three months pregnant with her first child, Keeva, and a few weeks earlier informed coach Eamonn Ryan that she wouldn't be available for the 2015 league campaign.

'I'm expecting in June, Eamonn,' she told him in a quiet corner of the Castlemartyr Golf Resort clubhouse at the team's holiday fundraiser.

'Ah congrats Angie … you'll be back for championship so!' he joked, before advising Walsh, as he would one of his own, to mind herself.

Courtesy taxis take them to the RTÉ Sports Awards, where Ryan is nominated for Manager of the Year and they for Team of the Year following an incredible ten-point comeback against Dublin in the 2014 All-Ireland final. The other nominees are the Irish men's rugby team for winning the Six Nations, the SSE Airtricity League champions Dundalk FC, and the All-Ireland-winning Kerry football, Kilkenny hurling and Cork camogie teams.

As they make their way to the pre-show drinks reception, O'Flynn, Cleary, Walsh and Corkery unanimously agree that the rugby team will win the public vote hands down. They've been here before, and although nominated again having won their ninth All-Ireland title in ten years, expectations of winning the award are zero. Instead, they turn their focus to getting a photograph with world number one golfer Rory McIlroy, who's there to collect the Sports Personality of the Year award, having won the 2014 Open and US PGA championships.

Other sports stars, including Irish soccer manager Martin O'Neill, IBF super bantamweight champion Carl Frampton and Ryder Cup captain Paul McGinley, flutter about, but all eyes are on how McIlroy carries himself in his stylish grey plaid suit.

Taking to their seats, Corkery, Cleary, O'Flynn and Walsh are in prime position in the front row. McIlroy is just inches away, and the countdown begins.

'Three, two, one, and we're live …' the production manager announces, pointing to presenter Darragh Maloney to take it away.

Video clips flash on the screen behind him of various guests, and when the Cork footballers appear lifting the

Brendan Martin Cup, the players holler and hoot. McIlroy turns and gives them a cheeky smile.

An emotional former Irish rugby captain, Brian O'Driscoll, is inducted into the RTÉ Sport Hall of Fame following a surprise announcement, and his parents, Frank and Geraldine, present him with his award. Afterwards, it's Eamonn Ryan's turn to be interviewed by Maloney and he's asked how the Rebels have won yet another All-Ireland.

'How have we been able to keep going?' Ryan repeats the question. 'We just have … and with the least amount of resources too,' he replies deadpan.

The crowd chuckle at Ryan's diplomatic jibe, of which any quick-witted Corkman would be proud. But the Manager of the Year award goes to the rugby coach Joe Schmidt for winning the Six Nations. As the New Zealander is interviewed, a production assistant taps Nollaig Cleary on the shoulder.

'Nollaig,' he whispers, 'ye've won the Team of the Year award, and you're to speak to Darragh.'

'Sorry?'

'You're to speak to Darragh when ye collect the award.'

'We won?' a puzzled Cleary asks.

'Yes. And you're to do the talking.'

'Ah, no, no, no … sure Briege is the captain,' Cleary replies, flustered, not knowing whether to believe what she's just been told.

'No, *you're* to speak to him.'

'Ah, no, no, no … sure Eamonn's the coach, ye have to speak to him.'

'We've spoken to him already!' he snaps, agitated by Cleary's objections, before vanishing back into the darkness.

Immediately, O'Flynn, Corkery and Walsh turn in Cleary's direction and quiz her. A *shush!* comes from behind them as they try to make sense of what's just happened.

'Are you sure that's what he said?' O'Flynn asks.

'He probably said *if* we win, Nol,' says Walsh.

'No, he said we won! I'm nearly sure of it,' Cleary insists frantically, now beginning to doubt herself.

Rory McIlroy turns around to see what the commotion is about. In unison, they smile at him.

The production assistant reappears, and the presumption is that it's to apologise, that in fact the Irish rugby team have won the award.

He taps Cleary on the shoulder again, leaning a little closer to her ear this time round. 'Oh, and by the way, act surprised!'

They don't need to act. They've finally been welcomed to the top table of Irish sport thanks to diehard sports fans, and it isn't out of sympathy, or anything else. The masses have finally recognised their achievements over the last decade, and every minute's been worth it for this moment alone.

27 per cent of the vote is for the Cork ladies footballers – 11 per cent more than the Irish rugby team.

In some ways the public vote means more than any of their nine All-Ireland wins, the most dramatic of which had come three months earlier, when, ten points down against Dublin with sixteen minutes left, they played out

L255, 432

the best comeback ever witnessed in Croke Park – a point by O'Flynn in the dying embers to win it 2–13 to 2–12.

The manner of that comeback solidified their greatness, and the fact that they're now the first female outfit to ever win the RTÉ Sports Team of the Year means so much.

As they make their way onto the stage, it's the happiest they've seen Eamonn Ryan. The man, the coach they've come to love. At seventy-three, he's fifty-six years older than the youngest squad recruit, but receiving tonight's award knocks four decades off him.

They veer backstage, out of sight, and begin their private celebrations. Hugging and jumping as one.

Sitting in the audience, Nollaig Cleary's husband, former Cork footballer Micheál Ó Crónín, can hear them celebrate behind the backdrop. He smiles to himself, knowing just how much this means to them.

•••

I had the privilege of following Cork's journey since Ryan's first training session in January 2004, first as a player on the fringes, then as a sports journalist. I have been both an insider and an outsider, which has allowed me to pen these pages and tell the story of one of the greatest GAA teams of all time. It is probable that we will never see the likes of them again.

Prior to Eamonn Ryan's involvement in 2004, Cork had never won a Munster senior championship title in the competition's thirty-year history, never mind a senior All-Ireland. After eleven years with Ryan at the helm, Cork accrued the Brendan Martin Cup ten times, nine division one national league titles and ten Munster championship titles. In 2016, under Ephie Fitzgerald, they added another All-Ireland.

But what many don't realise is the relentless journey Cork have been on to maintain their high standards. From suffering numerous hammerings at the hands of Kerry and Waterford in the eighties and nineties, a new culture created by Ryan helped Cork morph into a ladies football superpower. For more than a decade, they dominated the sport, winning twenty-nine titles out of a possible thirty-six come the end of 2015.

A total of ninety-one players would ply their trade under Ryan at one point or another, with forty-three having departed since 2005, all of whom have at least one All-Ireland medal.

Incredibly, since winning their first All-Ireland in 2005, come September 2015 they had lost just one championship game in the All-Ireland series – the 2010 quarter-final to Tyrone.

Leaving the pitch that day in Banagher, Co. Offaly, they were devastated, and for weeks after were unable to find it in themselves to make contact with one another. They weren't avoiding each other because of the defeat, but because they were ashamed about how they had let themselves, and Ryan, down in the months prior to the game.

In 2010 complacency had set in. Cork could have taken the easy option and laid the blame elsewhere, but instead they looked within. Those few weeks spent away from each other after the defeat to Tyrone was time spent soul-searching. The door was always open, to come or go, and Ryan would often say that being part of the team was 'a choice, not a sacrifice'. But that loss to Tyrone bruised their pride. They fell short of their own benchmark. That is what hurt the most, because it was they who had raised the bar for everyone else.

Their lack of ego aside, Cork are defined by the honest, diligent brand of football they play, which Ryan has humorously put down to them having 'small heads and small arses'. They're known, too, for an unparalleled ability to stare down adversity and come back from the edge of losing. From losing it all even.

What goes hand in hand with all they have done is *how* they have done it. They've grown up together, bonded together and been moulded by a father-like figure, who expected nothing but modesty in return throughout the entire process, his own mannerisms paving the way.

Ryan would say things like 'Appreciate what you have before time teaches you to appreciate what you had' or 'Attitude before aptitude, will get you to altitude'. Those things have forever stayed in his players' psyche.

But, most of all, from the first time they met Eamonn Ryan they were resolute in everything they did. Be that giving it their all on the field of play or in a simple drill; working as a unit; respecting Ryan and his selectors; coming back from eight, nine, even ten points down to win at the death; making their families and partners proud;

raising the profile of the game; being gracious in victory, and defeat; being the best they can be.

Relentless: this is their story.

1

THE FAMOUS FIVE,
AND A KERRYMAN

'Doubt is only removed by action.'
Conor McGregor

Goalkeeper Elaine Harte has solid hands, but tonight they're shaking. So too are her legs.

Sitting on a rickety bar stool in the back lounge of Murray's Bar in Macroom for the 2003 county board AGM, she's waited nearly two hours to hear who's been selected to oversee the county management teams for the following season. Aged just twenty-two, she's the only senior inter-county player present.

It's a poky old function room with faded upholstery, and from behind the empty bar a grumbling old ice machine interjects every now and then during the meeting.

Club delegates are crammed in, knowing sparks may very well fly over the course of the next few hours. For the first time in seven years, the senior manager's job is up for discussion, and strong personalities should add some drama on what would otherwise be a boring December night.

Charlie McLaughlin is the man who's been in charge of the Cork senior ladies football team since 1996, but not one piece of provincial silverware has been won in his seven-year reign. That, a few weeks previously, three Cork clubs – Donoughmore, Naomh Abán and Gabriel Rangers – won the senior, intermediate and junior All-Ireland club titles isn't helping McLaughlin's cause either. What is in his favour is the fact that the underage county teams he's involved in have been going well. Senior success, however, is what the mob is baying for.

It's a number of months since McLaughlin oversaw Cork's one-point loss to Kerry in the 2003 Munster senior championship semi-final, and the board made him aware in advance of tonight's meeting that a task group of five club delegates had been appointed to put in place the 2004 senior and junior county management teams. This is no coup.

Stephen Mullane of Liscarroll, John Thompson of Naomh Abán, Liz Ahern of Carrigtwohill, Ger Walsh of Donoughmore and Rockbán's Marie Mulcahy, mother of promising young player Valerie, have been tipping away in the background in the lead-up to tonight's meeting, searching for the reasons as to why the Cork senior team isn't progressing despite all the county's club success.

•••

Mulcahy signed up for the committee in a heartbeat.

'I was sick of it. We all knew the potential was there, if there was any bit of organisation. It was time to do something. We were tired of being hammered by the likes of Kerry and Waterford. The players weren't turning up to training, and what could you do with the four or five that did? How could you even win a match with that kind of carry on?'

Mulcahy established Rockbán LFC and was its secretary for ten years. Her eldest daughter, Valerie, had won two All-Ireland club medals at the turn of the millennium, and she knew that Cork had it in them if they got their act together.

The task group met once a week in the Commons Inn in Blackpool on the outskirts of Cork city. They were aware of the difficulty of the job, but something had to give. They knew what McLaughlin had achieved in his roles with the underage, but most senior club players in the county weren't willing to wear the jersey for him.

They approached Mossie Barrett, who, just weeks earlier, had coached Donoughmore to a second senior All-Ireland club title. Barrett wanted his own selectors, but the committee couldn't agree with that stipulation. Cork dual star Fiona O'Driscoll was also approached, but having recently retired, it was too soon for her to take up an inter-county coaching role.

A few others were in the mix, but as the committee delved further they realised the need to put in place someone who had no connections to Cork ladies football. Someone with no baggage and no agenda. It narrowed the pool of candidates considerably, and as the weeks drew closer to the AGM, their mettle was tested.

Committee member Liz Ahern confided in a friend at work in University College Cork about the group's dilemma. Maurice McNamara listened closely as Ahern queried the possibility of former Cork GAA stars such as Jimmy Barry Murphy and Larry Tompkins getting involved. McNamara was a shrewd Kerryman and a serious sports fan, with strong ties to the GAA teams in the university.

'I've someone in mind,' he told Ahern within minutes of the conversation commencing, 'but I can't tell you until I talk to him first.'

The following day, McNamara returned with a sheet of A4 paper, upon which sat a modest, five-line coaching biography. It read:

Eamonn Ryan (GAA Development Officer, UCC)
- Trained Cork minors through the nineties
- Selector for the Cork senior men's football panel for the last four years
- Coached UCC seniors
- Retired headmaster
- Has all coaching badges

Ahern was delighted with McNamara's proposal and the committee wasted no time in trying to meet with Ryan. It was now a week or so before the 2003 Cork ladies football board AGM, and Ryan agreed to at least hear them out at a meeting in the Powder Mills in Ballincollig.

He knew Charlie McLaughlin well, having worked with him on management teams before, and he was aware that the Donegal man was at the helm for Cork's last senior championship match a few months earlier. He listened, but under no circumstances would Ryan take the job with another manager *in situ*, despite the fact that McLaughlin had yet to be reappointed by the club delegates. Instead,

Ryan thanked the committee for their time and they headed their separate ways.

They were at a loss about what to do. With no names on the shortlist, all the task group could do was compose a statement with their recommendations to read out at the AGM.

•••

In Murray's Bar, committee member Liz Ahern takes to the floor to explain their findings. As the youngest member, AGMs and board meetings are relatively new territory, but Ahern's got bottle. She stands, and begins to read:

> This committee was set up with the stated objective of nominating a management structure for the Cork senior and junior teams.
>
> At our first meeting, the decision was taken to have discussions with a number of people nominated for the various positions, i.e. coach, selectors, liaison officers, etc. It became obvious in quite a short time that there was a large degree of dissatisfaction with the current structures and personalities involved. In fact, the more people we spoke with, the more this impression was compounded.
>
> A number of former officials stated that they would be more than willing to give their services to Cork ladies football but would not allow their names to go forward if the current management team was to remain in place for yet another year.
>
> This has placed the committee in a very invidious position, i.e. we believe that we can put an excellent management team

in place but there is no possibility that this can happen at this time. We regret to have to report that it is our unanimous feeling that most, if not all, of these problems stem from the current senior management.

After seven years, the state of our senior county ladies team is deplorable despite Cork clubs winning numerous All-Ireland club titles at junior, intermediate and senior level.

The senior Cork team's record is: All-Ireland championships: nil. Munster titles: nil. Despite having teams (Naomh Abán, Gabriel Rangers and Donoughmore) playing in all three All-Ireland finals, we contested no Munster final this year at either junior or senior level at county.

We feel that the time has come for change. We would appeal to the current management team to step aside for the sake of ladies football and allow us to nominate a new management structure which would be free of the politics and dissension that has become a feature of the current structure.

We feel that it is incumbent on us to put football first and to put our own petty differences to the side.

The unanimous decision of the committee is that we would like to be allowed to finish the job that we were elected to do and, to enable us to do so, we would ask the delegates at this AGM to encourage the senior management team to resign and not seek re-election.

There's an intake of breath as Ahern folds over the page and sits down. Delegates shuffle in their seats and mumble at the enormity of what's just been asked of them. Is this really happening? Is the man who has dominated Cork football at every level for more or less seven years being asked to step aside as manager of the Cork senior team?

A vote is taken on the committee's recommendation. Club representatives know it's time for a change, and the result is primarily in favour of the senior management team stepping down. The delegates have spoken. But McLaughlin refuses to step aside.

•••

Charlie McLaughlin was born in the small village of Creeslough in Donegal. From a family of seven, it didn't take him long to learn how to fight his corner, becoming a feisty centre-back, and lining out for Donegal at minor, U21 and senior level.

In 1969, as the Troubles kicked off in Northern Ireland, he left home aged sixteen. As a child, the political and religious unrest was never something explained to him, but instinctively he knew there was a divide. Years later, that divide would affect his family first-hand when his sister was badly injured in the Dublin and Monaghan Bombings on 17 May 1974, in which a series of co-ordinated car bombings took place in both the capital and in Co. Monaghan. Three bombs exploded in Dublin city centre during rush-hour traffic, and a fourth exploded in Monaghan ninety minutes later. A total of thirty-three civilians, aged from five months to eighty years, were killed between all the bombings, and three hundred, including McLaughlin's sister, were injured in what was the deadliest terrorist attack in the Republic's history.

At 5.32 p.m., while walking home from school on South Leinster Street near the railings of Trinity College, not far from Leinster House, a bomb hidden in a blue Austin 1800 Maxi – which was hijacked earlier that morning from a taxi company in Belfast – exploded. Despite being blown across two lanes of traffic and through a glass window, McLaughlin's sister survived.

Those difficult days made him the resilient man he is, and he quickly learned that life was too short to mince your words. Some folks don't like that about him, but it's never bothered him.

He sought adventure first in Dublin, where he lined out with the Crumlin-based St Enda's team for three years. Soon after, he made his mark in the senior domestic championship and was asked onto the Dublin inter-county panel, but being a proud Donegal man, McLaughlin declined. Emigration had been playing on his mind, and the plan was to move to America, but in 1975 he found himself playing football with Nemo Rangers in Cork, and four decades on he's still floating around the clubhouse in Trabeg.

A plasterer by trade, McLaughlin went on to win a Munster club championship with Nemo, but injury cut his career short. First he broke his collarbone, then his leg in a challenge match, before damaging his cruciate. He would never play again after that, but he'd do the next best thing and coach.

In 1996, the chairwoman of the Cork ladies football board, Ester Cahill, had heard of a football-mad Donegal fella who was coaching day and night across Cork, including the Ballygarvan and Cill na Martra junior football teams, Valley Rovers' intermediate footballers and the University College Cork (UCC) Sigerson team, while also being the masseur for the Cork senior and U21 footballers.

He must be good, Cahill decided and phoned McLaughlin to ask if he would coach the Cork senior ladies football team.

'I laughed at first to be honest, and then I said no,' McLaughlin remembers. 'But she pleaded with me to take just one session and show the girls what to do. It was on a pitch out on the Lee Road and there was about seven of them standing on the field waiting for me. They didn't have much talent, but they had a lot of heart, and that'll win out every time.'

Under the persuasive powers of Cahill, McLaughlin was reeled in with the offer of £30 a session. Three times a week, £90 was hardly worth his while, but he accepted.

Two years later, and with as much skill now as heart, Cork won the 1998 intermediate All-Ireland final against Laois, with McLaughlin and Pat O'Sullivan on the line. It was an emotional day. It was the first piece of silverware seventeen-year-old Karen Con O'Sullivan had won since her mother's tragic passing the year before.

On 18 May 1997, her mother, Joan, was driving Karen from their home in Castletownbere on the tiptoe of Ireland to Cork minor training in Donoughmore. It was a six-hour round trip for young Karen and her teammates, Susan Power and Emma Holland, but just minutes from arriving at the pitch, they were involved in an accident at Crean's Cross – one hundred yards from future Cork captain Juliet Murphy's house.

Sadly, Karen's mother was killed. A year later, however, O'Sullivan and Power both lined out at wing-forward, winning the All-Ireland intermediate football final in Duggan Park, Ballinasloe.

In 1999, McLaughlin was at the helm again when Cork won the division three league final against Kildare in Boherlahan, Tipperary. A few weeks later, he would oversee the first Cork victory over Kerry in the Munster senior championship, defeating the eleven-time All-Ireland champions in the provincial semi-final in Fitzgerald Stadium by a point. But it was a freak win. In the final in Dungarvan, Waterford drilled them by sixteen points, 6–12 to 2–8.

McLaughlin, though, was seeing progress. The previous year, Waterford had beaten them by twenty-four points. His vision now was to create a Cork Ladies Football School of Excellence and so he took up a development officer role with the county board and set about making the dream a reality with the help of Fr Liam Kelleher, Mary Power, Ted O'Donovan, Christy O'Sullivan and Sheila Quinlan.

At the very first session, ninety-eight girls turned up to the sports hall at Coláiste an Chroí Naofa boarding school in Carrignavar, and for the likes of future senior stars Rena Buckley, Geraldine O'Flynn and Bríd Stack, it was to be their university of football.

McLaughlin's School of Excellence would produce a conveyor belt of stars and underage All-Ireland and Munster titles for Cork. But with the underage set-up beginning to dominate priorities, the senior players began to have serious doubts about their importance, and the importance of the quest to win the county's first senior All-Ireland title.

•••

Elaine Harte rises from her rickety bar stool, her legs like jelly. She isn't one for putting her head above the parapet, but she knows this is what it'll take because there's no other senior player in the room to do the talking. She's only attending the meeting as a club delegate, but she knows she cannot hide.

Harte was the first girl to play on the boys' football team at Upper Glanmire NS. She played in goal for Ireland in soccer at underage level on an international stage, and won two All-Ireland club medals with Rockbán LFC – one in goal and one at full-forward. Taking her game to the next level is something she strives for. But that growth as a player has been stunted with Cork for the past number of years, and she's frustrated.

Softly spoken, Harte wasn't raised to make noise for the sake of it. She was raised to stand up for what she believed in, and the time is right.

'Look, I'm not here to speak on behalf of the players,' she begins. 'But what I can say is that we totally respect what Charlie has done with the underage teams and all the success he's brought them, but, after seven years at senior level, it's time for a change.'

All eyes are on McLaughlin, gauging what his reaction will be.

'How can you give out about things when you're one of the players who won't even come training?' he bellows towards the back of the room, his finger pointing with rage at Harte.

'Hang on a second, Charlie,' she replies, her voice shaking from the unexpected response. 'You knew I was working evenings and that I wouldn't be able to make some sessions. You'd arranged for different sessions with me and some of the backs, and that was the deal. I'd explained my work situation to you and that was the agreement we'd made.'

Someone in Harte's vicinity comes to her defence by saying McLaughlin has just made this personal, and Harte's eyes begin to fill up. 'Well, all I'll say is, if you're there next year, Charlie, I certainly won't be.'

It's all kicked off as predicted and the tension is excruciating.

The chairman calls order as everyone grapples with what's just happened. It's nearing midnight and the meeting is entering its fifth hour. The delegates are reminded of the recommendation: that the present senior management set-up move aside for the good of Cork football. McLaughlin reiterates that he's not bowing to the committee's recommendation and instead announces that he's putting himself forward again for the position of manager.

The five tasked with finding the new manager look at each other. They didn't expect that card to be played, and now they're caught in limbo, with no name to counteract McLaughlin's.

As it transpires, the committee members are sitting at the back of the room next to the Cork junior ladies football manager, Mary Collins, who arrived late to the meeting having been held up at a funeral in Millstreet. The previous year, Collins oversaw the juniors' first Munster final win in seven years and the chairman of the task group, Stephen Mullane, knows how sharp she is.

'Mary, you'll go up against him?' pleads Mullane.

It's the first Collins hears of it, and she's no more ready for what's being asked of her, but the seconds are ticking.

Desperation is spilling out of Mullane's eyes and Collins knows that the right thing to do is to say yes. Nothing will change otherwise and so Collins raises her arm.

'Through the chair, I'd like to put myself forward for the job too,' she spouts.

Not for the first time that night, things take an unexpected turn. Collins' proposal means a second vote must be taken. It's her versus McLaughlin, and pieces of paper are being frantically cut and distributed around the room.

The votes are collected and Collins lands herself the top job in the county at approximately 1.30 a.m. – six hours after the meeting commenced.

For McLaughlin, it's a kick in the gut.

'I felt rotten. Betrayed even. At the time, Cork ladies football was only going in one direction, and that was up.

If we kept doing the same thing all the time, only changing the drills as the players came up along to suit the physical aspects of the game, then we'd have got there at senior level.

'But, looking back, my communication with the older players was part of the problem. I know that now, but the thing was that the county board never looked at where we were coming from, only where we were going. You can put a very good roof on a house, but you'd be nowhere without a good foundation underneath it.'

But the players were part of the problem too.

2

HATING ON EACH OTHER

*'Our morale was a damp patch somewhere on the soles
of our boots ... we could either walk away, or we could
do something.'*
**Donal Óg Cusack
on the 2002 Cork hurling strike**

Here's how it was in Cork ladies football:

2001

In 2001, things began to unravel for McLaughlin. He'd
done well to take Cork to the 1998 and 2000 intermediate
All-Ireland finals, and the 1999 division three league final,
but in this, his fifth year, the players were finding the
approach stagnant.

There was no central training base, but the majority of
sessions took place in a rural townland called Castletown-
Kinneigh, 50 km west of Cork city, which meant a three-
hour round trip for those travelling from the east of the
county. Rarely were there enough bodies to even play a
game of backs and forwards, and team spirit was pretty
much non-existent.

McLaughlin moved the location of training to Nemo
Rangers in Cork city to try to counteract the falling
numbers, but invariably training started late, with players

strolling across the car park from the changing rooms, with no repercussions for their poor timekeeping. They warmed up themselves, moping through the motions – and that's how they played too.

As the county struggled at adult level, clubs were beginning to get their act together and soon their training became much more enticing to attend. Donoughmore were on the verge of winning their first senior All-Ireland club title in 2001, and for Juliet Murphy, and those like her, the approach of her club coach, Mossie Barrett, was far more beneficial to the improvement of her game.

'With Donoughmore, you were expected to do four laps of the pitch before training even started. It was a given,' Murphy reveals. 'Club training was so good that you'd not be bothered going to Cork sessions. Mossie Barrett had us doing winter training. He had us doing hill training and we would have gone through a wall for him. He was motivating and he built up a great rapport with the players. That sadly wasn't there with Cork.

'We were always serious with Donoughmore, and the players realised that what we were doing was what was needed to take us to the next level, and it was competitive.

'Mossie would say, "Right lads, we're gone in twenty minutes", and it was over with; whereas with Cork, you just never knew when a session would end.

'We had a professional set-up with the club too and we'd a good sponsor, but we owned it too, as players. We took on the responsibility. At the end of the day, you're talking about player fulfilment and self-actualisation. You go out and enjoy the game, and you come off wanting to learn more or improve. You didn't want to feel dejected going out in the first place, but sadly we felt like that with Cork.'

The little things became important to Murphy and there was a realisation that standards needed to be set and kept, and she would live by that rule for the rest of her career.

Barrett made a point of hanging up their Donoughmore jerseys around the dressing room before every game. It meant something. But, at a Cork game, oversized jerseys would be pulled out of a bag thrown in the middle of the floor. They might be washed, they might not. The players themselves would produce an array of different shorts and socks. There was no sense of unity and no sense of ownership.

The summer of 2001 epitomised the lack of direction and organisation. Midweek, the Cork senior team journeyed over the border to Abbeydorney to play Kerry in a Munster championship game. They travelled separately by car but agreed to meet in Ballygarry House in Tralee an hour or two before the game, but when McLaughlin got there, he was shocked to find that he didn't have a full team.

'I had been told by the county board that we'd have a team, but when we stopped, there was only a handful of players there. We started the game with thirteen, and two more players came late and started the second half, but it wasn't good enough.

'I asked the question afterwards why players wouldn't play and was told it was because their club teams were playing championship matches the next evening. That wasn't right. Players should have been given a few days, and I didn't blame them for not coming out to play.'

Ten minutes before a Munster senior championship match, players were introducing themselves to each other in the dressing room. It was agonisingly disjointed and there was no sense of ownership from the top down – from the county board, from the coach, from the players. No one was taking responsibility. There was no accountability either, but it was about to get worse.

During the warm-up at the following game against Waterford in Dungarvan, McLaughlin took underage players down from the stand to start in a Munster senior championship game ahead of players on the bench who had trained with the team, albeit sporadically. One of those in the stand was future All-Star defender Deirdre O'Reilly, who was there to watch her sister play, but instead she made her senior debut, aged fifteen.

McLaughlin's actions caused uproar among the clubs whose players were disregarded on the bench.

'It was reported to the county board after that players were taken down out of the stand to play,' McLaughlin recalls.

'Yes, they were, but it was reported in the wrong context. We notified players to travel to Waterford and Deirdre didn't realise she was part of the team and didn't bring her gear. So I asked where she was and somebody said she was in the stand, and my understanding was she was part of the team.'

O'Reilly remembers it thus:

'I was actually still only playing with the U16s and I had been lining out for the minors too, but that day I just went along to watch the seniors. The next thing someone came over to the stand and asked me to play, and sorted shorts and socks for me. I didn't really know what was happening.

'I had never played with the seniors before, but I just think there was a breakdown in communication.'

Either way, the incident proved how flimsily everything was thrown together, and McLaughlin's decision that night unfortunately sent the wrong message about teamwork to the squad, and in particular to the substitutes.

'It could have been harsh on the subs all right,' he reflects, almost fifteen years on.

'If we'd won, there might not have been the outcry there was. It's a hard job and I've definitely felt the backlash from it, but I'd be big enough to take it and I've learnt from it big time.'

In the aftermath, a number of fringe players walked, but McLaughlin saw it coming long before that.

'Some were playing other sports and we weren't top of their priority list. It was difficult, too, because of some of the hammerings we got. It's easier to keep going when you're winning, people follow where success is. But then there were the divides ...'

•••

Juliet Murphy tells how a club teammate once told her not to speak to a player from another club in the Cork dressing room. They laugh about it now, but that's how it was.

Clubs were now tasting provincial and national glory, and Murphy's Donoughmore were the most successful, winning their first senior All-Ireland club title in December 2001. On the day, they beat Ballyboden St Enda's of Dublin, with captain Mary O'Connor lifting the Dolores Tyrrell Memorial Cup, and a fourteen-year-old by the name of Rena Buckley starting in defence. Player of the Match was Donoughmore forward Ruth Anne Buckley, who months before quit the Cork set-up after she was one of the substitutes overlooked for Rockchapel's Deirdre O'Reilly that day in Dungarvan.

The same weekend Donoughmore claimed their senior All-Ireland club title, Rockchapel won the intermediate title, but there were no messages of congratulations sent between the two clubs. They despised each other, and their rivalry was tangible in the county team dressing room too. Donoughmore and Rockchapel county championship games were always explosive, with Mary Collins and her husband, Jessie, manning the line for 'The Rock', and Mossie Barrett, the Mourinho-like mastermind, doing the same for Donoughmore with his brother Tomás.

There's no denying it, Donoughmore were hated, and it wasn't just Rockchapel who hated them.

'The animosity in the county dressing room definitely stemmed from club,' recounts 2001 Donoughmore captain and dual star Mary O'Connor.

'From a camogie context, we could beat the crap out of

each other in a club camogie championship game, and the following night at Cork camogie training it wouldn't even be discussed. But there was something in ladies football where we weren't really able to forget about it.

'It was familiarity breeds contempt, too. You'd be loyal to your club and we were young, too. We didn't know any better.'

Donoughmore would arrive in convoy for their games, stopping first somewhere close by before entering the grounds together like a small army. It was their declaration that they had arrived, united. They were disliked for that, but they were ahead of the posse.

'We probably isolated ourselves a little,' admits Juliet Murphy, a thirteen-time Cork senior club championship medal winner with Donoughmore, 'but we weren't liked anyway. We were successful, so we were hated. We brought players in from outside the club and people didn't like that, and I can see why people hated us. To be honest, we'd a certain amount of arrogance about us, too, but the players were very honest, and we trained extremely hard for what we won.

'But it was really awkward in the Cork dressing room. I couldn't stand the sight of a maroon jersey. Any time we played Rockchapel it was almost always under lights, back in Millstreet, with the rain lashing down. It just magnified the entire situation.

'We hated them, and they us, but those nights were magical.'

2002

In 2002, things were still a mess. McLaughlin commenced his sixth season in charge, but there was still no provincial silverware. The reigning senior All-Ireland club champions Donoughmore had nineteen players representing Cork at all levels, but only three wore the red jersey at senior level. Things were fraying, and fraying fast.

Cork were now competing in division one, but only because the league had been revamped. The jump from division three didn't help matters. In the third round, Cork won their first ever game in the top flight – against Meath in Mountmellick – but they did so with a patchwork side.

The Cork junior team played beforehand, but with eight senior players unavailable to McLaughlin for one reason or another, the juniors were asked to volunteer as subs after just playing their own game. It was ragball rovers, but Cork managed to pull off the win, and it only showed what could be achieved if things were a little more coordinated.

More players evaporated after this, however, and the void grew bigger than ever in an already shredded panel. A challenge match was organised by the Cork senior management team against Donoughmore to try to find momentum from somewhere, but it turned out to be a farce. Donoughmore turned up with thirty players at their disposal, but Cork couldn't even muster a starting fifteen, and the club side had to lend bodies to what should be the county's flagship side.

The players who had walked from the senior squad

began to look elsewhere. They wanted to represent Cork, but not under a disorganised system as they saw it, and instead looked to the county's junior set-up.

However, it wasn't just the players who took action. Mary Collins of Rockchapel and Mossie Barrett of Donoughmore put their rivalry aside at club level and agreed to work together as selector and coach of the Cork junior team. In years to come, Eamonn Ryan would be singled out for breaking down the barriers of rivalry in the Cork dressing room, and to an extent he did, but it was the actions of Collins and Barrett in 2002 that first instigated a move towards cooperating together for the good of Cork football.

They combined to oversee Cork's first provincial adult title in seven years, beating Limerick in the Munster junior championship final in Emly. On the starting fifteen, there were six Donoughmore players and five Rockchapel, and they too had buried their hatred for one other. There wasn't exactly high-fiving, but there was a sense of relief – carrying all that baggage had become much too tiresome for everyone.

Cork scored five unanswered points to win, but the victory wasn't about raising cups, it was about raising the idea that a united approach was the only way of moving forward.

McLaughlin and the Cork seniors also reached the Munster final but wins along the way masked bigger issues. In their semi-final in Fitzgerald Stadium, they beat reigning champions Clare by a point. It was done with little or no training, but the fearless nature of the underage players recruited to fill in for those who had defected helped. Twenty-four hours beforehand, the Cork U16s won the All-Ireland against Galway, and in Fitzgerald Stadium in Killarney for the Munster senior semi-final, eight U16s were called upon – four started and two came on as subs.

Aged fifteen, and having just sat her Junior Cert, Geraldine O'Flynn made her senior debut for Cork. The night before, she hit her pillow as the MVP in the U16 All-Ireland final. Even at fifteen years of age, nothing fazed her and she kicked a memorable nine-point tally against Clare.

Come the final against Waterford, however, there was a worryingly large amount of underage players lining out, and their physicality was no match for the likes of Mary O'Donnell, Annalisa Crotty and Rebecca Hallahan. Almost half the Cork senior panel were aged sixteen or under, with Beara's Laura Power the youngest at fourteen. The 2002 All-Ireland finalists Mayo and Monaghan each had just one sixteen-year-old in their panels, but Cork still gave Waterford a fright.

The fearlessness of the underage stars, brought with them from McLaughlin's School of Excellence, and their medal-less elders, such as Juliet Murphy, Valerie Mulcahy and Elaine Harte, was beginning to bubble nicely. For the first time in a long time, people realised the need to blend youth and experience, and not rely on one over the other, but McLaughlin was still the reason many of the county's top players weren't lining out. And it took a Mayo man to bring it to the attention of Cork's sporting public.

In an article in the *Evening Echo* on 12 December 2002,

sports editor Liam Horan questioned why Cork had not yet won a Munster senior championship title despite all their domination at club level nationally. It came at a time when the GAA in the Rebel County was embroiled in the Cork hurlers' strike, with players demanding improved facilities in order to deliver at inter-county level. But this wasn't an incident in isolation. Had it not been for Irish soccer star Roy Keane's outburst over the unacceptable standard of facilities at the World Cup in Saipan earlier that summer, it's likely that neither the hurlers nor the ladies footballers would have sought to raise their own standards.

'I would give my right arm to be part of a successful Cork senior ladies team,' Murphy was quoted as saying. 'The talent is definitely there, but there's no camaraderie. Part of me thinks I should go for it no matter who's in charge. But there's no point when you're not going to get anywhere. The county board are happy to concentrate on underage, but we must try to win the senior now.'

It was out of character for Murphy, but she couldn't help herself. The frustration had become too much. She understood people were doing their best. She really got that, but sometimes your best isn't good enough.

McLaughlin declined to comment, but changes were afoot.

2003

The airing of Cork's dirty laundry by journalist Liam Horan was a wake-up call.

At the 2002 county board AGM, Cork men's football selector Timmy O'Callaghan of Mourneabbey was appointed to the senior ladies management team, as was Donoughmore's Frankie Honohan. An uncle-in-law of Juliet Murphy, Honohan was a selector for the 1984 All-Ireland-winning Cork junior men's football team, and his appointment, along with that of O'Callaghan, was an attempt to defuse what appeared, to some, to be a dictatorship.

Bar the Cork junior team, McLaughlin was involved in every other inter-county team, and the addition of O'Callaghan and Honohan was to bring a new dimension to the senior set-up alongside selectors Mary Power and Fr Liam Kelleher.

Competing in the 2003 division two league, the pressure was off, and with the back-room team freshened up, the stronger players in the county gradually began to come back out of the woodwork. Their commitment had marginally improved and they were turning up to games, at least. But there were still doubts as to the professionalism of the set-up, with one pre-game meal consisting of a fry-up in the legendary truckers' pit stop in Josephine's in Urlingford.

But they were winning matches and, with a little organisation and momentum, they reached the division two league final and beat Roscommon (2–8 to 1–7) in Cusack Park, Ennis, with Player of the Match Juliet Murphy lifting her first national trophy as captain of Cork, the first of seven that she would lift over the next four years. Dual star Mary O'Connor had been captain in many of the games en route to the final; however, she missed the final because she had to choose between the codes and opted to play in the division one camogie national league final against Galway in Páirc Uí Rinn. It was the first of many dual dilemmas that came her way.

Despite the changes and cooperation, however, there was still a feeling among the players that something had to give if Cork were to go to the next level.

'We won our own grade, but we weren't setting the world alight, and we were still crying out for change,' says Mary O'Connor.

'I remember there was a survey done by some of the players, and I thought, "This could be good – we could take this somewhere." We didn't want to upset people, and we didn't want to be singled out as troublemakers, but there was still such a strong urge for change.'

The players' survey took place between winning the 2003 division two league final and the opening round of the 2003 Munster senior championship, with forty-eight players across both the senior and junior panels taking part. From the results, a number of points were extracted which players brought to the attention of the county board in a signed letter.

Included was the request for a training weekend prior to the championship, a team bus for all championship games, a central training base, a female representative on each management team, for two selectors to be at every training session, for one member of the back-room team to be trained in first aid, and for specific days to be set for training.

In today's modern game, all of the above are a given. They were basic requests. Forty-two players signed their names in a collective plea for things to change and seventeen of these players went on to win senior All-Ireland medals with Cork when all those requests were implemented.

The 2003 Munster senior championship semi-final against Kerry in Carrigaline was to be Charlie McLaughlin's last game in charge of the Cork senior ladies footballers.

They did well to only lose by a point to Robbie Griffin's team, but another loss finally broke the senior players' spirit.

'I remember walking off the field afterwards and Charlie was next to me,' says Juliet Murphy. 'We'd won the 2003 league at that stage, and he said to me, "It's great now we'll be up in division one next year, and we'll be able to travel and stay away for matches." While he had a point, I knew we weren't going to do well in division one. It was getting much more serious and I knew the set-up wouldn't be able to take us any further.

'I appreciated what Charlie and the management team had done for us – we all did – but it just couldn't continue.'

3

THERE'S SOMETHING
ABOUT MARY

'I didn't want to be the sort of person who looked back and said, "I once had a chance but I didn't take it."'
Jonny Wilkinson

Driving home in the early hours of the morning following the 2003 county board AGM, Mary Collins' head is in a spin. It's her first night as manager of the Cork senior ladies team and already she's concocting ways to get out of it.

She's a strong-minded woman, matter-of-fact, and straight as a die. Born in Meelin in north Cork, into a family of six – four boys and two girls – Collins eats GAA for breakfast, lunch and dinner.

A dinger of a wing-forward back in the day, it was no surprise she was called on to line out for the first ever Cork ladies football team in 1974. Putting on that red jersey was the proudest moment of her playing career, but here she is, a mother of two teenage boys, working full-time, and the first ever female to be voted into a senior managerial position in the history of Cork ladies football.

The AGM was tense and the chairman of the task group set up to fill the position, Stephen Mullane, owes Collins big time, but he's a persuasive soul. When she phones him to hand in her notice less than twenty-four hours after being made manager, Mullane talks Collins into giving it a shot at least.

A production manager with the O'Connor Group in Newmarket, Collins' organisational skills are renowned. She can run a busy household with one eye closed, but it's the three-hour round trip to Cork for training that's giving her doubts about fully signing up for the job. It means leaving work in Newmarket at 5 p.m. and coming home at 11 p.m. twice a week, and on Sundays leaving at 7.30 a.m. For matches, she'll be gone all day.

But, after much humming and hawing, Collins has made her mind up. For the next twelve months she'll give it everything. She'll lead by example, set a precedent and never miss a training session. The players will need to see that the entire back-room team are in it with them – and besides, Collins doesn't do things by halves.

She realises the scale of the commitment that's needed and for days after she tries to pluck up the courage to tell her father, Willie Brosnan, of her decision. When she does, Willie's sitting on the couch watching television.

'Em, by the way, I'm the new manager of the Cork senior ladies,' Collins breaks it to her father.

'Ahh, for God's sake! What arro at?' he asks, sitting bolt upright.

She doesn't exactly know herself, but deep down her gut is telling her it's the right thing to do. Having managed Rockchapel to the intermediate and junior All-Ireland club titles alongside her husband, Jessie, Collins has seen the talent of adult players in the county week in and week out in an era when the county club championships are at an all-time high.

All this talk that the underage 'dream team' will bring senior success to Cork irked her somewhat. Was anyone looking at the likes of Valerie Mulcahy, Nollaig Cleary, Elaine Harte, Juliet Murphy, Aisling O'Connor and Deirdre O'Reilly, who were still all only in their early twenties?

All of them have the experience of winning club All-Irelands, they have level heads and are, in her eyes, complete footballers. They'll be the backbone, and the thought of seeing that talent go by the wayside has put a bee in her bonnet.

In the week that follows her appointment, Collins doesn't know who she'll be working with. Plans are still afoot to appoint a coach. Mullane and his committee only have one man in mind, and Eamonn Ryan agrees to meet them again in the Commons Inn, Blackpool.

Ryan has just relocated from his native Watergrasshill to his wife Pat's home in the Gaeltacht village of Ballingeary. Aged sixty-two, he has just undergone surgery, and a challenge such as this will be the new focus he needs.

Collins is greeted by Stephen Mullane, the Cork junior coach Ger Twomey – who will now double up as a selector with the senior management team – and Ryan. It's a brief enough meeting, but Collins is concerned.

'There's not a hope this is going to work,' she tells Mullane on the way home in the car.

Her first impression of Ryan is that he's very obstinate

and is going to be hard to deal with. In part she's right. Ryan does have a stubborn streak, but it works in the right way.

'You'll have to give it a bash now anyways,' Mullane tells her, and she nods in agreement.

On 14 January 2004, the county board officially announce Ryan as the new coach of the Cork senior ladies football team, and Eileen O'Brien, who has been involved with the underage teams, is appointed liaison officer to soften the transition.

The following Tuesday, Collins and O'Brien meet with county board chairman Steven Lynch to come up with a blueprint to get the best players in the county out again. At the Sandpit House on the back road between Mallow and Boherbue, they begin deliberations at 7.30 p.m. They spend hours going through each club with a fine-tooth comb and select the standout players they want to attend trials the following weekend. It isn't just talent they're looking for, it's personalities. Players whom they know will buy into the system and Collins' way of thinking.

At 1.45 a.m. they leave with a list of seventy-two players. The plan is to contact every player individually. It's Collins' plan and she has her reasons.

'It's a simple thing really. Making that call to a player, you're immediately saying to them, "We think you're good enough to wear the jersey." It gives them a lift. It gives them ownership.

'I'd tell it to them straight, and players knew what they were getting with me. As a manager you have to be above everything, all the rivalries and all that goes with it. Winning is your job, and you need the best players behind you to do that.'

From the outset, the players know they are dealing with a professional set-up, and communication is already much slicker. The following Sunday, 18 January 2004, seventy-plus players turn up and file into the dressing room at Stuake GAA pitch in Donoughmore to hear Eamonn Ryan's inaugural speech. Most haven't a clue who he is, but those whose parents are of a certain generation have assured their offspring that they'll be in safe hands given Ryan's playing days with the Cork footballers.

Juliet Murphy's father, Michael, has given his daughter the low-down before she is to meet him.

'We were chatting in the kitchen the night before our first training session, and Dad kept going on about how he couldn't believe we'd got Eamonn Ryan,' says Murphy.

'I had him built up in my head and I'd a good feeling about him because my father had spoken so highly of him. We googled him there and then, and he had his own Wikipedia page, so we knew we'd hit the jackpot!'

Elaine Harte's mother, Mary, is also good friends with Eamonn's sister, so she, too, has an inkling of what to expect, and in the car park before the first training session, Harte saunters up to tell Ryan of their connection.

'I remember thinking to myself "Don't make a fool of yourself now", because even before I spoke to him I was thinking about trying to impress him,' says Harte.

'I knew more or less straight away he wasn't going to

have a big chit-chat with me, and I didn't want to go too far. I just knew there was a line.

'He was an authoritative figure. He was a little stand-offish at first, but it wasn't that I couldn't talk to him. He was finding his feet and the players were doing the same, but from the first minute you could tell he knew what he was on about. You could listen to him all day. He was passionate, he was educated and he just knew how to talk to us.'

For three minutes Ryan speaks in the dressing room in Stuake. No more. Thirty-seven years older than the eldest there, Ryan senses a few players are bemused, if not amused, by his age profile. But, either way, he has them on the edge of their seats.

'The minute he walked in the door and started to talk, he'd won us over,' recalls Mary O'Connor. 'He was saying, "Well, ye want to try and achieve, yeah?" and we answered "Yes" because we'd been so sick of "Oh, we're playing a match next week and just turn up." Eamonn was talking down the line and talking about coming together and winning, and what he expected from us. We'd never heard stuff like that before and it blew us away.'

Four sets of jerseys are produced out on the pitch for the trial match. The senior All-Ireland club champions Donoughmore are to play a combination team of the other senior clubs in the county, while players from Gabriel Rangers, Naomh Abán and Beara are to play a selection from junior clubs.

For two hours they field, kick, hop and hope, looking

to impress this new 'God' they've been told will take them to the promised land. Ryan watches intently from the sideline. His arms folded at an angle, his head tilted, taking everything in. He doesn't let on, but he's not impressed.

'There was an awful lot of work to do on the skill side of things. An awful lot. I wasn't looking at the potential talent in them. That's not how I was thinking. It was about "How can I make this bunch better?" If they wanted to go further, then we'd have to work very hard. I didn't feel they were great players that day, that's for sure.'

He has no preconceptions of any player due to his lack of connections to the world of ladies football, but Mary Collins and selector Frankie Honohan are assisting, pointing out key players to watch. Their help is appreciated, as is that of additional selectors Ger Twomey and Timmy O'Callaghan, but Ryan will make up his own mind.

In general, he finds it hard to get to know people. His personality is distant by his own admission, but even so, players sense from day one that he's very approachable. Almost instinctively, all parties know there's a line. The management team's roles are clearly defined and all are freely welcome to make suggestions, but understandably it'll take some time for things to smoothly roll into motion.

•••

That day in Donoughmore was Ryan's first day in office and since then he has carried out almost one thousand sessions with the Cork ladies footballers. Every single session is documented in a variety of coloured notebooks, within which are scribbled numerous quotations from sports stars, nuggets garnered for his pre-game talks. Six players – Rena Buckley, Bríd Stack, Deirdre O'Reilly, Geraldine O'Flynn, Briege Corkery and Valerie Mulcahy – and selector Frankie Honohan have been on every step of the journey with him. But Mary Collins' contribution from 2004 to 2007 cannot be underestimated.

While Ryan was at his best on the training field, Collins dealt with everything off it. From the logistics, to speaking up at county board meetings, booking buses and hotels, dealing with whatever concerns players had and with parents or the LGFA, her workload was enormous.

The year before, in 2003, as a selector with the Cork juniors, Collins' own actions, putting aside her club rivalry with Mossie Barrett of Donoughmore, set an example that if you're playing with Cork, you leave your baggage at the door.

The previous set-up had been deeply factious. Players turned up sporadically and there was no camaraderie. All they knew then was rivalry – in the county dressing room and outside it. But here was Collins extending personal invites for trials to players of rival clubs. 'You're one of the best players in the county,' she openly told them, and meant it. With one statement, she had them all on an equal footing.

Her matter-of-fact style didn't allow room for any nonsense either, from players or parents. Invariably, Collins was in the firing line a lot more often because she was more accessible than Ryan, but she always rationalised things with total honesty regardless.

Naturally, it wasn't so straightforward. Early on in telling a player they hadn't been selected for a game because they'd only come back from injury, Collins was subsequently ignored by the player in question for a week. Parents initially had their tuppence-worth, too. In the 2006 All-Ireland win against Armagh, management made the call to replace a player who hadn't been playing well. In the aftermath, the player's father told Collins she cost his daughter an All-Star and, not only that, but he had a go at Collins' husband about it, too.

But soon, players and parents realised that decisions were genuinely made with the entire team's interest at heart, and nothing was personal. Of course it all came with the territory, and Collins knew that, but it wasn't easy. She was only able to do her best and at times it was an emotional roller coaster.

In her, the players had a mother figure, but one who didn't wrap them up in cotton wool. In her second year in charge in 2005, she felt the need to have a word with defender Bríd Stack. Living a half-mile apart, Collins would collect Stack every Sunday morning at 7.30 a.m., leaving Rockchapel for 9 a.m. training in Cork, but on one such car journey Collins was on edge. She had to speak her mind.

She could tell Stack had been out the night before. To be fair to Stack, it was a rare occurrence even in the early years, but Collins was all about maintaining standards, and she told Stack to 'cop herself on'. Now a multi-All-Star-winning defender, Bríd Stack believes that conversation made her the player she is today.

'Mary basically told me I'd got a big arse on myself! But that was the relationship we had. She cared so much for me. She just said, "You could be a great player but you need to get fitter." It was the best thing she ever said to me, and I wasn't offended because Mary was always a straight-talker.

'It was one of the reasons Cork did so well, because of her manner. If you weren't up to it, she'd tell you, and that was that,' says Stack.

Collins' attention to detail was key, too. In previous years, there was no uniformity as to how players togged out. There were no set shorts or socks. No set tracksuit or jacket. Nothing. But in 2004, the county board decided to unify all the inter-county teams with a clothing apparel deal with O'Neills that would see every player allocated a tracksuit, two polo shirts, a pair of socks and shorts. It was the first time it had been done across every grade, and the board was rowing in behind Collins' professional ways.

And she knew the significance of that, and applied it even further to the team. She would text players prior to games or tell them at the end of a training session what they were to wear to the next game or training session. Five-euro fines were dished out to those who didn't adhere. It was a small thing but it subtly made players realise they were representing something bigger than themselves. In essence it was character building.

The players saw, too, how Collins managed her time, juggling work and family life, yet never missing a training session. In that, they saw the sacrifices and the commitment she was making for them, and they knew she believed in them.

The fact, too, that Collins is still the only female to have managed the Cork team under Eamonn Ryan says a lot about what she brought to the table, but she wasn't the only female in the early years to play a vital part in fostering a bond of togetherness.

Liaison officer Eileen O'Brien is a lively spirit. One of those people whose energy could power a generator. Her involvement was vital in bringing the younger, underage players into the mix under Ryan – the likes of Bríd Stack, Angela Walsh, Briege Corkery and Geraldine O'Flynn. Her presence was a comfort to them, while her bubbly personality was something of a fascination to the older players who had yet to come to know her. But it didn't take them long to feed off her positivity.

At the same time, while O'Brien – who's married to inter-county referee Michael Collins – brought an element of fun, she never lost sight of the job to be done. On a team-training holiday to Lanzarote in 2006, for example, the players trained for hours in the searing heat on a synthetic grass pitch at El Campo Municipal, but they weren't in it alone. O'Brien joined in for the sprints, pushing them and driving them on as they baked in thirty-degree heat. She knew the players had to have the legs run off them, but it was tough watching them putting themselves through it, so, instead of asking Ryan to take things easy, O'Brien took part herself. Like Collins, she led by example.

They were all in it together. No matter what.

4

MASTERMIND

'Small minds are concerned with the extraordinary,
great minds with the ordinary.'
Blaise Pascal

It's 5.30 p.m. on a miserable February evening in 2004, and
Eamonn Ryan parks his car at the rear of Cork University
Hospital. He is halfway through three months of radium
treatment for prostate cancer, but not many know. It's exactly
a month since he stood on the sidelines in Donoughmore
for the trial games and his first full training session with the
Cork ladies footballers is later this evening in Liscarroll.

It's a fifty-five-minute drive away but he has every intention of making it. He is tired and what spurs him on is not
bravery, it's 'thickness really'. The fact that he'll soon be on
a pitch – where he's most at home – is keeping him going.

Soon, he's motoring along in the tiniest of cars, a white
2000 Daihatsu Cuore, which navigates the potholes of
north Cork surprisingly well for its modest size. He adores
that Cuore, which the players have nicknamed the 'Butter
Box'. For Ryan, it's his mobile office, a retreat in which he
can enjoy another passion of his – music. Not learning an
instrument is one of his biggest regrets, but in the Butter
Box he blares anything from classical to rock. It relaxes
him because tonight is important in terms of the players
getting a feel for his own genre of coaching. It's going to

be a challenge, but if he can get them to buy into how he operates, it'll be more enjoyable all round.

Facilities in Liscarroll are minimal. Just one floodlight is operating in a corner of the lopsided field, shedding whatever light it can on a new era in Cork ladies football. Ryan gets on with it regardless. He has a knack for improvising and making the best of situations, and in the years to come that same resilience will rub off on his players.

The minute Ryan blows the whistle, the players are mesmerised.

'It was so enjoyable,' Juliet Murphy recalls. 'We'd bare light and Eamonn was saying, "Careful now ... don't bump into each other, careful now." He was so nice and he'd say, "We'll try that with our left leg now," and he'd bring us in every so often and say something constructive or tweak something. He was so animated and we'd go back out and try and impress him again. We were all so enthusiastic.

'Whatever we did, he was praising us loads. We were like seven-year-olds. Praise meant so much to us, particularly the older girls. When it came to Cork we had no confidence in ourselves or in the set-up, and brick by brick Eamonn built it back up. He was telling us, "Ye're great footballers, great footballers." He'd say that quite a lot, whether he believed it or not at the time.'

For citóg Mary O'Connor, Ryan's arrival was like 'manna from heaven'.

'He'd break it down so simply for you and he was such a good communicator. You'd say to him, "Eamonn, did you see I kicked the ball with my right leg?" and he'd throw his eyes to heaven jokingly to say, "But yeah Mary, where did the ball go?" You'd be predictable in your game, but he challenged you to get better.'

Every drill has a purpose. Every technique is broken down, and everything is done with a ball in hand. The structure of the session is something they've never come across before. Although simple, the revelation to it all is the intensity with which Ryan wants drills done. They are short and snappy, yet quality is never to suffer.

'We always had a ball, everything was with the ball, even the warm-up,' says goalkeeper Elaine Harte. 'He'd say, "What's the point in having a corner-forward bored off their heads for thirty minutes playing backs and forwards and not touching the ball. You need to be touching the ball two to three hundred times in training to improve your skill, instead of just standing there waiting for a ball that might never come to you."'

Harte first came across Ryan a year earlier attending a coaching seminar. She thought then she had him figured out, but she wasn't even close.

'At the talk he was emphasising the importance of bringing competition into drills, no matter what age group you were working with. He gave the example of saying to kids, "Okay, twenty points in a minute is the world record, see if ye can beat it." Or for us he'd say, "I'd lads last week and they got this amount of points, see if ye can beat it." He did that in one of our first sessions and I remember thinking to myself, "Girls, he's only trying to get into our heads, he's only trying to get the competition going!" But it worked. Straight off we were striving to be better in everything we did. We thought we were beating fellas too, or were as good as them at least!'

Gradually Ryan asks one or two players for feedback about drills. It's his way of giving them a new sense of ownership. But even with three decades of coaching experience in the memory bank, he's still looking to improve. Subliminally, the players take note of that characteristic, and it's something they begin to do themselves over the next decade.

That eagerness to continually learn is key to the longevity of Cork's success. From Ryan's perspective, it has helped him bring a continual freshness, while the players will always find something new to work on in their individual games year in, year out. It is this approach of both player and coach, each never being satisfied, that has seen Cork raise the benchmark time and again.

Ryan wasn't fully aware of the factions that existed between the players when he first started, but he quickly became mindful of it.

'At that stage of my career I was very conscious about the importance of players getting on. While I wasn't aware of the full state of the conflict, I was aware that there wasn't a great sense of camaraderie in the first few months, but I didn't really know why.

'I didn't want to make a big deal out of fixing it. The only thing I did was make them work really hard, because now they saw that the person beside them was working as hard as they were, and gradually it hit home that they were all in this together.'

For Mary O'Connor, Ryan's actions soldered a new trust among the players. A trust that had long been broken and unaddressed.

'Before, you would arrive at Cork training and sit in your car and wait until someone else got out of theirs first before you did because you didn't want to talk to each other, and we probably didn't want to get to know each other either. You have to remember we were coming from an era when you went into the dressing room, put on your gear, played a match and went home. That was it. Sure you might never see the girl next to you again.

'People were half paranoid then because we didn't know or have faith in each other, but when Eamonn came along you knew the girl alongside you had trained really hard because you'd seen her do so.

'Once players saw that, they were committed. There was no one dodging and trust was automatically built up. If Eamonn had said, "Jump", we'd have said "How high?" He created a family situation where everyone relied on everybody else, and we all knew we needed each other.'

•••

The eldest in a family of six, Ryan was always the philosopher and would be seen immersed in a book for hours on end. He was also a grafter, and those two qualities moulded his coaching style.

Growing up in the rural village of Watergrasshill, outside Cork city, he would deliver coal with his father, Jim, with a hand truck, and mix grass seeds and load feedstuffs for delivery. When work was done he'd head off to the local playing field to watch the junior hurling team. One game against Watergrasshill's rivals Little Island in the forties stands out. As hurleys were dispensed with in the midst of a brawl, Ryan's younger brother Mick and his cousin gathered the opposition's hurleys and threw them over a nearby ditch as part of their contribution to the cause.

It was during this time that Ryan's love of sport, and all that went with it, was born. After work at weekends, he would cycle 24 km from Watergrasshill to Musgrave Park or the Mardyke in the city centre with his father to watch Irish rugby star Jack Kyle, or to watch former England soccer player Raich Carter in action with Cork Athletic FC. Later, when cars became more common, Ryan's mother, Mary, would join them – at a time when there were no women going to matches of any code.

Ryan queued for hours, too, to be in with a chance of watching former Manchester United star George Best playing in Flower Lodge in 1976. Cork hurling legend Christy Ring became a good friend when Ryan holidayed in Youghal during the summer months, and together they'd watch the sun set and talk sport.

Hurling was Ryan's first love. Having lived in Thurles for a few years as a young boy, when his father was transferred briefly to Tipperary with Sutton's Coals, he was swept up in the euphoria of Tipp's three in a row between 1949 and 1951. Any chance he got, he was up in the local Thurles Sarsfields GAA pitch running after the sliotar behind the goal of county goalkeeper Gerry Doyle, whose father was the legendary Tipperary hurler Jimmy Doyle.

Ryan himself would make his adult club debut as a goalkeeper just before his sixteenth birthday in a junior A game in 1957. Lining out in front of him were three of his childhood idols – Felix Sarsfield, Denis Dineen and John Flaherty – and Ryan was in his element. He'd made it, but the taste of victory saw him get carried away with himself and in the following game he conceded five goals in twenty minutes.

He would never let his head swell again, as a player or a coach.

It was hurling that made him tick, but football was where he'd make it as a player.

In the early sixties he caught the eye of the Cork football selectors and in 1963, aged twenty-five, he played both junior and senior for the Rebels. Three years later, in 1966, he was one of the stars in the Cork side that defeated Kerry – for the first time since 1957 – scoring three points from corner-forward. Concussion, however, saw him depart the senior football All-Ireland semi-final early against a Galway side bidding for three in a row. Without him Cork lost.

The following year, Cork retained the Munster title, then beat Cavan in the All-Ireland semi-final to face Meath in the final. It was Ryan's first time stepping out onto the field in Croke Park; however, the Royals won by a goal courtesy of Terry Kearns, who fisted a high incoming ball into the net of future Cork men's football coach Billy Morgan.

For Ryan, it was another lesson learned, but ironically he never had the ambition to win an All-Ireland. 'I dreamed as a young fella of playing with Cork but I never had the ambition to win an All-Ireland. It was always just about making the team. It's hard to explain, but it was a lack of ambition, and it was ambition.

'I was never disappointed with not winning an All-Ireland medal until one night I was out with former Cork football captain Larry Tompkins and some fellas joined us. I was blackguarding him saying, "They all know you, Larry", and he was saying that when you win an All-Ireland medal everyone knows you. Then it hit me that it was more important than I thought, but I would have been horribly disappointed if I hadn't played in an All-Ireland.'

Ryan studied at UCC, winning two Sigerson Cup medals during his time there. He'd return to his alma mater years later, after retiring from teaching, to become a GAA development officer. While in UCC, Ryan's leadership qualities were obvious, and he was selected to captain the 1967 combined universities team, a colleges All-Star team equivalent.

After he graduated, he studied at St Patrick's teaching college in Drumcondra, Dublin, where he played senior football and hurling with Erin's Hope GAA club. The summer before he qualified as a teacher, Ryan was tempted to go a different career route when he was offered a job as a trainee manager at Woolworths' store on Patrick Street in Cork city, with a weekly wage of £25. As a teacher he'd only earn £7 a week, but money wasn't going to sway him.

In that Woolworths offer, someone obviously saw Ryan's potential to manage, to rally and to get the best out of people.

He was always interested in business on a theoretical level, having studied economics, and many times throughout his coaching career he'd make the correlation between coaching a team and running a business. On reading the business pages of a national newspaper one day, Ryan was struck by the simplicity of how Kelly's Hotel in Rosslare had become so successful, and decided to use the same ideology to get the best out of his own players, and longevity with it.

'The owner had asked his staff to give what he called two "wow moments" a day to customers,' Ryan recounts. 'His mindset was, "I want to give these customers the best experience while they're here, so that they'll return to the hotel." It was a subliminal thing, but that's what the coach has to do. It's a selfish reason but, as a coach, if you can give the players the best experience, they'll return again and again.'

It was only when he qualified as a teacher that Ryan began to coach, but on reflection he admits he started too young. It meant his focus was split between playing and coaching, but eventually he went with the latter. Admittedly he was never a silky smooth player. He didn't train enough, and only learned his trade by 'banging up against fellas'.

'I came late to football and didn't start playing until I went to secondary school in Coláiste Íosagáin in Ballyvourney. You were playing against fellas from the wilds of west Cork and against Kerry fellas who lived for it, but I was never really coached. Maybe that's why I put such a huge emphasis on the actual teaching of skills, maybe too much at times.'

But his style paid off. Under his guidance, his hometown school, Watergrasshill NS, where he was teaching, won numerous Sciath na Scol titles. The local camogie team tasted glory, too. And between 1990 and 1994 he coached the Cork minor men's football team to three Munster titles and two All-Irelands.

In 1990, he coached Na Piarsaigh to their first Cork senior hurling championship title. He was also at the helm as a player/trainer when Watergrasshill won their first county hurling title in 1974, and involved with Ballingeary in 2006 when they won their first intermediate football title. A year earlier, in 2005, he was in charge when the Cork ladies footballers won their first division one national league and All-Ireland titles.

It's no coincidence that Ryan was on the scene when all four teams reached their respective holy grails. He has a way of instilling belief and creating a culture based on the attitude that diligence is the only way to make it to the top. He makes a commitment to be there every step of the way and equip players as best he can, but ultimately it's they who have to get it done. Having run a number of marathons in his time – including London, Dublin and Cork – Ryan knows there's always more in the tank, and he knows how to push players to the limit. But he also has an amazing ability to tap into a player's individual qualities and give them the freedom to express themselves on the pitch.

In 1983, when county teams had seen what he could do, he agreed to take charge of the Cork senior men's football team. They put an end to Kerry's dream of nine Munster titles in a row, while Ryan also trained the Cork junior footballers to win the provincial decider in 1988.

•••

Success had been sweet, but in the nineties Ryan craved more than just victories. He would immerse himself further in coaching literature and courses. In particular, a book by Rainer Martens called *Successful Coaching* fascinated him, while he also looked up to former Kerry footballer and manager Mick O'Dwyer. The two had coached an inter-provincial team in the early eighties, and Ryan was impressed by O'Dwyer's style.

'I just liked his approach. I won't say it was simplistic, but it was very down to earth and he seemed to have the players eating out of the palm of his hand, even though they were superstars. He just had a great way of relating to the players.'

Ryan also learned a lot from the literature produced by Pat Daly, the GAA's director of games development, and he took part in a course at the National Coaching and Training Centre (NCTC) in Limerick. There he enjoyed learning just as much by osmosis while mingling with the likes of former Irish soccer international John Devine and showjumper Gerry Mullins.

Ryan's appetite to learn got stronger and he began to look at how top teams in other sports trained. He would attend

Cork City FC training sessions and watch quietly in the corner. He would travel to Dublin to watch the Ballyboden hurlers train behind closed doors, or to Ballyduff in Kerry to watch their footballers. Always with a notebook in hand, he'd jot down eight points he could implement in his own sessions, with an asterisk emphasising a particular drill he could improve or manipulate to his advantage. Now, it is other coaches who are coming to see Ryan's sessions.

His knowledge also branches into sports psychology. 'It's only in the last thirty years that I subtly used psychology to try and get inside players' minds. All of it evolved slowly, but you'd learn by your mistakes, and I'd have no trouble admitting my mistakes either.

'I went from being an authoritarian coach to a player-coach. My job is to help people, to teach them, particularly on the technical side of the game, but I'd develop a situation where I'd try to have an empathy or sympathy with a player.

'By putting players at the centre of the whole thing and forgetting about yourself then, in almost some perverse way, you seem to get more satisfaction. Obviously you're doing all you can for the players' sake, and I think they reciprocate when they know you're genuine and that you've their best interests at heart. They're not just players that you use to further your own ambition, you're part of a group.

'Some might call it a psychological defect in that I find coaching therapeutic, but it can't all be about you if you want to get the best out of them. The more you put in yourself without looking for a spin-off, the more spin-off you'll actually get.'

A father of six – Jim, Deirdre, Don, Michelle and twins Jackie and Des – and a grandfather, Ryan is a family man. He has made huge sacrifices over the years to tend to the needs of his teams, being away from his family and his wife, Pat, and often missing milestones.

'The lads at home understand I'm not the full shilling. I'm near enough to it, but they'd appreciate it and begrudgingly they'd say fair play to you for doing it, but I don't think any of them would hold it against me.'

As a parent he would have been relatively strict, but once his children flew the nest, he figured he'd leave them off to their own devices. Never did he wrap them up in cotton wool or fill them with grand notions, no matter how proud he was of them. The same can be said of the Cork ladies footballers.

'I'd be slow to praise the players, but I'd praise them collectively all right. When you have six kids you can't be singling any of them out either. It's the same thing. They're all unique, all equally lovable, and they all have their own little idiosyncrasies,' says Ryan, whose approach has garnered so much respect despite minimal words of praise.

'He never singled anyone out. Never,' says Nollaig Cleary. 'That way players didn't think they were more important than others and it kept everyone on an even keel. I've played on other teams where coaches have had their favourites and, although not intentional, it causes consternation. Eamonn treated all of us the same.

'Teams by their very nature can have a lot of strong personalities and players can have the potential to go off, but Eamonn set the tone about being level-headed by his own mannerisms. That in itself automatically reined us all in, too.'

'You knew where you stood with him,' adds Cork's most prolific scorer, Valerie Mulcahy. 'Eamonn wasn't a *plamáser* and he didn't have favourites. He didn't overly chase anyone and that was needed because it set down a marker for everybody and in his eyes we were all on a par.'

That, says Ryan, took him a long time to figure out, but in doing so it harvested a plethora of individual leaders, who throughout the years took turns getting Cork over the line.

'It's just go out and play,' says Cleary, 'there was never any real tactics to it. Eamonn instilled such belief in us that we were the ones on the pitch making the decisions. We had done the hard work and because of that we trusted ourselves, and so did he. He allowed us to express ourselves. A lot of us had played other sports and he allowed us bring those facets to the set-up too and because of it we grew as much as people as we did players.

'Even when we were down ten points with sixteen minutes to go in the 2014 final, he wasn't roaring at us from the sideline. He knew we had it in us to make the decisions to lead ourselves. We were on the verge of an embarrassing loss, it would have been our first ever at Croke Park, but we had the leaders even when we were ten points down.'

There was a time when Ryan would have roared at players, but it was in a different era.

'It took me a long time to realise that way doesn't work. They're already under enough pressure, so your roaring is only adding to it. Of course there'll be times when you have to shout – if someone goes up the field completely and never comes back, you might have to shout then – but if you're doing it constantly it just adds to the confusion. The players have to work it out for themselves, within reason.'

It would take the Cork ladies footballers a number of months to see that they themselves were at the very centre of Ryan's methods, and gradually, too, they became aware of the sacrifices he was making for them. This was their quest, yet here was a man willing to do everything it took to make their dreams come true.

'He missed so much of his own life by being there for us at training and matches for over a decade,' says Juliet Murphy. 'At times he'd put us before his family, which can't have been easy for them, but he was infectious. I knew he was getting treatment when he first came on board and he was still coming to training, so he led by absolute example and through complete modesty. There was never an announcement that he wasn't feeling great, he just got on with it in his quiet, respectful way, and we responded to that. He was coming from such a genuine place and it made all the difference to us.'

5

THE MUNSTER MASH

*'You have to expect things of yourself
before you can do them.'*
Michael Jordan

Eamonn Ryan doesn't do pressure but today he's feeling it. After just a few sessions, it's match day, away to Munster champions Kerry in the opening game of the 2004 division one national league. It's Cork's first league game back in the top flight and the bus journey is quiet.

The younger apprentices are eager to appear mature and keep their usually bubbly chats to a minimum. The safety net that was the underage set-up is no more. There's nowhere else left to ply their trade but at senior level, and they realise they have no choice but to make it work. For the time being the older players sit next to their club teammates as rivalries still linger.

On the sideline in Cahersiveen, Ryan is feeling the eyes of the travelling Cork support (what little of it there is) on him in this, his first game in charge. It's nothing overt, but he can sense them looking at him a bit more intently than he's used to. Then again, he's admittedly insecure about a lot of things, and maybe the pressure is more intrinsic, but he wants it to go well.

In the dressing room, he goes about his pre-game routine as he has with dozens of teams before, but the process comes as a bit of a surprise to the players.

'I started laughing because it was like we were U12s,' says Elaine Harte. 'He made the starting fifteen stand up and lined us out there and then in the changing room, and I was thinking, "We know where we're playing. You don't need to show us, we're not that bad!"

'So I was first up and he said, "Watch the kickouts, make sure people can hear you" and he moved on to the six backs, then the midfielders and the forwards, and then the subs, so everyone was part of it.'

Multi-All-Ireland-winning dual star Mary O'Connor remembers being taken aback by Ryan's ways, too, but immediately she saw the benefits.

'I was like, "What the hell is he doing?", but it was the best thing. It made us see the bigger picture. Over the years then, if, for some reason, he didn't do that before a match we'd think there was something wrong, but it made you realise the unity of it too.'

In the first half in Con Keating Park things aren't going well. Cork trail by just five points but their performance is woeful. Fourteen of the starting team will go on to win All-Ireland medals in nineteen months, but for now there isn't a sniff of cohesion and their play is haphazard.

Back in the dressing room at half-time they expect Ryan to explode. There's an urgency to impress him, but their over-eagerness results in numerous errors. It's a long way yet from Skins and Under Armour, and the players vibrate in unison with the cold, water dripping from their eyelashes and steam rising from their limbs. They tried, but they know it's not good enough. As Ryan makes his way through the doorway, their eyes fixate on the concrete floor and they brace themselves for 'The Master' to dish out a harsh lesson.

'I was waiting for him to kill us,' says Elaine Harte. 'I let in a dodgy goal over my head and I was thinking, "He's going to tear shreds off me." But he was so calm and just said, "Okay, ye've messed up. There's nothing ye can do about it. Ye either fold or go back out and show them ye really want to play football." And I just thought to myself, "Thank God!"'

Having been outscored in the opening half, Cork match the Kingdom in the second. They play freer in themselves, knowing that Ryan just wants them to do their best, but they lose by seven points (2–6 to 2–13). It would be the first loss of just twenty-three in 151 league and championship games during Ryan's tenure, and they'd get a telling-off after all right, but Ryan wouldn't be the one to give it to them.

As the players traipse back into the dressing room in Cahersiveen, they're content that they didn't succumb to an unmerciful Kerry hiding like in other years. Sopping wet jerseys are removed in double-quick time and flung over shoulders onto the floor. Job done. But, as the mound of jerseys pile up, Mary O'Connor loses it.

'Lads!' she bellows, and everyone turns to her. 'Things are changing. We don't throw the Cork jersey on the ground any more. We earn those jerseys and we need to respect that. Fold them and put them back into the bag for the person kind enough to wash them for us. Our attitude needs to change, and it changes now!'

O'Connor is the only player to have won an All-Ireland medal with Cork, having won the 1995 junior All-Ireland against Tyrone, and her outburst leaves its mark.

'That was a massive turning point for us,' admits Harte. 'I can still remember it and the shame I felt having thrown the jersey on the ground. I was mortified having to pick it up, but it was a huge moment in realising what playing for Cork should actually be all about.'

For years the players moaned that the set-up wasn't professional enough, but here they were disrespecting the very thing they should be proud of. For the first time, they realised and acknowledged that they, too, were part of the problems under McLaughlin. As head coach he had to take the flack for a number of things, but to make him a scapegoat for the entire debacle wasn't a fair reflection. The players had a responsibility too.

'Our attitude had been wrong,' admits Juliet Murphy. 'If you were to ask any of the players I started out with, none of them I would say had a vision of walking out onto Croke Park in a Cork jersey. It's symbolic. It's what the greatest GAA players have done, but up until then we didn't have pride in the Cork jersey. We had an obligation ourselves and we realised it that day.'

The next few weeks are tumultuous in terms of results. They get their first ever win under Ryan, against Monaghan (3–9 to 0–7), and lose to reigning senior All-Ireland champions Mayo (1–8 to 2–13), but Ryan observes in his notebook that the players' decision-making is improving. It's not the only change that's occurring, however, as the three bus journeys to Cahersiveen, Mountmellick and Ballyline have resulted in a thawing of club rivalries.

'Travelling for six hours together, we had no choice but to get on!' says Juliet Murphy. 'With the rivalry thing, when you're playing against another club, you've to conjure up a hatred for them. That's what you do. You magnify that hatred for the purpose of motivating yourself, but on those trips we were slowly getting to know each other, and so too were our parents. That was a big thing actually, our parents. They had seen the potential in us all along. They'd seen us floundering, but they knew we had it in us if we were united.'

Slowly but surely the younger players begin to mingle with the older crew, and for 2003 Cork minor All-Ireland-winning captain Bríd Stack, it was essential.

'We were in awe of the likes of Juliet, Nollaig, Valerie and Elaine, and we'd go out of our way to make friends with them because we wanted to say Juliet Murphy and Valerie Mulcahy were our friends. I suppose that's what you do when you're young. We were trying to impress them and Eamonn at the same time, but they all led by such example that they pushed us to be better players.'

'We needed them too, though,' Murphy confides. 'The older gang knew we couldn't do it without them. The young ones just brought a new freshness. They were fearless, but at the same time they were so respectful. Even though there was never a lack of respect, we simply didn't know each other. They were chatty and friendly, and the more time we spent together, the more we learned about each other and our families. There wasn't one specific turning point when we all just became one, it was just a very natural process.'

Halfway through the league Cork have won just two of five games, against Monaghan and Longford, but on the training field Ryan is observing incremental improvements.

'They were starting to work really hard and were beginning to see, too, that we were making a bit of progress. Their attitude was never bad, but with every training session you could see the inches of improvement. The training was bogman stuff though, appalling actually, but they were happy to do it. At times you'd think basic drills were beneath you, but they never thought it. That was the big thing I was starting to notice, even though it was basic, there was never "Erra, this fella's behind the times" or "Why aren't we doing convoluted tactical stuff?" They were buying into it, and I was feeding off of that too.'

It's taken four months to get to this point, and although there's still a long way to go, they achieve what they set out to do and maintain division one status. They beat Meath in the quarter-final of the national league (3–13 to 0–13) before reversing their earlier defeat to title favourites Galway in the semi-final (0–8 to 0–6), and the result takes them and ladies football by surprise.

Ryan, Mary Collins, Frankie Honohan, Ger Twomey and Timmy O'Callaghan are only in the door, but already they've managed to bring Cork to the league final of the top tier – only the county's second ever appearance in the twenty-five years of the competition – and just twelve months after winning the division two title. Under the captaincy of Juliet Murphy, the players want to prove themselves at the highest level but have to do so against the best, Mayo.

However, turmoil is fermenting in the west.

The controversy stems from the senior All-Ireland final against Dublin the previous September, when Mayo opted to wear Azzurri gear in contravention of the LGFA's agreement with O'Neills that participants in championship semi-finals and finals must wear O'Neills apparel. During the subsequent seven months, there's been mediation, a vote of no confidence in the executive and a fine of €22,000 (albeit reduced to €2,200), which Mayo have failed to pay ahead of the 2004 league final, and they're thrown out of the competition a week before they're to face Cork.

Mayo captain Nuala O'Shea is woken by a phone call at 1.30 a.m. and is told the team has been ejected. The players are being punished for something that isn't their doing, but they cope admirably, as do their management team, who decide to train for the week as if they're in the league final anyway.

Common sense prevails and Mayo get the go-ahead, with the final set for 25 April 2004, as a triple header in Pearse Stadium in Galway alongside the national hurling league clash between Galway and Limerick, and the national football league semi-final replay between the Tribesmen and Tyrone – which liaison officer Eileen O'Brien's husband, Michael, will be officiating.

Like Mayo, Cork have their own problems off the field and are without a team sponsor on their jerseys for the live TG4 broadcast. The rawness of the Cork county board, but also of the players, is illustrated when Juliet Murphy ventures to St Stephen's Green in Dublin for the pre-game press call in jeans and a cheap Cork fleece she found thrown in the back of her wardrobe. She doesn't have a Cork jersey to call her own, and it's embarrassing.

In what minimal match previews there are, the game is flagged as David versus Goliath – Mayo, the dominant force in ladies football for the last five years, and Cork, the new guns.

The mood in the camp is calm and surprisingly nerves aren't a problem. It's uncharted territory, but for some reason the occasion isn't weighing them down. Upon arriving in the dressing room, league sponsors Suzuki and the LGFA have arranged jerseys and gear bags for the players, and they think they've made it.

Distracted, as the smell of freshly unwrapped plastic fills the room, they're protected from the mayhem that's ensuing outside. John O'Mahony's Galway have just secured a place in the national football league final, defeating Mickey Harte's Tyrone in extra time. The pitch is heaving with maroon and by the time Cork run out from under the tunnel an hour later than scheduled, there's still hundreds of Galway fans on the field.

In the warm-up, gaggles of spotty teenagers run alongside the players, taking the mick, while frenzied kids are causing all sorts of potential hazards.

But they are focused. Ryan has put it clearly: the Mayo players all have 'two hands, two legs and one brain', just like them. Mayo are not invincible.

At half-time Cork find themselves in front by six points (1–7 to 0–4) with the youngest player on the pitch, fifteen-year-old Amanda Murphy from Beara, netting for Cork in just her second league start. All watching are in awe of the fearless, fast style of football Eamonn Ryan has the challengers playing.

'I thought we'd the match won at half-time,' says Elaine Harte.

'I remember thinking, "Oh my God, we're Cork, and we're beating Mayo – what's that about?" We couldn't believe it and it totally affected us in the second half. We clammed up. They were Mayo and we began to fear them again because it was so far-fetched to be beating them.'

In the second half, Cora Staunton takes over, finishing with 1–10. For the last fifteen minutes Cork's fitness levels abate and Mayo's experience sees them win their second ever division one league title (1–13 to 1–11) against all the adversity that raged the week before.

As Nuala O'Shea collects the cup, Ryan huddles the Cork players together in the middle of the field.

'Look up and watch them getting the trophy,' he says. 'That's what we want to be doing, so remember this moment.'

Surprisingly, in the dressing room there isn't an over-whelming air of disappointment. Corner-back Niamh Keohane has been called to complete a drug test and, given her low hydration levels, the rest of the team decide to head off to the post-match meal down the road – leaving Keohane to get a lift on the Mayo bus.

'I don't know how she did it,' her Rockbán teammate Elaine Harte grins. 'I was so scared to even look at the Mayo girls when we were in the same room as them after! You'd be afraid to look in case one of them caught you. We had come to within two points of them, yet we were still in awe.

'We were there or thereabouts, but the thing was we were content with having just got there. Winning wasn't our aim so it was never really in our heads, but it set the ball rolling and people realised we were able to do this. If we could compete with the best, then we weren't very far off. Eventually we came round to not being happy with just competing, we wanted to win.'

'It took for us to be beaten to actually realise what we were capable of,' Mary O'Connor adds. 'It was a real turning point. We were inexperienced and young. It was only coming back on the bus we realised we'd left it behind us. Eamonn was really upset. Not at us, but that it had taken a defeat to bring us on, but that was all part of the character building.'

Ryan takes the blame for that first final loss, but, as O'Connor says, it's the foundation on which later successes were built.

'There were things I'd have done differently,' Ryan admits. 'There were changes I should have made and I didn't – one positional and one personnel. I can't say if it would have won the game, but thinking back, the players didn't even give a hint that I should have done something to rectify things. They never blamed me when things went wrong, and I was always grateful for that.'

•••

It's summertime and Cork are back in the Kingdom for the opening round of the 2004 Munster senior championship. They've worked hard the last two months, ironing out kinks since their league final loss, and a number of challenge matches against Charlie McLaughlin's Cork minors, Roscommon and Dublin have helped boost fitness levels.

When the ball is thrown in against Kerry in Killorglin, however, Cork are obliterated. Within thirty seconds Patrice Dennehy scores the home side's first goal, and by half-time Cork are fourteen points adrift (0–4 to 3–9). It's a nightmare. Three goals fly past Elaine Harte and Kerry All-Stars Geraldine O'Shea and Irish soccer international Kacey O'Driscoll are kicking points for practice. But, just like in Cahersiveen, Ryan doesn't raise his voice at half-time. The players are ashamed, but the call goes out from Ryan to get back to basics.

'Just concentrate on defence and work hard – harry, block, tackle – and we'll go from there,' he tells them.

It works. Cork keep Kerry to a single point in the second-half and manage to claw back eight points (1–11 to 3–11) but the loss has bruised their egos. They were hyped after coming so close to Mayo in the league final, but it was a harsh lesson not to lose the run of themselves.

In round two, they beat Clare in Doonbeg (3–16 to 1–6) to set up a semi-final clash against Waterford in Fraher Field, Dungarvan. It's nineteen years since Cork have beaten Waterford, with Michael Ryan – the former Waterford hurling manager – at the helm. A building contractor by trade, Ryan has built his own ladies football empire in the sunny south-east, winning the Brendan Martin Cup and division one NFL five times each. But he's wary of Cork's coming and organises for one of Waterford's rising stars, Mary O'Rourke, to fly back to Ireland from a J1 in New York for the game on 31 July. Joining her in the forward-line is future Six Nations rugby captain Niamh Briggs.

Again Cork start slow and trail at half-time, but defensively Bríd Stack and Angela Walsh are beginning to slowly fuse, as are the forwards, and they outscore the Déise in the second half and go on to win for the first time in almost two decades on a scoreline of 1–11 to 0–10. It's a massive win and highlights what they can achieve if they work hard.

They face Kerry again in the Munster final in Páirc Uí Rinn, Cork, on 15 August 2004, and this time they'll be ready for Geraldine O'Shea and Kacey O'Driscoll. Having been down by fourteen points at half-time, and losing by six, in the opening round of the championship five weeks earlier, Cork are complete underdogs. But they're women possessed. They shouldn't be in contention, but Ryan has zoned in on their kick and hand passing, and these minimal improvements see Cork stun the reigning champions into a 1–9 to 4–13 defeat.

Only twelve games into the job, and Eamonn Ryan, Mary Collins, Frankie Honohan, Ger Twomey and Timmy O'Callaghan have won Cork's first Munster senior championship title in the thirty-year history of the sport. Juliet Murphy steps up and receives the Dairygold Cup. The winners' inscription lists Kerry fourteen times and Waterford ten.

During their celebrations, Cork players impersonate the former German soccer star Jürgen Klinsmann, throwing themselves on their tummies across the pitch. In 2014, when they match Waterford's tally of ten Munster titles, Ryan reminds them that 'it's far from Klinsmanns' they are now.

For Elaine Harte, that inaugural Munster trophy was a moment of reckoning.

'It was our first senior cup, so it took precedence, but beating the kingpins Kerry was the icing on the cake. All that history of being hammered by them and Waterford, and here we were. All that hurt from being looked down upon as not a serious football county changed that day. The 2004 league final had been the door opening, and that Munster final win was us walking through it. We knew we'd arrived.'

Their resolve, too, was starting to take shape.

'All the little battles throughout the 2004 championship helped,' says Mary O'Connor. 'We were on fire that day in the Munster final. The younger ones had already beaten Kerry, so they'd no fear, and the older ones had so much resolve from sticking through the beatings, and that's what stood to us. Our resolve was huge because we felt we weren't really given any support outside of our own families and the management team, and now we wanted to win every match because we were doing it for ourselves.'

•••

The All-Ireland quarter-final against Mayo comes around quickly and Cork believe like never before. Mayo have just suffered a fourteen-point defeat in the 2004 Connacht senior championship final to Galway and word on the street is that the westerners are spiralling downwards. But Cork are cuter than to read into it.

The game is set for 12 p.m. on 28 August 2004, in Tullamore, and Ryan and Collins have decided it's best for the team to travel the day before. The bus departs the Silver Springs Moran Hotel outside Cork city; however, just five minutes down the road, the engine light comes on and the driver is forced to pull onto the hard shoulder. They wait for another bus and don't reach the hotel in Tullamore until just before midnight.

Although tired, many of the players don't sleep, and it's evident that something is off come throw-in the following afternoon. They're criminally wasteful with the ball, and despite a late splattering of scores, they lose by four points (1–7 to 1–11). For the first time in Ryan's reign, the players are genuinely devastated.

'We were heartbroken,' says Juliet Murphy. 'I remember walking towards the tunnel underneath the stand and talking to Eamonn. He knew we were really disappointed, but he alluded to how much we'd come on in just a few months. We both knew there was room for improvement, but you could tell, at that moment, there was a vision forming about winning an All-Ireland. We had a real chance if we just kept working hard.'

At the same time as Ryan and Murphy are conversing, selector Timmy O'Callaghan calls manager Mary Collins aside. He informs her that he won't be involved in 2005 and that it's time for him to move on, but wishes her luck and puts things in perspective.

'Mary, you'd be very foolish to walk away from this,' O'Callaghan warns her. 'There's definitely an All-Ireland in this team, and you've to stick with them because you're the woman to lead them.'

O'Callaghan is right. Collins is the woman pulling all the strings behind the scenes, and although she's always felt it would be a learning process, she now knows the dream is a real possibility.

6

PEAS & CARROTS

*'If you haven't learned the meaning of friendship, you
haven't learned anything.'*
Muhammad Ali

The atmosphere is nervous, pensive even, for it's the first time
Eamonn Ryan has called a team meeting. It's 22 October
2004, and the girls from Beara have travelled almost three
hours to the Commons Inn on the outskirts of Cork city
to be there. Crammed into the small function room, the
players sense this is serious as Ryan hands each of them a
four-page document. The title reads 'The Dream Becoming
A Reality'. Their eyes light up at once. He's staying, and
now the vision of winning an All-Ireland title is in black
and white. It's no longer something they're talking about,
he's just given them a map of how to get there. It reads:

Our Vision:
To bring Cork to the top of ladies football, and to the same
level as the men.

Our Philosophy:
To be the best in everything we do.

Our Style of Play:
To win.

Our Goal:
To win the All-Ireland.

Our Game Plan:
Blanket defence and attacking with speed and style.

Objectives:
1. Not to be bullied this season.
2. Dictate pace of every game.
3. Win every game.
4. Win as a team.

Players:
1. Commitment.
2. Look after properly.
3. Understanding of what's going on.
4. Total confidence.

Facts:
1. We are as good as what's out there.
2. We are feared by the teams out there.
3. When we want, we can destroy any team.
4. We're going to have the best set-up.

Requirements:
1. Proper training facilities.
2. Proper coaching set-up.
3. Total understanding of roles.
4. A team that wants to be the BEST.

They absorb every word. 'As a team we were feared by everyone out there,' page three reads, 'but we don't believe in ourselves.' The dream can become a reality if they want it bad enough, but they need to believe.

Management tell the players what's needed and expected. All-Ireland champions Galway trained more than a hundred times in 2004, while Cork had only done seventy sessions, and won just 65 per cent of their games. The players have to realise the sacrifices needed to get to the top. They have to be more committed, loyal to their teammates and play with pride in the jersey. There's to be no cliques, no gossip and what's said in the dressing room, stays in the dressing room.

Management will work on tactics and look to improve themselves, goalkeepers will be given specific coaching and the squad will get a proper kit. The Farm in Bishopstown is to be their primary training base, and they'll train three times a week – Wednesday, Friday and Sunday – no more. Ryan is conscious of the importance of rest, given players' club, college and dual responsibilities, and he stresses that strongly from the top of the room. They'll use O'Connor Coaches and travel collectively as a group, and look professional with the county board's unified gear across the board.

They're representing something much bigger now than just themselves and Ryan puts it to them that they'll have a few weeks to decide as individuals if they're willing to give the commitment in 2005 that's being asked of them. But Elaine Harte is torn. She wants to play but she's about to relocate to Tipperary to live with her husband-to-be, John Doyle, and for weeks the county's number one goalkeeper is in knots mulling over what to do. She's scared by the level of dedication management are requesting and doesn't think she'll be able to live up to what they're looking for.

It's now the first week in January 2005 and it's time to confirm her status to manager Mary Collins. She picks up the phone and makes the call.

'Mary, sorry now, but I don't think I'll be able to give the commitment ye're looking for this year because I'm moving to Tipp,' Harte explains.

There's a brief silence on the other end.

'Look, Elaine, you're not the first person to ring me and say the same thing,' Collins replies, 'but all I'll say to you is this: what will you do if you're sitting in the stand in September and we're playing in Croke Park?'

Without even inhaling, Harte responds. 'I'll see you at training.'

She's in. They're all in.

•••

The 2005 national league begins against Kerry in Dromtarriffe. Ryan has added the likes of Ciara Walsh, Angela's younger sister, Elaine O'Riordan, Caoimhe Creedon and Deirdre O'Reilly, Sinéad's younger sister, to the panel. He has upped his own game too, by making drills physically more demanding and adding in a punching game to toughen them up; it's paying off with a thirteen-point win over the Kingdom (5–9 to 2–5).

'I knew we'd get somewhere after winning the first league game against Kerry,' says Ryan. 'The girls had committed and I'd seen that they were genuine. Kerry were a nemesis and now we'd beaten them comprehensively. It was the best possible start to the league we could have got, and I sensed we were moving in the right direction.'

Cork are much more economical with the ball and cohesive in attack. In 2004 they averaged only four scorers in the league, but just two games into 2005 and already seventeen have made the scoresheet. Jim McEvoy has joined the back-room team and management are beginning to get into the rhythm of things too, despite an argument between manager Mary Collins and selector Frankie Honohan.

'It was during the course of a 2005 league game early on,' says Collins. 'Frankie has a very shrewd football brain, but Emer Walsh at corner-back had given away two balls, and I thought we should take her off. Frankie turned to me and said that it was only because the girl was from Donoughmore that I wanted her off.

'That got to me and I said to him afterwards that I never wanted to hear a statement like that again. I was entitled to my opinion and so was he. I didn't give a feck where she was from. She made two mistakes and I should be entitled to say it if I wanted.

'After that there was never a bad word between us. We were still just getting past our own club rivalry, and if we hadn't, it would never have worked. Like the girls, we were finding our way as well.'

Cork blow past Kildare (3–14 to 1–3) and Monaghan

(2–18 to 2–3), before losing to Galway by four points (0–11 to 0–7). It's a reminder that Cork have to continually strive to be the best in every game, and that just because they're winning doesn't make them any more entitled to get their hands on a trophy.

A one-point win over Mayo (2–10 to 2–9) is when the penny drops. Cork lost to them three times in 2004, and this victory is like winning an All-Ireland in itself. The rivalry officially commences as Mayo are issued five yellow cards, and it takes a free kick from Valerie Mulcahy in the last minute to get the win.

Off the field things are going well too, with the county board securing a sponsorship deal with telecommunications giant Smart Telecom. The previous October, O2 – who were then sponsors of the Cork men's hurling and football teams – rejected a proposal from the board; however, Smart are eager to align themselves with an up-and-coming team in the fastest-growing sport in Ireland and agree to a €10,000 deal over twelve months, with further bonuses of up to €5,000. The deal will eventually extend to €25,000 in 2006.

The timing's perfect as Cork defeat Roscommon in the quarter-final (5–13 to 0–7) and Waterford in the semifinal (6–11 to 2–6) to set up a showdown with Galway in the final at Dr Hyde Park, Roscommon.

The venue infuriates Cork supporters as it's only 80 km from the Galway border, but given that the team has a good chance, they venture to Roscommon with hopes of witnessing history. However, on 17 April 2005, the heavens open and a waterlogged pitch at Dr Hyde Park is deemed unplayable just half an hour before throw-in. The fans who've travelled from Castletownbere on the Beara Peninsula have to get back into their cars and drive 354 km home again, while the county board grapples with having to foot a bill for €3,000 given that the squad of twenty-seven and five selectors understandably stayed in a hotel the night before the game.

Under the general rules, the game has to be played at the same venue with the same referee, but the Cork county board calls on the LGFA to make an exception, and suggests the game be played as a double header before the Cork and Galway men's national hurling league game in Páirc Uí Rinn the following weekend in front of a large crowd of both sets of supporters.

Instead, the game is fixed for the Gaelic Grounds in Limerick a fortnight later, but the postponement is somewhat of a boost for Cork given that Galway will be missing their top forward, now Chelsea soccer star Niamh Fahey, who's on duty with the Irish U19 women's soccer team in Spain. That said, even if Fahey is present, nothing's going to stop Cork from winning their first division one national league title.

Galway are the reigning All-Ireland champions and Cork are the only side to have beaten them in 2004, but Ryan's players are much more astute a year on and physically leaner and fitter. Even when Briege Corkery is sent to the sin bin for the last ten minutes, they've got the stamina. There's no question in their minds that they're going to win, even with fourteen players, because losing back-to-back national league finals is not an option.

Galway suffer a thirteen-point demolition (2–13 to 0–6) and Cork captain Juliet Murphy accepts the trophy from President of the LGFA Geraldine Giles. Valerie Mulcahy is named Player of the Match with a tally of 2–2 and, having won her first bronze All-Star statuette just months previously, she's beginning to stand out as the go-to forward for Cork. It would be the first of seven Player of the Match awards she'd win between 2005 and 2015.

The players are given ten days off to celebrate, but things are fairly calm, with just one night on the town. When they return to training on 11 May 2005, it's all ball work, but Ryan calls a meeting afterwards.

'We've two of the three things we want to win won,' he tells the squad. 'The Munster title in 2004 and the division one league last month. The All-Ireland is the only title that eludes us now. Just think of that.

'You also have a chance to change the perception of ladies football. It's not something to be patronised, it's a serious game, skilfully played by serious players,' he adds, reminding them that they are representing something paramount.

Ryan breaks it to them how he's rated their league performance based on individual ratings and the overall result is 126/200, with the player average of 6.3 scribbled into his Aisling-branded notebook. The exercise is to show them that they're good, but there's more to do. There's always more.

'Your work ethic has got better, but no matter what other teams do, we must always strive to improve. Everything from here on out is in your hands,' he says.

He's subtly bringing them down a peg or two, and telling them to up their game again ahead of the championship.

They beat Kerry in the opening round of the Munster senior championship in Killorglin (2–14 to 2–7) despite scoring just a solitary point from four penalties; then Waterford (0–16 to 1–8), before seeing off Clare (5–28 to 1–2) in a game in which Nollaig Cleary scores 4–8. But, despite her personal tally, Ryan opts not to start Cleary in the Munster final against Kerry in Killarney. The younger sister of All-Ireland-winning Cork footballer John Cleary is at a loss to know what she has to do to make the cut, but there's no moaning. She must simply go out and do her talking on the pitch when given the chance.

Coming off the bench wearing number 17 against Kerry, Cleary scores 1–4, and she gets the nod to start in the All-Ireland quarter-final against Meath. The team announcement, however, is delayed given that dual stars Briege Corkery and Rena Buckley are playing the night before in a Cork senior camogie championship final. Ryan is relieved when the call comes through that they've both survived injury free, and less than twenty-four hours later, Corkery is running herself into the ground again, earning the Player of the Match award in Cork's win over Meath (2–19 to 3–10).

Chatting in the dressing room afterwards, fellow dual star Mary O'Connor congratulates Corkery on her county win with Cloughduv Camogie Club.

'Jeez, Briege, well done girl, pity you couldn't celebrate last night,' she says, but eighteen-year-old Corkery turns and replies in all seriousness, 'I know, sure I only got to have three or four pints!'

Corkery's young but she is a character in the making. It was her primary school teacher at Rusheen NS, Gerard Coakley, who first spotted her talent while she was playing in a Sciath na Scol game aged just seven. One inter-school game featured teams combined of boys and girls, with the girls allowed to pick the ball from the ground, as per LGFA rules. Sporting a short haircut, the whistle was blown a number of times against Corkery for picking the ball up, but at the turnaround Coakley took it upon himself to talk to the referee and let him know about his mistake. When he pointed at Corkery, the referee's disbelieving response was, 'Him? Sure he's not a girl!'

But, in the summer of 2005, Corkery's waiting on her Leaving Cert results and enjoying life. In the team meeting in The Farm before the start of the Munster championship, Ryan had told the players that he didn't mind them having a drink, but emphasised the importance of being able to remember what they did the next morning. Legend has it that Briege Corkery stood up and, with complete honesty, said, 'I have a pint bottle before every match and I intend on still having it.' Ryan responded by saying it wasn't his way, but if it was hers, so be it. There are no rules, just high expectations.

'Briege was a messer when she first started, but she was so young too,' recalls Mary O'Connor, 'but no question about it, she'd deliver every single day and play beyond all expectations.

'Juliet was aghast at Briegy's "super Sundays", but Juls was always the consummate professional and most of us tried to be like her in terms of how we prepared. But Briege is in a league of her own. Her genetics should just be tested and kept because we'll never see the likes of her again. She's a phenomenon.'

In the 130-plus games that Corkery's played for the Cork seniors between 2004 and 2015, she's delivered at the highest level 95 per cent of the time, and Ryan is quick to point out that fact.

'There's a misconception about Briege,' he says. 'There's a myth that she has a cavalier attitude. Now, she doesn't worry herself to death about things, but that's a plus, and she treats every game as if it's her last. She's never ever injured, and to think she's playing at the highest level in both codes for so many years. That's because she's responsible and looks after herself, and never misses training. She loves the craic, but she just adores being on the field.'

•••

The squad are growing closer with every session as the 2005 championship heats up, and Mary O'Connor and Caoimhe Creedon are nicknamed 'Peas and Carrots' because of the banter they're providing. O'Connor had opted out of playing in the 2005 national league, but ahead of the championship Ryan encouraged her to come back. On her

first night, a subtle wink from Juliet Murphy said it all –
they needed her and she needed them.

Commuting from Dublin, where she is based in her role
as acting CEO of the Camogie Association, O'Connor
has to make up for lost time and prove herself worthy of
a starting spot in the All-Ireland semi-final. At 4.15 p.m.
she departs her office in Croke Park and on hitting the
Watergrasshill toll bridge on the outskirts of Cork city half
an hour before training at 7 p.m., she knows she's motoring
well. Timekeeping is something the dual star prides herself
on, but time is still against her. There's nothing else to do
but change while driving, and somehow she manages to
Wonder-Woman it into a sports bra, jersey, shorts and
socks – much to the delight of one passing truck driver who
honks his horn and throws her a thumbs up as he passes.

Mayo are next in the All-Ireland semi-final and
O'Connor isn't the only one with a point to prove, with
the possibility of playing in Croker floating in the back of
the players' minds. The morning of the game, Ryan calls
out the starting team. Corner-back Niamh Keohane is
demoted to the bench with one of her best friends, Bríd
Stack, replacing her.

'It was horrible because we were mighty buddies all
the way up from underage,' says Bríd Stack. 'Obviously I
wanted to win my place back given how close we were to
making the All-Ireland final, but at the expense of one of
your friends is tough. Niamh was understandably upset,
but before going out onto the pitch she hugged me and
said, "Give it your best", and that meant so much.'

O'Connor hasn't made the cut either, while Valerie Mulcahy is sidelined too, given an ankle injury she picked up against Meath in the All-Ireland quarter-final.

From the start, Cork look nervous out on the field in O'Moore Park, Portlaoise, and Mayo – bidding to appear in their third All-Ireland final in four years – are well acclimatised. At half-time Cork trail by five points and despite the introduction of Mary O'Connor at half-time, they are still five points adrift with seven minutes remaining. On the substitutes' bench, Valerie Mulcahy is pleading in her head for management to call her and with time running out selector Ger Twomey indicates to her to warm up, injury or no injury.

Her free-taking left leg is strapped heavily, but it doesn't stop her raising three white flags to bring Cork within two points with three minutes left. Then, as the tension rises, Mayo's Ciara McDermott and Marcella Heffernan are sent to the sin bin, and Cork's belief goes into overdrive. Caoimhe Creedon capitalises on a poor kickout as cracks begin to emerge in Mayo's earlier calm exterior. Using her trademark shimmy, Creedon avoids the out-rushing defender and sends the ball over the bar. Tie game, 0–12 to 1–9.

The neon yellow digits on the scoreboard at the far side of the pitch now tick into the final minute, and as Mary O'Connor rises to contest a ball, out of the corner of her eye she spots her club teammate Juliet Murphy surging through from midfield. O'Connor manages to palm the ball down into Murphy's path, and with twenty-nine seconds on the clock, Murphy floats it high and between the posts, putting Cork in front by a point (0–13 to 1–9).

Mayo make one last surge down the left flank in front of the stand. Cork supporters roar at their players to get back and defend – Cora Staunton is on the verge of winning possession. Her mind is on nothing but scoring an equaliser. But, out of nowhere, defender Ciara Walsh shoots across to flick the ball out of Staunton's hands and over the sideline just seconds before the hooter sounds. And, although it is Murphy's winning point that will be forever etched in memories as the moment that Cork reached their first ever senior All-Ireland final, it is equally Walsh's commitment in stopping a late Mayo equaliser that secures them a place in the history books (0–13 to 1–9).

Arms wide open and tears of joy streaming down her face, Norita Kelly sprints the length of the pitch to join in the pile-up that's forming in front of Elaine Harte's goal. They've done it. They're headed for Croker and a date with Galway in a repeat of the national league final.

'The feeling was incredible. We'd been playing football for years and to get to Croke Park was unreal,' says Elaine Harte. 'It wasn't even being in an All-Ireland final; it was getting to play in Croke Park. For the weeks before the final, my mum said to me, "I've never seen you hold your head up so high." We were just so happy and on cloud nine for a week, but we'd to remind ourselves to calm down. We'd nothing won yet.'

7

THE EMBRACE

'If you are afraid of failure,
you don't deserve to be successful.'
Charles Barkley

It's mid-September and the rain has been pelting down all day in Donoughmore, where Cork training is taking place. Puddles pothole the pitch and football boots Michael-Flatley their way through, avoiding any threat of twisting an ankle.

Juliet Murphy extends the warm-up to limit the chances of someone getting injured before the All-Ireland final in three weeks' time and standing there stretching, rain running off the tip of her nose, an immense feeling of contentment comes over her.

'Lads,' she says, looking around at her twenty-six comrades, 'this weather is pure muck but there's nowhere else I'd rather be.'

Murphy doesn't speak for the sake of it, and when her forehead crinkles you know it's serious. Every sentence is reviewed before it ever leaves her lips, and those few words generate an electric surge through the group.

This is where they want to be. Together.

Preparations are about to take a turn for the worse, however. Two weeks before the final, on Friday 16 September 2005, only three players are at training; the rest are involved in club fixtures. Valerie Mulcahy (Rockbán), Caoimhe Creedon (Naomh Abán) and Nollaig Cleary (Gabriel Rangers) are the trio not obliged to play with their clubs.

With a week and a half to go, eighteen players are in action in club championships, and only six players can make Cork's fourth-last session before the All-Ireland final. Ryan is furious. So is Mary Collins, who contacts a number of county board officials to get games postponed, but cooperation isn't very forthcoming from the clubs she's told. Ryan is flabbergasted, but it's the card they've been dealt and, although maddened, they'll have to make do.

Not only does Ryan have to contend with club obligations, he also has five dual players involved in a senior camogie All-Ireland final – Mary O'Connor, Angela Walsh, Briege Corkery, Rena Buckley and Cathriona Foley – against Tipperary, fourteen days before the football final. It's not the ideal situation, but Ryan has a way of turning negatives into positives.

He organises for the squad to travel to Dublin to watch the camogie All-Ireland final and the team takes in a training session in Abbeyleix, Co. Laois, on the way. Ryan has also arranged a tour of the Croke Park dressing rooms with his connections, and a thirty-minute kickaround on the pitch once the fans file out of the stadium after the camogie finals.

The effect the visit has on the players is considerable.

'In terms of our preparation, that day was massive for us,' Elaine Harte recalls. 'Seeing the camogie team win too, there was a sense of "We can feel like this." We saw how devastated Tipp were and the contrast was huge. We knew, there and then, we never wanted to lose in Croke Park.

'When it came to the dressing rooms, we couldn't get over that each player had their own locker. Even the size of the shower area was a big deal because you wouldn't have to wait for six people to finish before the next batch could go in. It sounds silly, but that's what was going through our heads. By the time our final arrived, we were long over the wow factor of it all.'

The kickaround in Croke Park gives their plain Puma Kings, Adidas Predators and Copa Mundials a chance to meet the ryegrass surface, which causes much debate as to what studs to favour. But suddenly there's a dull smacking noise – the sound a size four O'Neills football makes when it connects with a face.

Juliet Murphy is on one knee, hunched over and slightly disorientated. Unfortunately for her, she happened to be in the trajectory of a football launched from the right boot of the strongest player on the panel, Deirdre O'Reilly. Despite a wobble or two, Murphy gets to her feet, but already the jokes are flying that she's overwhelmed by the surroundings!

Today signals the deadline, too, for talk about the All-Ireland banquet at the Citywest Hotel on the night of the final. It's a distraction they don't need, and there isn't to be any more talk of stilettos, Sally Hansen fake tan or Shellac nails.

The Rebel County is presently on a GAA high, with the

hurlers winning the Liam McCarthy Cup under captain Seán Óg Ó hAilpín three weeks previously and Elaine Burke lifting the O'Duffy Cup with the camógs. It's a tall ask for the ladies footballers to win the Brendan Martin Cup at the first time of asking, but if they do it, it'll be a first senior treble in the history of Cork GAA.

With a week to go, Ryan asks Cork hurling goalkeeper Donal Óg Cusack to speak to the players, to give them a bit of advice and inspire them if he could. Cusack is to be in Donoughmore at 10.45 a.m. a week before the final, and, after travelling over an hour from Cloyne, he speaks to them in the dressing room for ten minutes. His passion for the GAA is fizzing, and the players can nearly reach out and touch it. He wants them to win, but he wants them to achieve so much more than that, and the room hangs on every word that's coated in his thick east-Cork accent.

'You can never be satisfied with just one All-Ireland girls. This has to be the start of a much longer journey, remember that,' he tells them.

They haven't won anything yet, but Cusack can see, even then, the conviction to achieve burning in their eyes.

Sunday 2 October is creeping up, and for the remaining sessions Ryan marks out the exact width of the warm-up area in Croke Park so the players can visualise the tight confines they'll be operating in. At the last session in the Mardyke, he names the starting fifteen. Aged twenty-eight, thirteen years older than the youngest, Mary O'Connor doesn't make the cut and she's gutted. But this will be the tenth All-Ireland final she'll be involved in given her dual player repertoire, and Ryan calls on her for some words of wisdom.

'Mary, you've been here before, what should we watch out for?' Ryan asks.

O'Connor's head is doing somersaults. What should she say?

'Well … there's no point in being too psyched up before going out because the warm-up will take thirty minutes and you'll be just wasting energy. Don't get carried away by the crowd when you run out either, just stay focused,' she says.

But containing those levels of excitement on the biggest day of your career isn't so simple, and that's what O'Connor's getting at. They have to be disciplined in ways they've never known before.

Mary Collins issues orders that they're to wear their red polo shirts and navy O'Neills tracksuits to Kent Train Station on Saturday as they take the train to Dublin the afternoon before the final. On board, they entertain themselves with a homemade quiz, with selector Ger Twomey making a dashing, flamboyant quizmaster.

How many cows are on Frankie's farm?

How much money did assistant manager Jim McEvoy pocket in his Lotto win?

How many football boots does Valerie Mulcahy own?

In no time they're passing Portlaoise and are told who they'll be rooming with at the Red Cow Moran Hotel at Newlands Cross. On arrival, county board delegate Fr Terry O'Brien says Mass at 6 p.m. He's a balding, bubbly chap, whose sermon relaxes them perfectly.

After a buffet-style dinner, a team meeting is called in an intimate function room and Ryan informs them of the schedule for the next day. Other than that, they're free to do as they please for the evening.

Some sleep easily, others get just a few hours. For Galway's Niamh Fahey it's a late night as she arrives into Dublin Airport, having played in the FIFA U19 European Championship qualifiers in Estonia.

Tomorrow, Cork will have to be glued to her.

•••

In the morning, the players meet for breakfast and at 11 a.m. stroll to the nearby Ballymount Industrial Estate, loosening limbs and inhaling fresh air. Every year since, bar 2013 and 2014, they've followed that routine. Stopping outside a run-down unit in the estate, they huddle together. Each member of management speaks calmly for a minute or so before Ryan has the last say.

In his hands he unfolds a copy of a local Galway newspaper and reads the headline aloud – it suggests the Tribeswomen have the final already sewn up.

'They're legends in their own underpants,' he declares.

He means no disrespect to their opponents, but the chuckle from the audience is the reaction he's looking for. His one-liners are legendary and they never fail to register a giggle or two. He's an expert in keeping them calm. Nothing Ryan does is over the top, and the players follow by example.

In the lead-up to any game, Ryan pores over the papers

and finds an article, or a line from a book he's reading, that he can relate to the players, and he will always bring it back to real life. He is an intelligent man, but he is talking to intelligent people. There's no roaring or shouting, and every word he utters is pertinent to them. It's all about them.

They stroll back and eat lunch at 1 p.m., with the bus departing at 1.30 p.m. Gear bags and water bottles are loaded and, as the Garda escort arrives, the enormity of it hits them. Defenders Angela Walsh and Bríd Stack sit side by side. In a couple of hours they'll stand shoulder to shoulder in their first official team photograph in Croke Park, and for every final they'll play together afterwards it'll be the same routine.

'Something Inside So Strong' by Labi Siffre plays over the speakers.

Something inside so strong,
I know that I can make it,
Though you're doing me wrong, so wrong,
You thought that my pride was gone,
Oh, no, something inside so strong.

Manager Mary Collins and liaison officer Eileen O'Brien are at the front of the bus; out of the players' view, they're holding hands. They're overcome by it all but realise the importance of not looking overwhelmed for the players' sake. The closer the bus gets to Jones' Road, the more frequent sniffles become and soon the majority are in tears. Stack and Walsh are silently comforting one another now.

Not a word is spoken but their hands are on each other's knees for support.

'You'd be looking out the window crying, not wanting to make eye contact with anyone,' says Stack, 'yet you know the person beside you is crying, and the person behind you and in front of you is, because the odd sniffle is a giveaway, and you know at that point there's no going back.'

Valerie Mulcahy is emotional too, but there are no tears. She chats quietly to the player beside her, but assistant manager Jim McEvoy glares at her to be quiet.

'Having a chat was my coping mechanism,' says Mulcahy. 'It was my way of dealing with the build-up, trying to keep things as normal as possible if I could. Everyone will deal with it differently. It's a very emotional journey, but at the same time, it's where I wanted to be.'

The bus pulls into the concrete underbelly of the Hogan Stand in Croke Park. It's dimmer and darker than they expect and there's nowhere to hide now. Officials direct them towards Dressing Room One. Bríd Stack positions her gear bag neatly in the locker next to her clubmate Deirdre O'Reilly, with Mary O'Connor flanking her on the other side. Angela Walsh is doing the same across the room and that exact seating arrangement will remain standard for the next five years until O'Connor's last final in 2009.

The awe-factor of their surroundings has long dissipated and they make their way out the tunnel to sit in the stand and watch the junior All-Ireland final between Sligo and Armagh.

'I remember turning around when I got out and being

so nervous,' says Stack. 'I couldn't even look into the crowd. As we were sitting there, the Galway team came out and their captain, Aoibeann Daly, turned and gave a small wave to someone in the crowd, and I thought, "How's she doing that – waving?" I couldn't even make eye contact, not to mind lift my eyes off the floor!'

Elaine Harte is enduring the same trepidation and the butterflies are flapping.

'In my head, I'm saying, "Don't look up into the stand and don't get engrossed in the moment." You have to appreciate it, obviously, and take it all in, but I didn't want to be acting the maggot, jumping around with the excitement of it all.'

Galway on the other hand look like they're at home. It's twelve months since they won their first senior All-Ireland title. In 2004, they were unaware of the unwritten rule in ladies football that fake tan is to be worn on All-Ireland final day, but today, with headphones in and sunglasses on, they're looking ever so bronzed as they glide behind the goal at the canal end during half-time of the junior final.

Eamonn Ryan is watching from the sideline, attentive to their every move.

'I knew then we'd beat them. I didn't think their heads were in the right place. Not that I knew for certain, I just had a feeling. They weren't being cocky or arrogant, they're a lovely bunch, but I just sensed a vibe of complacency. They'd won the year before and were after beating Mayo a few times since, who, like us, were their nemesis, and maybe that had got to their heads.

'I watched them walking around and I thought to myself, "We're going to win this." I wouldn't be like that normally, I'd be more the glass is half empty, but our crowd looked much more serious.'

Back in the dressing room, Ryan makes a point of presenting each player with their jersey. Assistant manager Jim McEvoy, who spent time as logistics manager with the Cork senior hurlers, suggested he do so. Alone for a few minutes, with no officials floating about, management and players huddle together. With arms tightly squeezed around shoulders and waists, Ryan presents number 30 and works his way down to number 1; the captain is always last to accept her jersey. The exchange with Juliet Murphy is a powerful one. A sensitive one.

'Anyone who gets to an All-Ireland final deserves to have their jersey presented to them. This isn't just a day out in Dublin, you've already achieved something by getting here,' Ryan tells them.

In his pre-match talk, he asks the players if any of them noticed the man in the wheelchair on the footpath in Phibsboro on the way. They had.

'Well, there's worse things in life than losing today,' Ryan says matter-of-factly, and heads straight for the door.

In front of 23,358 fans, Dublin referee Tony Clarke gets the final underway, but Cork's start is miserable. The pace and space is something they've never encountered, and in midfield the industrious Norita Kelly can't even catch her breath.

Despite this breathless start, at half-time Cork trail by

only a point (0–3 to 0–4) and Ryan knows they're within touching distance. He's confident about how they're doing, but at the same time he's concerned that the players might lose heart because they're not converting their chances. But The Master keeps the instructions simple.

'Keep doing what you're doing, but every player has to become a defender now,' he stresses.

In Galway's previous five games, they've scored sixteen goals, and Niamh Fahey is posing a threat. But, with every mini-defensive battle won by Cork in the second half, fuses of belief begin to ignite across the pitch.

Nollaig Cleary's left leg adds another point to the scoreboard. She can't get over the fact that she's actually kicked a point in Croke Park. For the next few minutes she secretly smiles to herself, content with her moment in the limelight. Had she been taken off there and then, it wouldn't have bothered her too much, for she thought she'd made it. But momentum is swinging fast in Cork's favour and Cleary wants more. She senses, as they all do, that the game needs to be closed out.

Valerie Mulcahy is loving it, living the dream, and Galway coach Richard Bowles has to call future two-time Six Nations winner Claire Molloy from the stand, with instructions to stop number thirteen from doing any more damage. Molloy's introduction works, but a deliciously placed penalty on the fifty-first minute by Mulcahy means Galway's hopes of back-to-back titles are diminishing.

The full-time hooter pierces the Dublin skyline and the pixels on the screen to the left of Hill 16 flicker 'Cork 1–11,

Galway 0–8'. Almost instantly, thousands of supporters flood the pitch, like paper clips to a magnet, and no sooner has goalkeeper Elaine Harte thrown her hands in the air than there's a teenage boy running straight for her, jumping and cheering in her face. She doesn't have a clue who he is, but the joy in his voice says it all.

She manages to find a few of the backs to celebrate with, but the crowd is literally running at them from all directions. Rubbing their heads, patting their backs. It's mayhem. Things start to get a little rough, so they negotiate their way across the pitch towards the Hogan Stand. Wearing tracksuit pants makes it easier for Harte to blend in and avoid more attention, but by the time she makes it over, a mini army of security men have formed a ring in front of the Hogan Stand steps.

The biggest one of them happens to be staring down at Harte, before returning his stern gaze over her head to scan the crowd. She waits a second to see if he'll let her pass. Surely there's no secret password?

'I'm a player,' she chirps up to the base of his chin.

He doesn't flinch.

Grabbing her white Smart Telecom-branded top, Harte raises her voice a little higher, 'Look, look – my jersey, my jersey!'

He looks – but, no, he still doesn't believe her.

The others are climbing the steps towards the Brendan Martin Cup now and she's pleading with him.

'My jersey, my jersey – Look! My boots, my boots!'

'Boots?' he croaks.

'Yeah! Boots! Boots! They're my boots! I'm the Cork goalkeeper!'

And with that, he let her through.

•••

In the presence of the Irish president Mary McAleese, Juliet Murphy hoists the cup over her head, her eyes on the heavens above. She's played here once before as an eleven-year-old girl in the 1991 INTO Mini Sevens. All the struggles to reach this moment have been worth it for Cork's most athletic player ever. After thirty years in the wilderness, Cork have won their first senior All-Ireland title, and with it complete what the media will soon label 'The Rebel Treble' – as they join Tipperary and Galway in the elite group of counties who have won all four senior All-Ireland titles in men's and ladies GAA.

Cup in hand, Murphy manages to find Eamonn Ryan in the tunnel and they embrace. Murphy's head dips into Ryan's right shoulder and his hand fastens securely around the back of her neck. He beams with pride and Murphy does too.

It's Mary O'Connor's first senior football All-Ireland medal after eleven years of trying, but the emotion is initially a bittersweet one. Her honesty is refreshing.

'In truth, initially, part of me was devastated because I hadn't been picked to start. I came on as a sub after twenty-five minutes but I found it hard to be happy because I hadn't actually started. But that was selfish of me. I thought of where I'd come from, not having played in the league, and of course where we'd come from as a team.

'I wasn't long copping myself on. Of course we were delighted, but I don't think we realised the magnitude of what that victory meant, even to those of us who'd been around a while. I think deep down we all craved so much more than just one title.'

The private celebrations commence in the warm-up area, with champagne spraying across its synthetic grass. The five double All-Ireland-winning dual players indicate that a trip to Quinn's Bar around the corner is the done thing. They would only have an hour or so to share a well-earned drink with supporters before departing to get ready for the All-Ireland final banquet at the Citywest Hotel later that night. But rounding the players up at Quinn's was a task manager Mary Collins hadn't envisaged as part of the job.

'Trying to get them all back on the bus was a complete nightmare! Frankie was saying, "They're like a herd of cows – you put one lot of them in, and they're gone out the other door!"' Collins remembers with a chuckle.

The bus from the Red Cow to Citywest is like a moving nightclub. Once there, they join the junior teams, Armagh and Sligo, and also teams from North America, Canada, Britain, London, Europe, New York and Australasia that have taken part in an International Ladies Football Tournament in Dublin in the week running up to All-Ireland final day.

Sadly for Cork, the gloss of their first win is overshadowed by the attention given to the international teams for the majority of the function. A disappointed Galway player's father makes note of it and approaches a member of the Cork management team. 'Did ye win an All-Ireland today?' he asks sarcastically. 'Coz Jaysus I'd swear 'twas some foreign team won it!'

The players carry on celebrating regardless. The following morning heads are sore as they regroup in the reception at the hotel, reading the morning's papers, disseminating match reports and smiling at accompanying photographs as they wait for a Garda escort to take them to Our Lady's Children's Hospital in Crumlin.

Beaming county board officers put the wheels in motion for the homecoming to Cork and the 5 p.m. train from Heuston Station is booked. Iarnród Éireann has decked the entire train in red and white, and as they pull out of the station the first song is sung, and they don't stop singing until the two-and-a-half-hour journey comes to an end in the Rebel County.

At Mallow Train Station they step onto the concourse and wave to the crowd, before heading for Kent Station in the city. Hundreds are gathered and RTÉ television cameras record Mary Collins and Juliet Murphy carrying the Brendan Martin Cup onto Cork soil, before an open-top bus takes the team through the city as far as the Imperial Hotel on the South Mall, where the Lord Mayor of Cork, Councillor Deirdre Clune, greets them on a makeshift stage.

Autographs are signed, hugs and high fives are dished

out, but time is pushing on and they must leave for Juliet Murphy's home club in Donoughmore, where bonfires blaze at the crossroads and hundreds have already descended on Pat Barry's Bar. They've celebrated All-Irelands in ladies football in Donoughmore before, but they've never celebrated the biggest one of all.

Somehow, when everything dies down at 5 a.m., Mary O'Connor lands herself in a bush walking the country roads back to Murphy's house, but she finds her way eventually. Murphy's parents, Michael and Mary, have sacrificed any chance of sleep, having donated their bedroom to accommodate the squad's arrival. Instead, they sit at the kitchen table drinking coffee until it's time to turn on the hob and feed whatever bodies surface in the morning for a fry.

Others headed off earlier in the night, with Norita Kelly, a trainee accountant, and Angela Walsh, a substitute teacher, working the next morning. Defender Norma Kelly, a bank teller by profession, wisely booked off a few days in advance for celebratory purposes. But Mary Collins is peeved upon hearing a rumour that a high-profile Kerry footballer working with Kelly was allegedly given a week's holidays with pay despite losing his respective All-Ireland football final the week before. It's pure speculation, but, nonetheless, even the thought of it has irked Collins no end.

8

SAND, SWEAT AND SUNBURN

'There is no way around the hard work. Embrace it.'
Roger Federer

Armagh's Maebh Moriarty crumbles hard and fast. The collision with Briege Corkery happens right in front of the Cork dugout during the 2006 division one quarter-final, and there's no mistaking the cracking sound. The daughter of former Armagh centre-back Paddy Moriarty has broken her leg.

Cork physio Michael Cotter springs from the timber bench and Moriarty's protruding femur says it all. Although in agony, the Clann Éireann woman lies motionless in the cold February air for the next thirty-five minutes. A mound of hoodies and jackets is all she has to shield her from shock before the ambulance takes her to the Midland Regional Hospital in Portlaoise.

There was no malicious intent from Corkery, it's just one of those horrid, inexplicable injuries that happen when least expected.

The quarter-final resumes as soon as the ambulance trundles off the pitch in Ratheniska, Co. Laois, and a win for Cork signifies an entire year unbeaten – seventeen victories on the trot. In a matter of weeks they retain the league title against first-time finalists Meath, and it's Cork's fifth final win out of six in two years under coach Eamonn Ryan.

His intention now, however, is to take the team on a training holiday to Lanzarote before the Munster championship begins. Ryan's been to Puerto del Carmen before with the Cork senior men's football team and the objective is the same as it was then: to bring the squad back down to earth. The funny thing is, the players aren't remotely above themselves, but Ryan is a deep thinker, pragmatic, wary even, and he's not giving complacency an inch.

They spend a week in the sun, but for five days, twenty-seven ladies train like animals. Winning habits have dissolved the bedrock of rivalry that existed for so many years in the senior set-up, but now it's burning calf muscles and aching limbs during beach sessions that galvanises them.

On the first day after checking in, the squad arrive down to the pool, like a large family of country bumpkins, milk-bottle in colour, with no notion of slathering on a bit of suncream. A typical Irish contingent on the continent. Ryan requested that each player pack their own football and they begin their own game of ball at the poolside.

Midfielder Norita Kelly makes a run for the water to catch a kick pass, but as she pushes off on her right leg it suddenly loses its grip on the tiles and flies backwards, high into the air, with nothing to stop her from smacking her head on the concrete ground. Everything turns to slow motion as Kelly begins her descent. But the momentum of her run takes her a fraction beyond the kerbing of the pool and she crash-lands into the water. She surfaces smiling, with ball in hand. Kelly earns the nickname 'Slipper' for the remainder of their sojourn, but Cork are lucky their midfield anchor hasn't suffered a serious head injury.

That night, dinner is in the hotel restaurant, but by the time the dessert menus appear, there's no sign of Ryan. An hour later he returns, drizzled in sweat. He's walked a couple of miles in search of the perfect spot on Playa de Los Pocillos beach where the team can train the following day. Mary Collins relays instructions for players to be in the hotel foyer at 9 a.m. and collectively they'll retrace Ryan's footsteps. After a fifteen-minute walk, they arrive at the smoothest part of the beach, sheltered perfectly by a nearby rock face, and everything is already laid out – cones, ladders, balls and more cones.

Ryan's been up since the crack of dawn preparing for the session, and the team trains for the next three hours, with water breaks dotted in between. The girls' leg muscles are overflowing with lactic acid from treading in the sinking sand – but the sand is giving way to their determination. Their faces stew in sweat as salt specks crystallise on the corner of their mouths. Everything stings.

After cooling down in the sea for twenty minutes, they wander back, red raw, to the hotel for a bite to eat and a siesta before a pool session at 4 p.m.

The following day they return to their private plot and perspire all over again. The players are dreading it, however, because they know Ryan's famous 'three-track' or 'All-Black' runs are about to be unleashed. An exercise in cardiovascular stamina, three-track runs consist of three tracks – 21 metres, 40 metres and 80 metres – which are sprinted. Divided into groups, the older players are cute enough to do the toughest run first. They sprint 21 metres, three times and back. Then the next group take off, sprinting 40 metres out and back twice, and then both groups unite to sprint the final 80 metres and back. The catch is they only have thirty seconds to complete each run and, not only that, they'll do three sets with just ninety seconds to recover between each set.

It's tough going any day, but in thirty-degree heat in June it's torture. Ryan's taking training to a whole new level, a level that will see Cork deliver an unbeaten season in 2006, the only one under Ryan's reign.

That evening, sunburn melts into the players' pores. Some are worse than others, and Laura Power and Claire O'Donoghue's feet are destroyed. Rena Buckley goes by the name 'Patches' for her naive attempt to apply suncream. Bríd Stack has had to ask selector Frankie Honohan and his wife, Nell, for their natural manuka honey remedy to regulate her body temperature, given that lying in her bikini on the cold tiles of her bedroom floor hasn't done much to alleviate her condition.

For the next two days, Stack is forced to wear an Argentina soccer jersey because it's the only thing she can find with long sleeves to protect her from the sun.

The squad relax and cool down on their balconies for an hour or two, watching the sunset, before strolling to a nearby restaurant for dinner where Mary Collins issues rehydration orders. The players are yet to have their one night off during which they're allowed to drink, but at the end of dinner a singsong commences without a drop of alcohol in sight.

It lasts an hour and a half, with Rena 'Patches' Buckley lashing out 'Bold Thady Quill' and Caoimhe Creedon serenading the warm evening air with 'Caledonia'. Ryan loves a singsong as much as the next person, but he's getting tetchy the longer it lingers on, eager to plan the following day's session.

For ramblin', for rovin', for football or courtin',
For drinkin' black porter as fast as you'd fill ...

Two wealthy Englishmen are quietly observing the team from the corner of the restaurant and, after an hour or so, they signal to Ryan to join them and ask about the singing Irish troupe. He duly fills them in and the English gents can't get over how self-contained and grounded the team is. They're involved in sport in the United Kingdom, but they've never seen unity like it. The girls aren't looking for attention, they're just enjoying each other's company, enjoying life, and the fact they're all on the same football team is a bonus. The rivalries have now long evaporated.

I don't know if you can see,
The changes that have come over me
In these last few days I've been afraid,
That I might drift away
I've been telling old stories, singing songs,
That make me think about where I've come from ...

They hand Ryan a €50 note to buy a round of drinks for the team and wish him luck, but instead Ryan asks the barman to put it towards the bill for dinner.

The evening is a snapshot of what Cork will become known for off the field in the next decade; how they touch so many people's – even strangers' – lives just by how they carry themselves. This is Ryan's third year driving the chariot, but it's at that moment he realises he needn't ever worry about the players getting ahead of themselves.

'There was never a hint of it in their demeanour,' he says. 'It's one of those things I noted then because I get very touchy if anyone gets above themselves. If they started to get notions about their own greatness, the next thing they'd do is get judgemental and the natural follow-on then is to find fault with others, with us, the management, with one another; but they've never done that.

'The thing about ego, too, is that you've to realise it can quickly make shit of you. You have to subjugate it. Not kill it, subjugate it.'

Although training is energy sapping, the players are enjoying every minute. Ryan's varied the sessions, including two at the local football stadium, El Campo Municipal, where they play twelve-a-side rugby the length of the field. Games of soccer are also organised for beach sessions but, much to the surprise of onlookers, this athletic-looking bunch are hopeless.

'Only two or three could play soccer while the rest of us were just mulluckers,' laughs Bríd Stack. 'We set up goals and Angela would just hoof the ball down the pitch, and as the ball's coming through the air we're all panicking about how not to handle it. The next thing, Geraldine [O'Flynn] comes out of nowhere and volleys it into the back of the net … with her hand!'

Ten years on, O'Flynn is still in Stack's phone book as 'Geraldino'!

But the training holiday isn't without a blip. One night two players decide to sneak out on the town without permission and it isn't long before Ryan and selector Ger Twomey notice they haven't returned from dinner with the rest of the squad. In the early hours of the morning, they manage to find the culprits, but there's no repercussions because Ryan has no rules. The father in him just wanted to make sure they got home safely. The following morning, however, their teammates aren't long revealing how worried management were, and the duo apologise to manager Mary Collins.

To this day, the players will not divulge who the culprits were, such is their loyalty to each other. Soon after that incident, they agree on a saying to reiterate their commitment to the cause – 'you're either on the train, or you're off of it'. It was time to get back on track.

•••

The opening round of the 2006 TG4 Munster senior championship against Waterford is set for 7.30 p.m. in Dungarvan but, despite all the hard work done in Lanzarote, things are out of Eamonn Ryan's control. At 1.30 p.m., 80 km down the road in a place called Callan in Kilkenny, seven dual players – Angela Walsh, Briege Corkery, Rena Buckley, Mary O'Connor, Cathriona Foley, Regina Curtin and Elaine O'Riordan – are lining out in the All-Ireland senior camogie championship against the Cats, and Ryan must sweat it out to see if they'll come through injury free. Communication has been good between Ryan and Cork camogie manager John Cronin, but fixture clashes are something neither have their say in.

Player welfare wasn't debated then as much as it is now, but for the players themselves it's more of an inconvenience than anything. They want to be out on the field, starting for both teams preferably, so they're not going to rock the boat or moan about it. They're out almost seven nights a week between club, college and county training, and their commitment is only ever truly seen by their families and loved ones. They try to make every training session they can, and social lives and relationships are put on hold. Today, gear bags are packed along with lunch boxes of pasta and chicken to eat en route to game two, and that's just how they roll.

Mary O'Connor's been playing both codes since she was seventeen and doubling up is second nature to her. She plays her part in beating Waterford in Dungarvan with the footballers, but the two sides will meet again in the Munster final in the Gaelic Grounds, Limerick. O'Connor, however, is struggling with her confidence.

It's hard to believe given the strong exterior her war face paints, but deep down, one of the greatest dual players in the history of the GAA is suffering.

O'Connor had twenty-one possessions in the subsequent Munster football final but didn't score a single point, and to say she's having a crisis of confidence is an understatement.

'Confidence was never my friend,' O'Connor reveals. 'Throughout my whole career I worried about what people thought of me as a footballer and that was my biggest problem. I was very introverted and people probably thought I was strange, but I just didn't have as much faith in myself when it came to football. Camogie was different because as a defender I knew I could just work really hard, but in football, as a forward, I felt I needed to be scoring.

'I didn't approach Eamonn about it because I was embarrassed. I thought he might think, "Who's this one now? Would she ever cop on? She's been around for years", but he could see himself I was struggling.

'He has a fantastic empathy with players. If you made a mistake, or if you weren't going well, he had an ingenious way of empathising with you. Maybe it's because he played himself, but players appreciated that and it's another reason why we gave him our all.'

O'Connor is brutal, too, for dwelling on missed chances and could spend an entire match embroiled in an internal struggle while the game passed her by, but a simple anecdote from Ryan one day changes all that. During a cool-down after a training session, he tells the players about former Newcastle United star Alan Shearer's approach to missed chances.

'Shearer has scored 283 goals in his career, including a record 260 in the Premier League, but he's missed thousands of chances,' he says. 'But Shearer's way of not getting bogged down by the misses is to give himself ten seconds to think about the opportunity he's just fluffed. Ten seconds, that's it, and he moves on.'

In the aftermath of the Munster final, however, Ryan and selector Ger Twomey can see O'Connor's conflict written all over her face. They don't say a thing, but instead call on the services of long-serving cameraman Pat Lynch to compile video clips of the good things O'Connor did over the sixty minutes of the final so she can see for herself how valuable her contribution is. This, in a time when video analysis was in its infancy. They do the same for other players in need of a pick-me-up.

Cork might be the reigning league and All-Ireland champions, but every high-achieving athlete has their insecurities, and in Ryan's own understanding and subtle way, he'll help his players any way he can.

At the next training session, O'Connor starts counting to ten.

•••

Mayo are next in the All-Ireland quarter-final but with it comes two curveballs for manager Mary Collins. The first is thrown her way in the warm-up. Briege Corkery is whizzing around cones, giving and going. Her luminous yellow bib is trying to keep up with her and she's ready for this one. The sweat is already twinkling across her forehead, but today she's wearing a white headband tasked to soak up the residue.

Rena Buckley can't help but look at her. There's something different. 'That's odd,' Buckley thinks to herself, 'Briege never wears headbands.'

A photographer appears to have noticed too, and calls Corkery to the sideline to take a picture. She smiles, as he asks her to turn the headband around. On the front, in red print, it reads 'Corona Extra'.

The photographer has been tipped off by the marketing firm responsible for asking Corkery to wear the headband to promote the drinks company Corona, for which a few euro is thrown her way. She was asked to wear it and obliged, not foreseeing the furore it would cause.

The following day, the photograph adorns the front of the sports pages with the headline 'Corkery enjoys the limelight'. She didn't see any harm in it given that Cork hurlers Niall McCarthy and Kieran Murphy both wore Corona-branded football boots, and what's the difference if she wears a headband?

Mary Collins' blood is boiling. She's been caught on the hop and it isn't yet known if any action will be taken against Cork following their win against Mayo (2–12 to 1–11) as a consequence of Corkery's wardrobe faux pas. According to Rule 40 in the official ladies football rulebook at the time, 'Markings allowed on playing gear, kit bags, etc., shall be manufacturers or sponsors names, crest or logo … individuals in breach of the rules shall be liable to suspension.' However, the question is asked whether headbands come under the term 'playing gear'. They don't and Corkery is given a pardon.

Collins has more woes, however. At the final whistle the same day against Mayo in O'Moore Park, Portlaoise, she's approached by the CEO of the LGFA, Helen O'Rourke, and the then president, Geraldine Giles.

'I didn't know anything about the Briege situation until after the game, and they were livid over it,' says Collins. 'But they were cross with me too, because we wore the national league final jerseys the same day, which had league sponsors "Suzuki" written across the back of them, and of course, this was the TG4-sponsored championship being shown live on TG4.

'Outside the dressing room they were flying questions at me and I didn't have a clue what they were on about. But then I realised. They had every right to be angry, but we only had one set of jerseys. They couldn't believe it. We were All-Ireland and league champions, and all we had was one set of free jerseys that we got in the league final. In hindsight we should've thought of it, but we just brought the jerseys we had and that was it.'

It's just as well that a few weeks earlier the team decided not to allow TG4's cameras to follow them for the purpose of a documentary on the 2006 championship campaign. Ryan had been approached about it and he put the request to the players. It was their call.

Following a challenge match in the University of Limerick, the players sat in the dressing room and debated the pros and cons of the documentary. No one was in doubt as to the excellent coverage the Irish broadcaster and the likes of Gráinne McElwain, Micheál Ó Domhnaill, Brian

Tyers and Rónán Ó Coisdealbha give to the sport, and this was a chance for the players to promote the game they love.

But the count came in and the vote was no. The thought of cameras entering their world – a world that's secret and sacred to them – didn't sit well. And besides, they were wary – wary of themselves, that they might not retain their All-Ireland title.

There's always an element of self-doubt, even to this day. Ryan regularly plants the seed. There's a fine line between being confident and cocky, and it's that droplet of doubt that's the slim difference, and Ryan is a pro, knowing the exact moment to turn the tap on, or turn it off.

Against Laois in the All-Ireland semi-final, there's no stopping them, and Cork win 1–12 to 0–8, but Ryan is suspicious of the youthful Armagh side they'll face in the All-Ireland final in Croke Park. So cautious in fact, he runs his players into the ground in the lead-up.

9

THE STARS ALIGN

'A good player can play great when the feeling is upon him; whereas, a great player can play great when he wants to.'
Bob Torrance

The hype goes up another notch at the press night in the Mardyke Arena ahead of the 2006 All-Ireland final. Reporters sit in the sports complex's foyer, teasing answers out of the players.

'What is it Cork have to do to retain the All-Ireland?' Like Stepford wives, the answers are more or less the same – 'Respect Armagh.'

They've been listening to Eamonn Ryan, who's anxious about how they'll fare against the northerners. The squad have absorbed his cautiousness. At the same time, they're more comfortable with the media attention the second time around. They now know what interviews entail and enjoy the opportunity to promote their sport, a sport that's beginning to attract the attention of diehard GAA fans for its less cynical style of play.

Forward Regina Curtin is asked to write a diary piece for a local Cork daily newspaper to give an insight into a player's preparations ahead of an All-Ireland final, and she happily puts pen to paper:

Sunday, 24 September 2006

It's one week to All-Ireland final day. I wake early because I'm used to it with Sunday morning training sessions, but today is different. The Cork senior camogie club championship semi-finals are on and because of the involvement of a few of our squad, the footballers decided to have training after so everyone will be present, even if they're not training.

I arrive in Glanmire at 4.30 p.m. for training at 5 p.m. Michael Cotter, our physical therapist, is setting up to meet the walking wounded. Val is first up, then me, and the list continues. I get my rub and some painful treatment for my elbow. I'm recovering from an arm break but I keep reminding myself 'no pain, no gain'.

Juls and the gang have started the warm-up so I fall in and there's a definite energy in the air.

I look around at the girls, we all look focused and the vibe is good.

Training is light and we finish with a game. The bibs are given out and I'm on the yellow team, marking Sinéad (O'Reilly) – 'Lots of running then', I think to myself. The game is lively and the girls are pushing hard. The team's still not named so places are up for grabs and we all want to make an impression.

The surface is heavy, but it's not surprising after all the rain. We're still adjusting to the greasy ball and the damper autumn conditions, but the game has some good passages of play. We finish with sprints, keeping the feet sharp I guess, and Juls takes us for the cooldown.

Management have organised a meal at the Silver Springs Moran Hotel, and afterwards we watch a few video clips of Armagh's semi-final win over Galway.

We discuss how Armagh could threaten us. A few opinions are voiced and we leave the room knowing Armagh will be tough opposition. We respect that, and we know it will come down to who wants it more.

I go home feeling drained, but satisfied. The excitement is starting to creep in.

Monday, 25 September

I wake early again. My first duty is a gym session. My elbow is progressing nicely. Jim (McEvoy) collects me and we head to the Kingsley Hotel for a weights session. I want to maximise my chances for Sunday so I'm making every effort to squeeze as much out of my arm as possible. The session is intense and my arm feels like jelly by the end of it and, as I stand under the shower, my arm is shaking.

Normally in the evening I might go for a run or maybe just a walk, but I decide to get as much rest as possible especially after the previous three weeks of intense training. After coming out of the cast, I feel that I've lost a considerable amount of fitness so a lot of work needs to be done if I stand any chance against the girls from the North.

I go to bed early as tomorrow we're jetting off to Dublin for some pre-match interviews. I rest my head on my pillow and ponder on the thought of being in Donoughmore this night next week, hopefully celebrating at a homecoming.

Tuesday, 26 September

The alarm beeped at 7 a.m. and I'm ten minutes behind schedule, arriving late to Cork Airport. I abandon the car and run like I'm possessed to the departures lounge.

Jim (McEvoy), Juliet (Murphy), Caoimhe (Creedon) and myself land in Dublin, where we head straight to Croke Park. We change into our gear and make our way down to the sideline. There we meet Rena (Buckley), who is already in Dublin because of college.

The next hour or so passes quickly with photos being snapped and TV crews and radio stations getting the final thoughts of both camps. I must admit my involvement was minor. Juliet, however, is bombarded with microphones and different recording devices. She's coolness personified and I admire her composure. Caoimhe and Rena capably oblige to do interviews *as Gaeilge* for TG4 and soon enough the formalities are done.

All that's left to do is collect the kit for Sunday and leave for the airport. The flight is delayed due to bad weather, but thankfully we land back safely in Cork Airport, and head straight to training in The Farm. The session started at 6.30 p.m. and we make it out onto the field fifteen minutes late. The mood is good. The tempo is high, and you can tell we're definitely preparing for battle.

Wednesday, 27 September

I wake with palpitations, having dreamt about the game. The result was in our favour. Maybe it's a sign?

We've training tonight again, and it's the last trip of the

year to The Farm before Sunday's showdown. How time flies. It seems it all began only weeks ago, yet a successful league campaign and a summer of championship has passed. A feeling of finality and nostalgia comes over me as I drive there. This is our last training session in the year, and it'll all boil down to just sixty minutes.

Training is light, and I sense that Sunday can't come quick enough for us. We're ready.

Eamonn calls us into the meeting room after and Cork hurler Seán Óg Ó hAilpín is standing there waiting to speak to us.

He mentions three things about his match preparation that stick in my mind:

1. Never underestimate your teammates – they're the ones you'll look to if you're in trouble on Sunday.
2. Never underestimate your opposition – complacency can cost you games.
3. Never underestimate the prize – after all, it's what we've been training for, for the last nine months.

Thursday, 28 September

I wake up with a giddy feeling. Jim and I are heading on another expedition to Dublin. My mission is to hopefully curtail the flamboyant and downright cheeky Dustin the Turkey on RTÉ.

It's been arranged that an Armagh and Cork representative go on live television and challenge the 'bird' himself, or at least try and get a word in edgeways. We fly to

Dublin Airport and kill some time at St Stephen's Green Shopping Centre, where we spot former President of the United States, Bill Clinton, who's there to carry out a book signing. I manage to get around some security men and before I know it, I'm shaking Bill's hand!

At RTÉ, we're greeted by the Ladies Gaelic Football Association's PR representatives. I'm introduced to Armagh's Patricia McEvoy, and we're whisked off to make-up. The show goes well, and it's over before we know it. Dustin asks what celebrity I'd have as the Cork captain, and of course I had to say Bill, having met him that morning!

On the train journey home, I begin thinking, and hoping, that on the next train back to Cork I'll be surrounded by my teammates, but more importantly that the Brendan Martin Cup will be with us.

Friday, 29 September

Today is the day of final preparations. The sun peeps through the curtains. The day is fresh and I decide to check the weather forecast. I'm hoping Sunday will be dry, at least for the game. I'm trying to decide which boots would be most suitable – long studs, multi studs or blades. It's been a talking point at the last few training sessions.

My day's duties include collecting fruit for the weekend, a trip to the dentist, and a visit to the beauty salon. The only interruptions are a few phone calls from my dad. I think he's starting to get nervous. It's funny really how it's not just your own life that becomes so involved in these occasions, but your family gets sucked into the build-up as well.

Messages and well wishes are flying in, and it's only now it's hitting me. I find that I get so used to training, playing games and then some more training, that sometimes I forget the significance of being part of such big All-Ireland weekends. It makes me realise how lucky I am to have these moments in my sporting career.

A few of us have dinner and strangely enough the game isn't mentioned. It's Val's turn to cook. We reckon she might burn something, but in fairness she proves us all wrong and it's a gorgeous meal.

I head home and pack my gear bag. The weekend is finally here.

Saturday, 30 September

I arrive at Kent Train Station at 1 p.m. for the 1.30 p.m. departure.

Cork camogie captain Joanne O'Callaghan is there to kindly see us off, along with a few family members and friends.

On board, there's another quirky quiz like last year. The prize – a sick note from training from Dr Lucy Fleming – is definitely worth winning!

We arrive in Dublin at 4.15 p.m. and a bus takes us to the Red Cow Moran Hotel. Armagh are opting to travel down tomorrow morning before the game, while the junior teams, Sligo and Leitrim, are staying in the Citywest Hotel, where the banquet will be held tomorrow night.

We chill for an hour or two in our rooms. I'm bunking with Donoughmore's Aisling O'Connor and we head downstairs for Mass at 6.15 p.m. County board PRO Fr Terry O'Brien says Mass before we dig in to dinner. After, we have a meeting at 9.30 p.m. Eamonn is the only one to speak, and we absorb everything he says.

One more sleep.

•••

At half-time in the All-Ireland final, the dressing room has suddenly shrunk. Armagh are leading the reigning champions 1–4 to 0–3, courtesy of a rocket of a goal from Mairéad Tennyson; but they shouldn't be.

Agitated, Eamonn Ryan shuffles from foot to foot. His brother-in-law, Tim Murphy, hands him the stats for the first half and they don't read well. Murphy's been a godsend this year, helping to take Cork's game to the next level, but today the players' legs are stuck to the sod of Croke Park.

A gentle soul, Murphy operates in the background, but the manner in which he delivers the stats to Ryan is perfect. His method isn't hi-tech or convoluted, it's professional and as concise as you can get. Thanks to Murphy, Cork now have a record of where they're going wrong, and right, and his analysis supplies them with the ammo they need to rectify the situation.

Murphy's stats indicate a rake of wides but the kickouts are also causing problems. Cork have lost four of their first five, with one point coming directly from a kickout. Ryan is annoyed. Not at the copious errors, but at the simple fact that the players aren't doing themselves justice.

In the second half they have no choice but to.

Twelve minutes after the restart, Nollaig Cleary pounces on a missed shot off the crossbar and makes no mistake, putting the ball into the back of Fionnuala McAtamney's net. Her conviction rallies her compatriots and Cork lead 1–5 to 1–4; but with seven minutes left, it's back to a tie game.

Amanda Murphy – who is playing in her twelfth All-Ireland final, aged just seventeen – pops up with a cracking point to put Cork ahead by one again. Then wing-back Geraldine O'Flynn begins another concealed run up the left flank in front of the Cusack Stand. Armagh fans scream to warn of her attack, as though she's a pantomime villain. O'Flynn's right boot connects with a pass and as the ball ascends time stands still. It's direct – over the crossbar – and she turns and pumps her fists towards the crowd (1–7 to 1–5).

Inspired by O'Flynn's movements is seventeen-year-old Ciara O'Sullivan, who is watching in the stand and will one day captain Cork, but Armagh's Mairéad Tennyson isn't done yet and she points to bring Jacqui Clarke's side back within one. Defensively, however, Cork hold out to win their twenty-fifth championship game on the trot – and with it back-to-back All-Ireland titles (1–7 to 1–6).

The dual stars also complete a first historic double-double having beaten Galway the previous fortnight, and this year round Mary O'Connor is delighted to start and finish in her first senior All-Ireland football final.

In the press zone, Ryan realises how close his side came to losing the Brendan Martin Cup, but takes full responsibility for his side's near self-destruction.

'I made the team edgy and we didn't play well because of it,' he tells the gaggle of journalists. 'I did an extra night of training last week because we were hot favourites and I didn't like the feel of that. I spoke too much about respecting Armagh. Everything was my fault and I know I messed up. All my yapping transmitted a pressure onto the players that I shouldn't have. But somehow the stars aligned for us.'

•••

Ladies football is on a high, with the 2006 final proving such a great advert for the game, and it's only going to get better. In the weeks that follow, the LGFA hosts the inaugural Ladies International Rules series. Earlier in the year, LGFA officials met with the Australian Football League during the O'Neills/TG4 All-Star trip to Singapore, and it was agreed that two ladies international rules games would take place in November 2006, one in Breffni Park, Cavan, and one in Parnell Park, Dublin.

Four Cork players – Angela Walsh, Juliet Murphy, Rena Buckley and Norita Kelly – are selected by Irish team boss, former Armagh men's football captain Jarlath Burns; a surprise choice given that Cork's Eamonn Ryan has won back-to-back All-Irelands in the association's premiere competition.

The first game is broadcast live at 4.30 p.m. on Tuesday 31 October, which is another puzzling decision for fans. However, given that it's the exact time that TG4 made its first broadcast a decade earlier, it's a sweet gesture.

Nothing but tumbleweeds blow across Breffni Park in game one. The Australians are on a hiding to nothing, as TG4 presenters scramble for words to soften the escalating cricket score (130–15). And, even with Jarlath Burns swapping the entire backs with the forwards in the second act, the twenty-five-player Irish selection are unstoppable.

The second leg in Parnell Park, Dublin is much closer (39–18) but nonetheless the damage to the series has been done. It shouldn't have come as a surprise to anyone, however, that amateur ladies footballers could mix it up with some of the toughest footie players in Oz, because that's where the standard of the sport is going.

In reality, it's Cork's two-year dominance that's having a knock-on effect on the game as a whole. They're continuously raising the bar and other counties are now beginning to follow suit. Soon the competition will get much tougher.

10

DUDE, WHERE'S MY HOTEL?

'We're not invincible. No team is invincible.'
Frank Lampard

Ciara Walsh sits in the departures lounge at Cork Airport. Her gear bag between her legs, she reclines and leafs through the pages of a physiology book. Her older sister, Angela, dropped her off at the set-down area and, given how frantic the weekend's been, a seat is a welcome friend.

This is her weekly routine, commuting back and forth to Newcastle in England, where she's studying physiotherapy at Northumbria University. Not one cent does she get for travel expenses, but no one does. The previous two seasons she drove two hours from Carlow IT to The Farm twice weekly for training, so it's much of a muchness. Her parents, Donie and Kathleen, toil the land in east Cork to fund the air miles, but they know how much their daughter loves wearing the red jersey, and she appreciates their generosity.

Competition for places is increasing and twenty-year-old Walsh isn't willing to surrender her spot. For the first time in two years, Ryan has extended his squad – including another sticky defender in Linda Barrett, future captain Amy O'Shea, sixteen-year-old Rhona Ní Bhuachalla and Laura MacMahon, sister of Cork footballer Kevin.

Things need freshening up in 2007. Talks of league and championship three in a rows are mentioned in the press, but no one predicts the quest will come to a spectacular end in the national league semi-final in Banagher, Offaly. After a thirty-one-game winning streak, spanning twenty-six months, Frank Browne's Mayo are the ones to topple Cork (4–12 to 2–12).

Referee Joe Murray puts his lips to the whistle, and Mayo's Martha Carter clenches her fists and lets out a roar, while all Bríd Stack can do is bite the collar of her jersey as she looks down in disgust at the Offaly turf. This one hurts.

'It felt like we had lost an All-Ireland,' remembers Stack. 'We couldn't believe we'd lost a game, but afterwards it was like a load was lifted off our shoulders. We were always going to be beaten some day. It happened, so we moved on. But what we took from it was so important; we realised we could be beaten. It was a reality check, but a fresh start all over again.'

Ryan and co. are oblivious to their winning streak statistic until the inevitable happens. Ryan has had so many disappointments in his coaching career that he doesn't do records. Neither does he look beyond the next game, and after the loss to Mayo that ethos is further engrained in the psyche of the players.

Like the summer before, he's pencilled in a training holiday, only this time it comes a day after the Munster semi-final against Kerry in Beaufort. It's Cork's first competitive game since crashing out of the national league, and they're struggling again today. It takes two goals by citógs Mary O'Connor and Valerie Mulcahy, twenty-seven seconds apart in the closing minutes, to save face (3–12 to

1–13). Kerry coach Robbie Griffin has come very close to cracking them.

In the subsequent media coverage, Cork are deemed 'jammy dodgers' for their Houdiniesque escape, and the squad doesn't take kindly to such candour. The lip service has faded now for the two-time senior All-Ireland champions and they must quickly learn to take the positives with the negatives. Increased coverage has seen their profile rise, and if they play poorly, they must accept it will be reported on.

Deep down the players know their performance against Kerry wasn't good enough. Ryan does too, and twenty-four hours after the game they're already tearing through three-track runs at their warm-weather training camp in Benalmádena, Málaga. Everyone has a point to prove, the team as a whole and as individuals, so much so that players are overlooking injury.

Returning from a beach session on the second day, Mary O'Connor's flip-flops deceive her as she climbs the steps to her hotel room. She stumbles and hits her knee on the ridge of the marble steps, and a red tributary pours from the gash above her kneecap.

A Scottish couple passing ask if she's okay, but O'Connor opts to play it cool. 'Oh, yeah, yeah, I'm grand!' she says, with her palm over the wound.

Rooming with Juliet Murphy, O'Connor scans the horizon to see if she's anywhere nearby, but there's no sign of her. With bloodied hands, O'Connor fumbles her phone out of her pocket and texts Murphy.

'I think my training holiday is over.' Send.

She waits a minute for a reply, hoping her captain will come to the rescue as she's done so many times on the pitch, but nothing. O'Connor can't dwell any longer and hobbles to the lobby, bent over awkwardly with her hand still applying pressure to her knee.

The receptionist takes one look and shrieks.

'Ambulancia! Ambulancia!'

Mortified, O'Connor braves a smile.

'Sí señorita.'

The eight stitches aren't so bad. In fact, they're less painful than the thought of missing out on proving herself worthy of a starting place in the upcoming Munster final against Waterford, and she gets minimal sleep. The following morning as manager Mary Collins mans the sidelines at training on the all-weather pitch at Campo de Fútbol de Césped Natural, O'Connor makes a beeline for her.

'I'm okay to train this morning,' she blurts out.

Collins looks out over the top of her sunglasses and her eyes work their way down to O'Connor's knee.

'If you fall over, you're going to rip those stitches!'

'I don't care,' O'Connor replies. 'I'm not missing out!'

The training is tougher than the previous year. Much tougher. Between sprints, Valerie Mulcahy reminds herself that if they want to be number one, they must train like number two. She's giving it everything she's got. Last year wasn't her best, and being substituted after forty-three minutes in the All-Ireland final against Armagh made it all the worse. Outside of football, too, things had been tough.

In her private life, Mulcahy had been coming to terms with her sexuality. But this year she has decided to be true to herself.

'I told a few of the older players I trusted first that I was gay and they were really supportive. It's tough because the GAA community is big, yet small at the same time, and I was a little paranoid because I didn't want people to think that my sexuality was all there was to me.

'It just became known then within the team and I wasn't treated any differently. No one made an issue of it and it felt good to come out and not have to keep holding it all in.'

In Málaga, the weight of those worries are visibly gone from Mulcahy's shoulders and she's immersed in training.

Juliet Murphy is another who is raising the bar. Every session, the former Irish basketball international relishes the challenge of striving for more. It's in her genetic make-up; and the little details in Ryan's training sessions – like having everyone start in line for a run – allow for few shortcuts.

Today, however, Murphy is on edge. Energy levels are low in the group considering the heat, and concentration levels are even lower. Mentally, this lack of group energy and concentration is torture for Murphy. She can't conceal her frustration anymore and she lets rip. It's a rare occurrence, but instantly the players' application escalates.

'If Juls is upset, there's a reason for it,' says Bríd Stack. 'To hear her shout would send shivers down your spine and immediately people's work rate goes up ten thousand per cent. That's the effect she had on us. She never tolerates low standards because her own expectations are so high. She really made us buy into that as a group, and every now and again we needed her to get upset.'

Upon their return from Málaga, Cork win their fourth successive Munster championship title, against Waterford in Fitzgerald Stadium, Killarney (3–7 to 1–6), and they begin the quest to retain the Brendan Martin Cup in a new piloted Champions League-like format. They see off Galway (2–13 to 1–11), Monaghan (4–11 to 0–11) and Roscommon (2–21 to 0–2) in their group, Dublin in the quarter-final (3–17 to 1–4) and Laois in the semi-final for the second year running (4–14 to 0–6), to set up a revenge clash with Mayo in the All-Ireland final in Croke Park.

This is the one the players want. It's the grudge match fans want, but there's also an element of history attached. Kerry are the only county to have won three successive senior All-Ireland titles in the association's twenty-four-year history. Mayo, Waterford and Tipperary have all tried and failed, but Cork are on the verge of matching it.

Ryan doesn't ban talk of three in a row when speaking to the press – what's the point in prohibiting something that's naturally being brought up in the build-up? If anything, speaking about it normalises it. The players aren't getting caught up in it either; they're fully operating on next-game mode – the national league semi-final loss to Mayo earlier in the spring taught them to stick to this.

One aspect Ryan doesn't discuss is Mayo's biggest scoring threat, Cora Staunton. The Carnacon woman has scored 3–44 in the 2007 championship to date, but Ryan's looking at the bigger picture. Mayo have thirty All-Stars between them, Cork have eleven. To win, they'll have to beat the team, not the woman.

However, the night before the All-Ireland final, in the far corner of the bar in the Moran Hotel, there's a heated discussion brewing between management.

The last night at training Ryan announced the starting fifteen in the dressing rooms in The Farm, with Amanda Murphy coming in at full-forward instead of Mary O'Connor, who suffered a knee injury in a challenge match two weeks earlier.

Management tend to make their team selection based on what they've seen in the three training sessions before the final and they'll almost always reach their decision by consensus. If things are close, they'll pick different teams, rate players and compare the results to decipher the finer margins. This time they're all agreed on the starting fifteen to face Mayo, but there's been no talk of who'll mark Cora Staunton at centre-forward. Ryan's plan is to make the announcement in the dressing room before the game, but Mary Collins isn't content with such short notice.

She believes Rockchapel's Bríd Stack is the woman to mark Staunton, seeing as she's played centre-back all year, while Frankie Honohan wants Donoughmore's Rena Buckley to get the nod. Each is understandably vouching for who they know best.

'Could we not give Bríd a chance?' Collins asks, red in the face – from perseverance as much as agitation. 'She's played centre-back all year, Rena hasn't, and you're giving the message to a player straight off that they're not up to it. We all know that's not true, but that's what you'd be telling her! After ten minutes, if it's not working out, we can move Rena onto Cora then.'

Ger Twomey sides with Collins. It's the right thing to trust Stack from the off as they've done all year. If Staunton's on form, then they'll adjust accordingly.

They're agreed, but it's not over yet. Collins knows Stack's temperament, having managed her to two club All-Ireland titles.

'Eamonn, you've to tell Bríd tonight,' Collins advises Ryan. 'If it was Deirdre O'Reilly you wouldn't have to tell her, but I guarantee you it'll be better if you tell Bríd tonight that she's marking Cora.'

•••

It's 10 p.m. and there's a brief knock on Stack's hotel room door. She peers through the eyehole and sees Ryan standing solo in the corridor.

'Just to let you know, you're marking Cora tomorrow Bríd,' he says, without fuss or fanfare.

'Grand job, Eamonn,' she nods, and closes the door.

Stack's more at ease now and there's no more wondering. She knows what she has to do and she sleeps better because of it. Collins has called it spot on, but no one knows yet that it's to be her last game in charge of Cork.

•••

The morning of the All-Ireland, there's usually nerves floating about, but not today. Instead, the players are taking it all in, appreciating the moment. Their team song, 'Don't Give Up 'Til It's Over' by The Dubliners, is seeping through the speakers on the bus.

> *Don't give up 'til it's over, don't quit if you can*
> *The weight on your shoulder will make you a stronger man*
> *Grasp your nettle tightly, though it will burn*
> *Treat your failures lightly, your luck is bound to turn.*

For the first time in three years, Juliet Murphy finds a seat down the back. She doesn't want to get caught up in the Garda escort or see the hustle and bustle of fans as they near the stadium. She wants to focus completely. It's a special day in another sense. Her grandfather, Jack O'Sullivan, is making his first trip to Croke Park, aged ninety, and the *Evening Echo* newspaper has kindly offered the Cork captain its corporate box so O'Sullivan can enjoy the occasion in comfort.

The presentation of the jerseys in the dressing room is as emotional as always, but when Ryan presents the injured Mary O'Connor with the number 14 jersey, the applause rings off the dressing-room walls. Her teammates know how much she has given to the game for so many years, how much she deserves to be on the field and how cruel it is that she will not be.

Cork save their most flamboyant football for Mayo. Every other day the sides meet it's a battle of attrition more than great displays of football, but Cork are in the mood for making history.

Bursting through the Connacht champions' line just before half-time, however, Cork midfielder Norita Kelly finds herself in uncharted territory in the forward-line. Latching onto a long ball in, with one Mayo defender on her tail, Kelly lands and turns to take off, but her leg buckles. Immediately she grabs her knee and from the burning sensation Kelly knows she's ruptured her cruciate.

Unfortunately for Mayo, a penalty is incorrectly given despite no contact being made with Kelly. Valerie Mulcahy obliges, giving Cork a six-point lead (1–6 to 0–3) at the turnaround.

Kelly's departure forces Ryan to make a few positional changes and Deirdre O'Reilly moves from corner-forward to midfield and sixteen-year-old Rhona Ní Bhuachalla comes on in attack. It's her first appearance in Croke Park but it very nearly didn't come to pass. The night before, Ní Bhuachalla and her club teammate Anita Thompson failed to turn up for the team meeting. Ryan wasn't impressed. Their timing was off and when they realised it was too late, both teenagers were distraught.

Two years previously, in 2005, aged fourteen, Ní Bhuachalla had witnessed the euphoria of Cork's first ever senior All-Ireland win and TG4's cameras picked up on her smile in the crowd, waving a red and white flag. Now Ní Bhuachalla is terrified she's blown her chance of playing in Croke Park due to bad timekeeping, but Ryan calls her to come on.

In the dressing room at half-time, Ryan doesn't have much to say. His players' performance is more or less where it needs to be, but they know there's no way they can ease up. In 2004 they were six points up against Mayo in their first national final and lost, and they're not going to let it happen again.

Mulcahy scores a second goal just after the restart but, as predicted, Mayo make a comeback with two green flags of their own (2–11 to 2–6). It isn't enough to claw back victory on what has been a torrid day for captain Christina Heffernan's side.

High in a corporate box, ninety-year-old Jack O'Sullivan watches his granddaughter make history, climbing the steps of the Hogan Stand for the third successive September. Murphy asks the injured Mary O'Connor to lift the Brendan Martin Cup with her. It signifies the friendship and solidarity in the squad – a harmony brought about by one man in particular.

'There's no words to describe you, Eamonn,' Murphy declares in her acceptance speech, her voice trembling. 'You're just unbelievable!'

It's the first time in any of her three speeches that Murphy's let herself go and she speaks to the 21,327 fans in the stand as if they're good friends. Meanwhile, Bríd Stack is awarded Player of the Match for containing Cora Staunton. Mary Collins had nailed it.

That night, the injured Norita Kelly and Mary O'Connor clump into the Citywest Hotel for the All-Ireland banquet with their crutches. Upstairs on the landing three hairdressers cater to the Mayo players' needs, but upstyles are the least of Kelly and O'Connor's worries. Recovery awaits in the coming weeks, but for now they'll celebrate like never before.

•••

Prior to the final, a trip to Castletownbere was promised by the team to Amanda Murphy if they won the All-Ireland. It's only fair because three times a week for as many years, Murphy's father, Mike, would collect her at the gates of the Scoil Phobail Bhéara and drive his daughter 160 km to training, before returning home at 11 p.m. Her commitment, and that of her parents, Mike and Margaret, is immense and this is the team's way of saying thanks.

The morning after the homecoming in Donoughmore, the players surface and head for Pat Barry's Bar for one drink before departing in convoy for the extreme west of the county. It'll take three hours, but an hour or so from Castletownbere they pass the first bonfire blazing in their honour. For the remainder of the journey, bonfires roar, flares are fired and messages of 'Up Cork' are splattered across the road in red and white paint.

A Garda car offers to meet them in Glengarriff, and Norma Kelly and Deirdre O'Reilly are enjoying the banter. Kelly parks herself in the passenger seat of the Garda car with the driver's hat on her head, while O'Reilly waves a Cork flag out the back window. Soon, the liquid levels catch up with Kelly and she requests the squad car to pull over for a toilet stop. The convoy comes to a halt and out she hops to run to the nearest house. Ringing the doorbell, she asks the homeowner can she use the bathroom.

'Oh, you play with Cork? Ah sure work away girl, the toilet's all yours!'

When they finally arrive in Castletownbere, Amanda Murphy is honoured by the people who know her best, before the party moves to a local bar. Juliet Murphy and Eamonn Ryan, however, venture quietly across the road to another pub on hearing that the All-Ireland final is on repeat since Sunday evening, and The Master and pupil relive the game all over again.

'You'll have a drink, Juliet?'

'Go on so Eamonn, sure I will.'

They sit in silence, watching the game and smiling.

Soon word gets back to the others that the match is being shown and the rest of the players filter across the main street. The decibels go up a few notches with their arrival and they sing and cheer, absorbing every second of the celebrations, for these are the best they've ever had.

The barman shouts out, 'What do ye want in the cup?'

'Oh, we don't fill it,' someone replies.

'What? Ye don't fill it?' he asks.

'No. Someone in Croke Park told us in 2005 that it would damage the sterling silver if we filled it, and Brendan's worth a lot to us!'

And it was then one of the newer players on the squad pipes up. 'One of the Galway girls I go to college with told me they filled it in every pub they went to when they won it in 2004.'

A burst of laughter erupts and nearly takes the roof off the place. Some are doubled over laughing at their naivety. For three years, they failed to fill the cup, and the consensus is that tonight they'll make up for lost time.

The party continues in the Beacon Nightclub in the Beara Bay Hotel, above which the players have kindly been given accommodation for free, but Norita Kelly is struggling because she can't find her crutches. Instead, she props herself up against the bar counter and hops on one leg to the music.

As the early hours of the morning drift in, Mairéad Kelly, Laura MacMahon and Norma Kelly are the last ones standing. They gather their gear bags and, armed with their hotel key card, head off out the road, ready to rest their weary heads. Twenty minutes pass and there's no sign of the hotel. An hour later and there's still no sign of it. Their feet are achy now, from the walking as much as the dancing, and eventually a car passes them. It stops and the driver rolls down his window.

'Girls, are ye okay?'

'We can't find our hotel,' says McMahon, showing him the room key card, with Beara Bay Hotel printed on it.

'And where were ye earlier?' he asks.

'The Beacon Nightclub.'

'Sure, that's part of the hotel, that's where ye're staying!'

•••

The Cork senior team ahead of their first division one national league final appearance under Eamonn Ryan in 2004. They lost to Mayo in Pearse Stadium, Galway, 1–13 to 1–11. *Picture: Mary White*

The Cork team ahead of the 2005 division one national league final against Galway in the Gaelic Grounds, Limerick. *Picture: Mary White*

Cork captain Juliet Murphy celebrates kicking the winning point in the dying seconds of the 2005 All-Ireland semi-final against Mayo in Portlaoise. In the background is her club teammate Aisling O'Connor of Donoughmore.
© *INPHO/Andrew Paton*

Cork's Norita Kelly in action against Annette Clarke of Galway in the 2005 All-Ireland final. Kelly was the best fielder of the ball during Cork's reign, partnering Juliet Murphy in midfield. © *INPHO/Donall Farmer*

The Cork substitutes count down the clock in the final seconds of the 2005 All-Ireland final. Victory over Galway ensured the county's first senior All-Ireland title. *Picture: Denis Minihane (Irish Examiner)*

Eamonn Ryan hugs captain Juliet Murphy after winning Cork's first senior All-Ireland title in 2005. *Picture: Denis Minihane (Irish Examiner)*

Captain Juliet Murphy and manager Mary Collins carry the Brendan Martin Cup after arriving into Kent Station, Cork, for their homecoming in 2005. Also pictured is coach Eamonn Ryan and liaison officer Eileen Collins. *Picture: Ger Bonus (Evening Echo)*

Cork's five All-Star winners in 2005 – Briege Corkery, Angela Walsh, Valerie Mulcahy, Juliet Murphy and Deirdre O'Reilly. *Picture: Mary White*

Briege Corkery, wearing the Corona-branded headband that landed her in a spot of trouble prior to the 2006 All-Ireland quarter-final against Mayo. *Picture: Adrian Melia Photography*

Bríd Stack celebrates Cork's 2006 one-point win over Armagh with team manager Mary Collins.

Angela Walsh, second from left, with the Brendan Martin Cup, her father Donie, her mother Kathleen and her younger sister Ciara.

The team taking in a training session at Campo de Fútbol de Césped in Benalmádena in 2007. Included is manager Mary Collins and selector Ger Twomey.

An injured Mary O'Connor awaits the Cork team's arrival onto the pitch in Croke Park ahead of the 2007 All-Ireland final against Mayo. She suffered a serious knee injury just two weeks before the final. *Picture: Eddie O'Hare (Evening Echo)*

Mayo's Cora Staunton is hunted by Juliet Murphy, Deirdre O'Reilly and
Player of the Match, Bríd Stack, in the 2007 All-Ireland final.
© *INPHO/Lorraine O'Sullivan*

Amanda Murphy in action against Mayo's Martha Carter in the 2007
All-Ireland final. It was to become Murphy's twelfth All-Ireland final win at
only seventeen years of age. © *INPHO/James Crombie*

Back row: Amanda Murphy, Norma Kelly, Mairéad Kelly, Briege Corkery, Anita Thompson, Elaine Harte, Valerie Mulcahy, Caoimhe Creedon, Amy O'Shea and Anne-Marie Walsh; front row: Laura MacMahon, Angela Walsh, Norita Kelly, Rhona Ní Bhuachalla, Rena Buckley, Bríd Stack, Geraldine O'Flynn, Nollaig Cleary and Ciara Walsh, attending a New York Knicks game in Madison Square Garden on their team holiday in 2008.

Valerie Mulcahy is red carded in the final moments of the 2008 All-Ireland semi-final against Tyrone by referee Liam McDonagh. The incident led to Tyrone captain Maura Kelly coming to Mulcahy's defence ahead of a disciplinary hearing, which eventually ruled she could play in the All-Ireland final.
© INPHO/Lorraine O'Sullivan

Bríd Stack and Angela Walsh with Laura Mai Cahill from Cork during their visit to Our Lady's Hospital for Sick Children in Dublin in 2008. Sadly Laura Mai passed away a few months later.

Captain Mary O'Connor in action in the 2009 All-Ireland final against Dublin's Sorcha Furlong. O'Connor famously stated in her acceptance speech, acknowledging Cork's first five in a row, 'Kilkenny, we see your four and raise you one!' © *INPHO/James Crombie*

Elaine Harte and goalkeeping coach Kieran Dwyer celebrate Cork's 2009 All-Ireland final win over Dublin. *Picture: Brian Lougheed (Evening Echo)*

A distraught Laura MacMahon walks off the field after Cork lose the 2010
All-Ireland quarter-final to Tyrone. It was Cork's only defeat in the All-
Ireland series in a decade.
© INPHO/Cathal Noonan

Cork celebrate winning the 2011 All-Ireland final against Monaghan in the warm-up area in Croke Park. It signalled their return, having lost the 2010 quarter-final to Tyrone.

Ciara O'Sullivan in action against Donegal in the 2012 All-Ireland quarter-final in Dr Hyde Park. Cork went on to win on a scoreline of 8–27 to 0–2.
© *INPHO/Morgan Treacy*

Above: Angela Walsh sprays champagne in the dressing room following Cork's win over Monaghan in the 2013 All-Ireland final.

Left: Eamonn Ryan with Juliet Murphy, Elaine Harte, Briege Corkery and Bríd Stack after winning the 2013 All-Ireland final against Monaghan. All four had played in every minute of Cork's eight All-Ireland final wins since 2005. *Picture: Mary White*

Eamonn Ryan and Nollaig Cleary share a joke at her wedding in the Rochestown Park Hotel, Cork, in 2013. *Picture: David Keane (Evening Echo)*

Retired Cork player Juliet Murphy doing commentary for TG4 during the 2014 All-Ireland final between Cork and Dublin. *Picture: Eddie O'Hare (Evening Echo)*

Nollaig Cleary, Briege Corkery, Eamonn Ryan, Geraldine O'Flynn and Angela Walsh collecting the 2014 RTÉ Sports Team of the Year award. Winning by public vote was huge, and it was the first time a female team won the award. © *INPHO/Cathal Noonan*

Rena Buckley puts in a block against Dublin's Niamh McEvoy during their national league clash in CIT in 2015. Blocking is a simple skill coach Eamonn Ryan has asked his players to rehearse time and again over the years.
Picture: AnoisPhotography.com

The most successful GAA players ever, Briege Corkery and Rena Buckley, in action against Louise Ward of Galway in the 2015 All-Ireland quarter-final at the Gaelic Grounds. Together they have amassed thirty-two senior All-Ireland medals, sixteen each – six in camogie and ten in ladies football.
© INPHO/Ryan Byrne

Eamonn Ryan and his son Don gather the players in the corner of the pitch in Semple Stadium following their 2015 qualifier win against Meath to discuss pulling out of the championship due to ongoing dual star fixture clashes. *Picture: AnoisPhotography.com*

Former Cork full-back Angela Walsh (*left*) with her daughter Keeva and goalkeeper Elaine Harte (*right*) with her daughter Aoibheann, with team liaison officer Bridget O'Brien, who knitted their daughters SuperValu-branded tops for the 2015 All-Ireland quarter-final against Galway.
Picture: AnoisPhotography.com

Geraldine O'Flynn is escorted off the pitch by Cork physio Brian O'Connell having injured her knee fifteen minutes into the 2015 final.
Picture: AnoisPhotography.com

Orla Finn contests an aerial ball against two Dublin players in the 2015 All-Ireland final, with defenders Aisling Barrett and Róisín Phelan looking on.
Picture: AnoisPhotography.com

After winning the 2015 senior All-Ireland final against Dublin. All eight members of the Cork team pictured have been there since Cork won their first of ten titles in 2005. From left: Deirdre O'Reilly, Briege Corkery, Geraldine O'Flynn, selector Frank Honohan, coach Eamonn Ryan, Valerie Mulcahy, Bríd Stack and Rena Buckley. *Picture: AnoisPhotography.com*

Ephie Fitzgerald, who replaced Eamonn Ryan in January 2016, on the sideline ahead of his first All-Ireland final as the Cork ladies football manager. Also pictured is Hannah Looney, Angela Crowley, Mike Carroll, Bridget O'Brien, James Masters, Frank Honohan and Pat O'Leary.
Picture: AnoisPhotography.com

The 2016 senior All-Ireland-winning Cork team who defeated Dublin to claim the county's eleventh All-Ireland title in twelve years.
Picture: AnoisPhotography.com

Captain Ciara O'Sullivan (10) of Mourneabbey leads Cork out onto the field for the 2018 All-Ireland final against Dublin in Croke Park, where a record attendance of 50,141 was set. *Picture: Magda Lukas*

Mary White interviews Eamonn Ryan following Cork's division one national league final replay win against Galway in 2015. *Picture: AnoisPhotography.com*

The following January, Mary Collins is at a loss. She had given up three years of her life for Cork ladies football and sacrificed time with her family in the process. But now she felt it was the right time to step away. Her bravery to stand up at the county board meeting in late 2003 was the start of an incredible journey, which saw her oversee Cork's first ever Munster senior championship title, first division one national league title and first senior All-Ireland title, as well as four successive provincial titles.

But now, since stepping down, she's at sea. She misses the players all so much and the craic on the bus to matches.

To fill the void she becomes manager of the Rockchapel men's football team, on which her two sons are playing. She owes them her time, but it's not the same.

On the night she realises the enormity of what she's stepped away from with the Cork set-up, she's watching the lads' training session down at the local pitch. But before it even gets underway there's excuses galore for fellas missing and, when it does start, everything is done at a much lower intensity than what she's accustomed to.

In the far-off pitch, under whatever light they have, she can see Geraldine O'Flynn and Bríd Stack doing their individual winter training for the upcoming season, and they're going flat out.

Collins calls a halt to the men's session.

'Lads,' she says, 'would ye just stop for a minute and go down there and watch Ger and Bríd. That's what training is!'

The players are annoyed at her for saying it, but the

truth hurts. Mary Collins, however, is hurting just as much. She's heartbroken.

11

LIFE, DEATH AND GRATITUDE

*'Sport teaches you character, it teaches you to play by
the rules, it teaches you to know what it feels like to win
and lose – it teaches you about life.'*
Billie Jean King

Briege Corkery saunters up to the counter at Ski Dubai
with Bríd Stack, Angela Walsh, Juliet Murphy and
Deirdre O'Reilly sheepishly tagging behind her. They're
part of the 2008 LGFA O'Neills/TG4 All-Star touring
group staying in the Le Méridien Mina Seyahi beach
resort, and having sand-boarded in the desert yesterday,
they've decided to go the opposite end of the spectrum
today.

Rena Buckley, Valerie Mulcahy and Nollaig Cleary
take the relaxing option and lunch at the seven-star Burj
Al Arab hotel.

'And have ye skied before madam?' the gent behind the
counter at Ski Dubai asks Briege Corkery.

'Oh, yeah, we're kind of intermediate, like,' she smiles
covertly.

Ski passes secured, they swap their O'Neills shorts
for snowsuits and head for the baby slope. Corkery, the
youngest, is the calmest of the lot.

'Sure, we'll just figure it out as we go along,' she assures
her elders.

In just a matter of minutes, Corkery's got to grips with the baby slope as the others slide gingerly across the snow.

'Feck this!' she says, heading in the direction of the intermediate slope in search of a bigger challenge.

The other four watch her take off, as fearless as if on one of her characteristic bursts up the pitch. But, from the wings, a marshal appears, frantically waving his hands over his head.

'Snow plough! Snow plough!' he yelps.

Corkery sees it and turns as fast as she can, twirling her body to change direction and avoid hitting the plough head on. The girls are in convulsions at the distressed marshal, but Corkery's athleticism allows her to adjust her trajectory safely out of harm's way – albeit tangled up in some orange safety netting!

Corkery's valour impresses her defensive colleagues and Deirdre O'Reilly and Angela Walsh decide to give it a whirl, crashing wildly into the mats at the base of the slope, much to the amusement of two seasoned Canadian skiers looking on.

'You guys are crazy, eh!'

'Ah this is mighty craic, lads!' beams Walsh, who's now getting into the spirit of things and decides to report back to Bríd Stack and Juliet Murphy on the beginners' slope.

'Lads, it's deadly!'

'Come on up for a look. There's ski lifts that take you the whole way up and back down again. Just come up on the lift with me, watch us and come back down!'

Apprehensive, but intrigued, Stack and Murphy hop

onto the ski chair and snuggle either side of Walsh on their ascent. Approaching the top, Walsh prepares to jump.

'Right girls, see ye at the botttttommmm!'

They happily wave her off as the lift trundles on around the corner, but suddenly it comes to an abrupt halt and they're left dangling high above the resort. The emergency button has been activated and the same marshal is back again, roaring up at them.

'Get down! Get down!'

'Ah here, don't say we were supposed to get off, Bríd?' Murphy asks, with a hint of panic in her voice.

'I don't know,' says Stack, 'but I'm going to feckin' kill Angie when I see her!'

The resort comes to a standstill and skiers take in the commotion.

'Get down! Get down!'

'We can't ski! We can't ski!' they respond in unison.

The order comes back that they've no option but to jump to get down onto the slope, and Stack is fit to kill her best friend for landing her in it. It's quite a height, but once they hit ground they begin to thaw a little. But, with no ski poles, they realise there's no way of navigating their way back down the incline.

'Scoot down on your bums,' Walsh shouts up, but it's far too steep to attempt.

The marshal informs them there's only one way down and points to a bright orange, canoe-type stretcher. Stack and Murphy look at each other in disgust. With no choice, they climb in and, holding onto the front, the marshal takes off down the slope with two All-Stars strapped tightly inside.

They're mortified, and their teammates assure them that they won't mention the incident to anyone. When they arrive back to the hotel, however, they're bombarded with questions about which Cork players were badly injured in a skiing accident and had to be lifted off the slopes. Unknown to them, a group of Croke Park officials had witnessed the entire episode while having lunch overlooking the resort.

Adventure is never very far away, and a few weeks later, on the Cork team holiday in New York, things don't go exactly to plan either. As part of their visit, the All-Ireland champions are to play an exhibition game at Gaelic Park on West 240th Street and Broadway in the Bronx. Nollaig Cleary spent many a summer evening playing football there on a J1 visa, where she met her future husband, Micheál Ó Crónín, and won two New York championships. But her one-stop-too-soon subway directions have left some of her teammates wandering aimlessly around the Bronx. They thought they'd hit the jackpot when they spotted a large shamrock painted on the side of a building, but it was just an off-licence whose owner had never heard of 'Garlic Park'!

•••

Life is good in the spring of 2008. There's a new dynamic forming among management as the departure of Mary Collins and Eileen O'Brien means it's the first year a female isn't involved in the team, and the older players panic initially. They know how much Collins had professionalised the set-up off the training field and they fear that things may revert to disorganised chaos. But they need not have been worried, as new selectors Noel 'Dip' O'Connor and Justin McCarthy are more than capable. O'Connor oversaw Inch Rovers' first Cork senior county championship title win in 2007, while McCarthy's precision and knowledge of rising inter-county stars, from his work with underage teams, means one eye will be on the future.

The five-year captaincy of Juliet Murphy also comes to an end. Full-back Angela Walsh is her successor, given that her club, Inch Rovers, had claimed the county title. Like Murphy, Walsh played sport at a high level internationally – with the U19 Irish volleyball team at the 2003 World Youth Games – and the twenty-one-year-old's maturity is a carbon copy of her predecessor's. If there's one thing Murphy's taught her, it's to never get caught up in being captain. Just play your own game. That's how Murphy led and garnered so much respect. Walsh intends to do the same.

The league goes well, with the aim being to win back the division one title they had relinquished to Mayo in the 2007 league semi-final in Banagher. The incentive, however, is much bigger than just pride, with the players learning that Tim Murphy, their stats man and Eamonn Ryan's brother-in-law, has been diagnosed with cancer. The team is staying in the Louis Fitzgerald Hotel in Dublin ahead of a league game against Monaghan when they hear. It's a bolt from the blue, and it's the first time real life has encroached on their bubble. With Tim Murphy firmly in the back of their minds, they win the league final against Kerry (6–13 to 2–10) in Ennis, and beat them again in the championship provincial decider (1–23 to 2–7) in Páirc Uí Rinn.

Galway prove tough in the All-Ireland quarter-final (2–11 to 1–7) and only for the heroics of former Irish international soccer goalkeeper Elaine Harte, Cork wouldn't be in the semi-final against Tyrone. Ryan knows the team is going through a bad patch. Their average shooting success is 63 per cent and during training before the game he enquires as to how many of them had watched the 2008 Champions League final between Chelsea and Manchester United. He asks what they thought of John Terry's performance, and they quickly make fun of the Chelsea defender's missed penalty. Served him right they said.

'Yeah, but he'll still get paid £90,000 the next week,' Ryan reminds them.

It's his subtle way of saying, if you miss a score, if you miss a chance, don't be too hard on yourself, you'll still come out the other side. His point resonates and they're far more efficient in the All-Ireland semi-final against Tyrone, but it's a game remembered for the wrong reasons.

Cork are nineteen points in front (4–18 to 0–11) with thirty seconds left on the clock in Tullamore, when Sligo referee Liam McDonagh blows for a free out against Valerie Mulcahy. She's been turning the screw on Tyrone all day, working hard defensively as much as offensively, and adds 1–5 to her championship total of 4–14 to date. But it's a soft free she gives away.

'Ah, for fuck's sake,' Mulcahy mumbles, frustrated with herself as much as with the call.

But McDonagh misinterprets what she says and reaches for the red card in his pocket. Mulcahy can't believe her eyes. A red means she'll potentially miss the All-Ireland final against Monaghan in three weeks' time.

Motionless, hands on her hips, Mulcahy tries to take it in, as Nollaig Cleary appears at her shoulder. 'What the hell was that for Val?' she asks.

'I dunno! I don't have a clue!'

TG4 commentator Robbie Griffin is just as confused. 'It would be a tragedy if Mulcahy were to miss the final,' he tells Brian Tyers *as Gaeilge* during the live transmission. 'At best, it would have been a yellow card. I didn't see her do anything wrong, but she may have said something out of frustration, but it was certainly no more than a yellow card. Valerie plays by the rules and it would be a crying shame if she's to miss the final.'

On the sideline Eamonn Ryan is as dumbfounded, and on his return to Ballingeary in the early hours he begins to build a case for the disciplinary hearing. First thing the following morning, he picks up the phone to ring Frank Murphy, the secretary of the Cork men's county board. He could easily tell Ryan to paddle his own canoe, but he is more than helpful, poring over the rulebook and offering advice. Attempts, too, are made to source a lip-reader to watch video footage of the match in a bid to prove that what Mulcahy said wasn't offensive.

In the meantime, a Croke Park official makes contact

with the Rockbán forward to put it to her about the seriousness of the situation.

'You do realise that if you appeal the red card and it's not successful, you won't be able to play in the final?' they ask.

Mulcahy understands all right, but she's not going to lie down without a fight and certainly not when she knows in her heart she's been wronged. But the strongest support comes from the least expected avenue: their opponents.

Tyrone captain and full-back Maura Kelly – now married to football star Ryan McMenamin – was within earshot when McDonagh issued the red card. She could easily sabotage Cork's bid for four in a row at a time when many are crying out for new holders of the Brendan Martin Cup. But the St McCartan's woman is better than that, and ahead of the appeal she takes time to write a letter endorsing the Cork full-forward's version of events. Mulcahy is forever indebted to her for the gesture.

At the disciplinary hearing the following week, on Monday 15 September, in a hotel in Tullamore, Offaly, the three-time All-Star is accompanied by manager Jim McEvoy, Nollaig Cleary and Eamonn Ryan, for whom it's a seven-hour round journey from west Cork.

The same night, Mulcahy's Rockbán teammate, Cathriona Foley is returning to Leeside with the O'Duffy Cup as captain of the Cork senior camogie team, having won the All-Ireland. The party follows on to Foley's local pub in Carrignavar and Mulcahy would have been the first one there to congratulate her, but she misses out on one of the proudest night's in her club's history – a club her mother, Marie, helped establish.

Instead, she's sat across from a handful of LGFA officials, her stomach in knots. They inform her that it's been reported that she said 'fuck you, ref', but she pleads her case and a two-week ban is handed down.

'It was the worst experience of my life sitting in that room,' Mulcahy reflects. 'I'd be lying if I said I was delighted with the two weeks. Don't get me wrong, I was thrilled to be playing in the All-Ireland final, that meant everything to me, but I was still very disappointed with the decision.

'I knew myself I had done nothing wrong. Hand on heart, I didn't deserve that red card and yet I had to "serve time", which also included missing a championship game with my club, and on the sideline that night I just felt so helpless.'

But things are put into perspective for Mulcahy in the week leading up to the All-Ireland final.

Stats man Tim Murphy has taken a turn for the worse and is moved to Marymount Hospice. Mulcahy, captain Angela Walsh and Bríd Stack pay him a visit with a card signed by all the team. A gentleman of the highest order, he's given them so much of his time and it's their time to be there for him.

'Go out and win it now,' he tells them, with as much conviction as he can muster.

They can see he's weakened a lot since they last saw him and it hits them he won't be with them for much longer.

The Saturday morning before the All-Ireland final, Eamonn Ryan also calls to see his brother-in-law, before departing that afternoon for the capital. At home now, surrounded by his family and loving wife, Mary, Tim's struggling, but all he's talking about is the match, offering Ryan statistical advice on how to counteract the Ulster champions, Monaghan.

On the bus journey up, the girls can see Ryan isn't himself. They know how close he is to Tim and, although he tries to mask it, they can sense his torment. He could be somewhere else, with his family, with his sister, yet here he is with them and it means so much.

That night the players cram into Angela Walsh's room at the hotel. 'We're not going out to win tomorrow for us,' she says, 'we're doing it for Tim and for Eamonn.'

They all instinctively felt it during the day, but verbalising makes it real. It isn't about them, it's about those closest to them.

In the huddle before throw-in, Walsh reminds the team of the pact they made the night before. Emotion pumps profusely in their veins and, with every shoulder squeezed, their belief is fortified. They win 4–13 to 0–11 and Mulcahy is named Player of the Match for her contribution of 3–2. She had a point to prove after what happened in Tullamore.

Too superstitious, Walsh didn't prepare a speech and for a split second panics. There are 20,000 or so people in the stadium and only a handful know what the team has endured in recent weeks and days. Walsh holds it together, for everyone.

At home in Cork city, Tim Murphy's drifting in and out of consciousness. His family are by his bedside telling him how the game is going, keeping him informed of who's doing well and how things are panning out, and when they tell him that Walsh has lifted the Brendan Martin Cup, he smiles.

'Good girl, Angela, good girl.'

They would be some of the last words he'd say.

•••

It's the first year Cork haven't travelled to Dublin for the All-Ireland final by train. Instead they go by bus with Cormac O'Connor of O'Connor Coaches – a gentle soul with the patience of a saint. But, on their way back to Cork on Monday afternoon with the Brendan Martin Cup, whilst having a few celebratory drinks in the back room of The Eagle's Rest in Portlaoise, news trickles through that Tim Murphy has passed away. The players are in no doubt that he hung on to see them win.

Ryan understandably skips the homecoming, but he, his wife, Pat, and their family are on the players' minds. They have mixed emotions but know Tim would want them to celebrate because he knew as much as anyone how hard they had worked to get to the top.

The party heads for Killeagh and forty-four lodgers bunk in at captain Angela Walsh's house. Eight laugh their way to sleep in the attic, while the only space left for Rhona Ní Bhuachalla to lay her head is in the bottom of a wardrobe.

Bar the first in 2005, the homecomings in the city are always timid affairs, with a couple of hundred making the effort to welcome the team home. The players' preference would be to head straight to the captain's home club. The nights in Donoughmore were always good, while Brendan Martin himself – after whom the senior All-Ireland cup is named – joined in on the celebrations one year in Ballydesmond in north Cork when the party had to continue in candlelight after the generator packed up. The same night, defender Rena Buckley intentionally strapped her ankles for the devilment ahead.

The next evening, on Tuesday 30 September, the squad reunite for Tim Murphy's removal, to support his wife Mary, sons Donal and Barry, and daughter Niamh, at the funeral home opposite Páirc Uí Rinn, where Tim had watched Cork win their first Munster senior title in 2004.

The last few days have been emotional and it has made the players realise how important family and loved ones were on their journey to a fourth All-Ireland title. For some, the odyssey began before any silverware was won. Standing on boggy sidelines in obscure places, braving the cold in rusty stands or sitting on damp chewing-gum-covered concrete seats. The likes of the Murphys, the Walshs, the Kellys, the Corkerys, the Buckleys, the Mulcahys, boyfriends, girlfriends, husbands-to-be, wives-to-be; or the likes of Jim Ryan, younger brother of Eamonn, Tommy Seaward, or former Cork hurler Tony Connolly and his grandson Chris, whose sheer love of sport saw them follow the team the length and breadth of the country for over a decade.

Eamonn Ryan is a genius at keeping the players grounded, but the contribution of their families and partners in keeping them so level-headed can't be underestimated.

They're the ones who believed in their potential on days when Waterford and Kerry hammered them out the gate. Amid deep-rooted club rivalries, it was the unifying actions of their parents huddled together in stands that softened the edges. The parents got to know one another and their daughters followed suit. They kept an admirable distance from Ryan, too, and he from them. Some could count on one hand how many times they've had full-blown conversations with him. A former school principal, Ryan mastered how to handle parents and they quickly came to respect how he went about his business.

Of course, the odd parent queried a decision over the years, but selectors were usually the ones who'd get the earful. Ryan, rarely so. But it was the system you had to buy into, and if you didn't, the door was always open.

But Tim Murphy's passing was poignant. He had been their secret weapon – and they will never forget.

12

THE UNSUNG HERO

*'Two things define you. Your patience when you have
nothing, and your attitude when you have everything.'*
Anonymous

Eamonn Ryan is mid-sentence giving a talk to the
Ballyboden St Enda's hurlers in Dublin, when a thought
crosses his mind. He's speaking about how physical Gaelic
games have become. 'You can pump iron for hours, but if
you don't have the skill to put the ball over the bar, then
where are you at?' he asks. The word 'physical' reminds him
of someone, and on the back of his hand he writes the
letters 'GOC'.

Probably the most athletic camogie player ever, Cork's
Gemma O'Connor is as physical as they come, yet just as
skilful. She only started playing football at a high level in
her twenties with Donoughmore, but her athleticism and
strength could bring a hardiness to the 2009 panel. Ryan's
not sure yet where he could play her, but with seven players
departing – including nineteen-year-old Amanda Murphy
– he's thinking outside the box.

As he leaves the podium, he excuses himself and steps
outside to ring O'Connor. She's the first and only player
he's gone to this length to reel in. She agrees to attend the
first session, which nearly always falls on 16 January – the
birthday of Ryan's firstborn, Jim – but after a handful of

sessions, O'Connor is forced to call it quits because of work commitments as a corporal in the Irish Army.

Other than that, not much else has changed come the start of 2009. The majority of the back-room team is still in place, for now, although later in the year manager Jim McEvoy will part ways with the squad, while Eamonn Ryan's son, Don, has offered to assist his father as the team's new statistician.

Mary O'Connor of Inch Rovers is the new captain, but it nearly didn't come to pass. Sixteen months earlier she suffered a serious knee injury just two weeks before the 2007 All-Ireland final and was told she'd never play inter-county football or camogie again. It happened in a challenge match with the footballers just days after losing the camogie All-Ireland final to Wexford. Her body in general was achy, and the second she jumped for the ball, she knew she was in trouble.

Lying in agony on a dressing room table in Macroom, she argues with the paramedic not to cut her sock. It's her lucky sock. But that's all he has time to do before a call comes in over the radio to attend to a cardiac arrest in the village.

So they improvise.

O'Connor's Santa Fe jeep is converted into an ambulance and as she lies on her back with her head against the driver's seat, the team doctor, Dr Lucy Fleming, begins the forty-minute journey to the South Infirmary Hospital in Cork city. For hours O'Connor waits in A&E for an MRI scan. Her knee swollen, her heart deflated, she knows this isn't going to end well. The following day, Cork GAA doctor Con Murphy phones to confirm her worst fears, while a deeper scan by Dr Tadhg O'Sullivan in the Whitfield Clinic in Waterford shows she's suffered a lateral collateral coronary knee ligament injury. In layman's terms, she has torn ligaments and muscle straight off the bone, and 90 per cent of her knee is bruised. The injury is as bad, if not worse, than if she did her cruciate.

Devastated, that night she cries herself to sleep. Having trained all year, to stumble at the final hurdle is a kick in the teeth. But after fourteen years of playing both codes at the highest level, and now aged thirty, her body is screaming for a time out.

In the dressing room for the 2007 All-Ireland, O'Connor sat teary-eyed. Briege Corkery put her hand on her shoulder as if to say, we've got your back. Mary Collins spoke highly of her when presenting her with the number 14 jersey, Eamonn Ryan made sure she was in the team photograph, while captain Juliet Murphy handed her a folded piece of paper of encouragement.

'As I'm writing this, I'm doing that lactic drain thing you told me about … I know tomorrow will be hard, but we're all there for you …' it begins. It's typical Murphy, caring and thoughtful, and to this day O'Connor carries the note in her wallet.

Although 2007 was an extremely difficult time, it was her teammates who mentally carried her through her recovery. She purchased an aqua belt and twice a day for three months she ran lengths of the swimming pool at the

Aura Leisure Centre in Youghal, before going to see world famous physical therapist Ger Hartmann in Limerick. Hartmann had worked with the likes of Sonia O'Sullivan, Paula Radcliffe, Kelly Holmes and Moses Kiptanui, and within a couple of months of following his exercises, O'Connor was back running. But there were obstacles.

'After the 2007 All-Ireland celebrations I got quite irritable. People who know me say I get very cranky over sport anyway, but I was introverted and intense about sport because I felt that was the only thing I was good at.

'Then I got despondent and went into myself. I wasn't bordering on depression or anything, but I knew I wasn't happy with myself because everything was difficult. I had my work to focus on, but when you're so active and so motivated all the time, and to be suddenly struck down and you can't do anything and you can't drive, you're just sitting at home thinking. That got to me.

'You start to reflect on the year and try to look at the positives … like the jersey presentation, the way Mary Collins spoke about me, Eamonn ringing, the girls' text messages, and you feel part of something.

'You have to focus on getting right, and what you're going to do when you do get right. I said to myself, once I got back, I was going to create the best version of myself and 2008 turned out to be my best playing year in camogie and football in terms of consistency. In hindsight, the injury actually prolonged my career because I was forced to give my body a rest.'

A year and a half later, O'Connor's leading Cork out

onto the field for the 2009 national league final against Mayo. It hasn't been their most aesthetically pleasing campaign, losing back-to-back games for the first time in seven years, but it's another reality check on their pilgrimage. They cannot take winning for granted.

A new sponsor is sourced with the help of former GAA president Christy Cooney just in time for the televised final, with businessman Denis Desmond's MCD Concerts firm coming on-board in a five-figure sponsorship deal.

Cork dispatch Mayo (1–10 to 0–11), and after featuring in thirty-one All-Ireland finals (ten in football and twenty-one in camogie) Mary O'Connor is finally a winning Cork captain.

•••

Back on the training field, the bond among the players is as strong as ever. Over the course of the last few years they've matured, both individually and as a group. They've learned how to handle themselves, and situations, and with that maturity comes the realisation that they're important role models for the next generation.

Their togetherness stems from a very simple weekly ritual. For the last number of years, selector Frankie Honohan has nourished their limbs after every Sunday morning training session. The Donoughmore man's contribution to this success story has always been overlooked, but the players have never underestimated his importance.

Every Friday, Honohan sources chicken carcasses and boils them to make stock for his homemade vegetable soup.

The carcasses don't cost a penny, and more often than not he uses his own vegetables – potatoes, carrots, onions, leeks, celery and cauliflower – but the time he dedicates to the task is priceless.

Everything must be organic, and he's never once changed the recipe for fear of upsetting the routine. On Saturday morning he prepares the vegetables, and if he's busy elsewhere on the farm, then his wife, Nell, takes over, before baking scones or brown bread.

It's another early start for Honohan on Sunday as he heats the soup to save time later on, before transporting it into the back of his car with all his other cuisine paraphernalia and he heads for training in The Farm.

With thirty minutes remaining in the session, Honohan disappears into a secondary dressing room with a bottle of gas and a stove he's brought from home. He reheats the soup and lays out scones, bread and cups for when the girls come in off the field.

In sync, management and players mingle, courtesy of Honohan's unsung generosity.

'It's easier for them to relax when their tummies are full,' says Honohan. 'I'm not sure how it started really. I've never made soup for any other team I've been involved in. I think after some cold morning one January one of the players joked that they'd love soup, and the next week I just brought everything along, and it's been happening ever since.'

To the girls, he means everything.

'Frankie's effort to the cause is incredible, and he'll never know how grateful we are to him,' says Bríd Stack. 'The only thing that's not organic is the cup! But Frankie is the type of guy who'd give you the shirt off his back, and his wife, Nell, can't be forgotten either. They'd have put all the Rockchapel girls up a few times for the homecoming celebrations to Donoughmore, and he'd make us all onion soup and we'd be drinking it at five in the morning! Even then, he was still looking after us, making sure we were all okay, and we owe him and Nell so much.'

Sunday training brunch was a new concept for Ryan, too, but its value plays an enormous role in Cork's success.

'Frankie's contribution will never be fully appreciated. It's of far more benefit than going to the fanciest hotel in town and having a meal. The players sit down and relax and get to know each other more. You'd find that someone from the east of Cork is talking shite to someone from the west of Cork, and a selector could be listening, or even talking more shite, but the dynamic that's created is super.

'It sounds very agricultural but it's great. Another team might think you should have caterers, and because you hadn't, you were unprofessional. But it's the ambiance it creates.

'The girls are all dolly birds and could arrive dressed to kill after being at some function, but then they come into the dressing room after training in their tracksuits and they're like little ones from fifth class.

'It's an understated part of our success and it hasn't got the appreciation it should have, and if I ever move on to another team, 'twill be one of the things I'd be hoping to bring.'

Honohan's culinary skills aside, his football brain is even more beneficial. Time and again he has spotted things in play that others have not. Tactically he's on the ball too, and if Cork did not have Honohan's knowledge from the very start, it's questionable how far they would have gotten.

•••

In the summer of 2009, Cork claim their sixth provincial title in a row, against Kerry (6–15 to 0–9). They go on to hammer Kildare by twenty-nine points in the quarter-final (4–23 to 0–6), before being put to the pin of their collar by Mayo in the semi-final: a goal by Briege Corkery with fifty-five seconds remaining ensuring their return to Croke Park (3–10 to 1–9).

But there's somewhat of a sideshow playing out on Leeside. The Cork GAA board has fixed the men's senior county football championship final for Sunday 27 September, on the same afternoon as the ladies bid for their fifth successive All-Ireland title, with St Finbarr's in action against Clonakilty. Supporters are disappointed with the timing of the fixture, especially given that the Fermanagh county board has moved its county SFC final between Derryconnelly and Roslea to the Saturday night with their ladies in the intermediate All-Ireland against Clare on the Sunday. Not only that, but Antrim, who are facing Limerick in the junior ladies final, refixed their men's SFC decider for Saturday also.

Unfortunately, the respect for the reigning senior All-

Ireland champions in their home county isn't, as yet, as substantial as they'd like it to be.

Cork are facing a Dublin side desperate to get their hands on the Brendan Martin Cup for the first time. They've worked hard under a high-profile back-room team – five-time All-Ireland-winning Waterford manager Michael Ryan, three-time O'Connor Cup coach Gerry McGill and Olympic athlete trainer Jim Kilty – and the vibe is that this is their year.

The morning before the final, Eamonn Ryan visits the grave of his brother-in-law, Tim. He says a quick prayer and asks his former statsman to give the girls guidance from the heavens above because he knows they'll need it. Juliet Murphy and Briege Corkery are on antibiotics and Ryan's worried they won't hold up, while the bookies have Cork 1/11 favourites and Dublin at 6/1, and that perceived disparity is also unsettling him.

Cork lead three times, Dublin six, and they're on par as many times, in front of a crowd of 20,600 – the majority of whom are brandishing sky blue colours. At half-time Cork trail by a point (1–2 to 0–6) and the Dubs' attack looks much more sinister. So much so that Ryan moves midfielder Juliet Murphy to centre-back, where she's never played before, to cut off the supply line. Nine minutes after the restart, full-forward Amy O'Shea fractures her ribs and departs on a motorised stretcher, and Cork are struggling to get points on the board. Valerie Mulcahy's free taking is keeping them in it, but with time running out, Murphy's getting tetchy.

She knows she's lost at centre-back and during a break in play sprints towards the sideline. 'Eamonn, move me back into midfield please! I'll be able to do something for you there!' she pleads with Ryan. He gives her a nod of approval and off she goes.

Murphy is his first lieutenant on the field and he believes in her implicitly. He isn't remotely offended by her request, because he's trained her and the entire panel to think for themselves and take responsibility. Murphy has never questioned Ryan's instructions before, but she knows in her heart that if she stays where she is she'll be no use to anyone.

With six minutes remaining and trailing by a point, captain Mary O'Connor's legs have gone. Shattered, she signals to the bench to take her off. It doesn't matter if she's captain or not, she just wants to win.

Within seconds, her replacement, Mairéad Kelly, kicks the equaliser, before Nollaig Cleary's left boot fires over the next point with one minute and thirty-five seconds left on the clock (1–9 to 0–11).

Winning the next kickout is vital and Geraldine O'Flynn pounces on it. For the next ninety-five seconds, Cork keep possession, with Juliet Murphy doing that shuffle she does when holding the ball up. Like playing a zone offence in basketball, she dictates a pass-and-move format. They create a string of thirty-nine hand passes amid a chorus of boos from the Dublin supporters, but they don't care. They can't even hear them their focus is so intense. It's all about using their heads, and that sequence of play is now revered across the realm of Gaelic games.

For the first time in her sixteen-year inter-county career, and with twelve All-Ireland medals to her name, Mary O'Connor lifts the Brendan Martin Cup as Cork captain. Until this season, she's kept herself to herself, her shyness making her generally reserved, but this year she's learned to be more vocal.

'Kilkenny, we see your four and raise you one!' she shouts, referring to the Kilkenny hurlers' recent four in a row win under Brian Cody.

Her acceptance speech goes on as long as the celebrations in Killeagh the following night, but it has been a long time coming for her personally. And, unknown to her then, it would be her last time in Croke Park with the footballers.

'People gave me grief about the speech, but I'd been thinking so long and hard about it. It was a bit of tongue in cheek really and it was my one opportunity to be up there.

'But the first minute after the final whistle is the best. That feeling of satisfaction and relief, and you're all sharing it together. And the craic in the dressing room … silly stuff, jumping around, throwing water … we're grown women but you just can't help but feel like a child in your element.'

Things, however, would turn sour in the aftermath for Eamonn Ryan. During the course of the game, he allegedly had a run-in with an official, who reported the incident to the referee, and Ryan is given an eight-week suspension at a follow-up disciplinary meeting in Tullamore.

'It was alleged that I told an official, a guy in a yellow bib, to go away,' Ryan recalls. 'They claimed I said it in unparliamentary language, but I didn't. I just told him to go away. I was a bit hard done by. You might have wondered if I kicked him would I have only got four weeks? I wasn't happy about it, but the sun is still shining and life goes on.'

13

ANNUS HORRIBILIS

*'Hard work beats talent
when talent doesn't work hard.'*
Tim Notke

The quad bike in front is spraying specks of rubbish like slurry back on top of Nollaig Cleary. She clings to the handlebars, grateful for her sunglasses. They're the only protection she's got zooming through mounds of household waste on a cross-country expedition during the team holiday in Tunisia.

When it's Norita Kelly's turn, Cleary reluctantly hands over her 'protective goggles' – health and safety isn't exactly a priority on the tour operator's list.

It takes one day for the first victim to fall with diarrhoea. Then there's the vomiting, and it signals the start of Cork's *annus horribilis* in 2010.

One by one, the players drop. The majority are curled up in their hotel rooms and, with two to a room, the bathroom visits are becoming ever more awkward. Toilets are working overtime, and those in dire straits request a single room. Laura McMahon is so ill she has to be given an injection to help her stop getting sick. And, while those bedridden are miserable, the rain is making it unpleasant for those not yet afflicted, too.

Flying into Dublin Airport on Saturday 20 February

can't come fast enough, but in the morning they have to drive from the capital to Inniskeen in Monaghan for a national league tie. As it stands, Ryan won't be able to field a team, but luck is on their side when a call comes through that the game is off due to a frozen pitch. Those with iron stomachs who are left standing celebrate with a rare fry.

On the bus home, Laura MacMahon is still green, and blood tests later show she had salmonella.

When all are recuperated, Cork go on to win their fifth national league title in six years, beating Galway (2–10 to 1–9) to complete their first ever national league three in a row. It's an even more special day for Mairéad Kelly who, after seven years in the squad, makes her first start in a final.

Despite the win, something isn't sitting right with Ryan. The edge that saw Cork win five successive All-Irelands the previous September isn't as sharp and absences from training aren't been communicated as clearly to management. The players' focus is diluted and their intensity in training is ebbing.

They haven't let their guard down for years and there are whispers that players are drinking when they normally wouldn't. Adventures are had to the Galway Races during the championship, and holidays are also taken at a time that's usually sacred. Angela Walsh heads to Australia for five weeks to spend time with her partner, Kevin, who left Ireland during the recession to find work; this is understandable as they haven't seen each other for months and life outside football must go on.

Even Juliet Murphy, the polished professional, is taking shortcuts. She's not doing as much in the gym, and every now and again stays out late on a Saturday night. Although no alcohol is ever consumed, the tiredness makes it a minor battle to get through training the next morning. Rest and recovery are subtly put to one side. She's giving more of her time to others now, too, agreeing to be a trainer on RTÉ's *Celebrity Bainisteoir* for wedding planner and contestant Franc. The selfish streak that's needed to be the best isn't as taut as it once was.

But it's not just Murphy, it's the majority. They're getting fractionally complacent, and however little they're taking their foot off the pedal individually, it's mounting up.

Captain Rena Buckley has a quiet word with Eamonn Ryan. She's concerned. His enthusiasm hasn't wavered in the slightest, but the players haven't upped their game remotely since the previous autumn. He can see it for himself, and on Sunday 27 June calls the thirty-one players on the squad into the green dressing room block in The Farm for a meeting.

A film of subliminal complacency had now settled over them. They beat Kerry the week before in the Munster semi-final by five points (2–8 to 1–6) – a game which the dual players featured in at 3 p.m. in CIT, having already played Kilkenny in a senior camogie championship match in Páirc Uí Rinn fifteen minutes away at 1 p.m. Although it wasn't a bad result, Ryan needs to rein the team in.

Armed with an A4 sheet of paper with handwritten

notes, Ryan informs the players of where he thinks it's going wrong. They listen, but it doesn't sink in as much as it should. They defeat Clare in the Munster final (5–13 to 2–9), but in the subsequent training session, eleven are missing. The dual players are excused for recovery purposes because on the day of the provincial final they were once again forced to play two games within a matter of hours. The fixtures clash saw them first line out in a senior camogie championship match against Galway at 2 p.m. in Athenry before having to travel to Castletownroche, 413 km away in north Cork to play in the Munster SFC final at 5 p.m. A police escort was organised to get Mary O'Connor and Rena Buckley from Galway to the Cork–Limerick border in time to make the second game. Their friend, Tommy Seward, drove O'Connor and Buckley as the escort whizzed through weekend traffic, but it was a situation that never should have arisen. The players were annoyed by the inconvenience, but opted not to speak publicly about the dangers of playing two senior inter-county games in a matter of hours, not to mention having to resort to getting a high-speed escort.

First eleven, then twelve were missing from training; then fifteen. The absenteeism is much too high for Ryan's liking. A few of the older players meet among themselves. They know they must re-stabilise their focus, but the discussions aren't as frank as they should be and things are left unsaid.

There's a six-week window now between the Munster final and the All-Ireland quarter-final against Tyrone, and

Ryan carries out a beep test, which is a twenty-metre shuttle run test. Only half the squad are present. It's a warning sign that he's worried about their fitness, and there are chinks in their armour.

•••

Meanwhile in Tyrone, a young man in his early twenties by the name of Niall Colton is reinvigorating a side that lost to Cork by eighteen points in the fourth round of the national league (3–13 to 0–4) earlier in the spring. The Red Hands managed to score just four points that day, but Colton's been busy transforming them ahead of the championship.

The players like him. He's passionate and he's rekindled their love of football. From tyre bags, to pull sleds, to hill sprints, their effort has multiplied tenfold since February.

A cousin of centre-back Neamh Woods, this is new territory for Colton, but he's feeding off his players' energy and they off his. A picture board of photographs of the team, which includes an inspiring Muhammad Ali quote, is made and carried onto the bus for every game. It's a small touch, but it's potent.

Twenty-four hours after each game they play, Colton has it dissected and analysed in full. Burning the midnight oil, the next day at training he presents the players with charts of where the opposition scored from; where they have to get tighter in defence; where they won and lost kickouts; and where they gave possession away. Every base is covered.

The physical work has taken care of itself, but the

paperwork is moulding them into a well-oiled unit on the field. With just twenty-three players on the panel, it's the tightest Tyrone team there's been in some time. They've come through the qualifier against Sligo, and ahead of the quarter-final have played three more competitive games than Cork, their last just a fortnight ago; Cork's was six weeks ago.

The Tuesday night before facing the reigning champions, Colton's ladies are hopping off the ground. So much so, they know that they're going to win. The return of Neamh Woods from Boston for the game is an added boost.

For Cork, forward Mairéad Kelly has flown in from the Women's Rugby World Cup in Surrey, England, having featured for Ireland against the host nation the night before. Angela Walsh also returns to the starting line-up for the team after her trip to Australia, despite not having played a competitive game since the league final in May.

With a quarter of an hour gone in Banagher, Cork are dealt two blows. In the tenth minute, Ciara O'Sullivan snaps her cruciate. Six minutes later, so too does 2010 Munster Player of the Year Geraldine O'Flynn, who just a week before kicked fourteen points from play in a club championship game. She opts to play on, but her knee only holds out for a couple of minutes. Cork, however, still manage to lead by six points at the turnaround (0–11 to 0–5).

In Colton's dressing room, Tyrone still believe. It's not that they believe in beating Cork, it's that they know what it takes to win this match. For the first time in a long time, they believe in themselves.

The game takes on a darker hue in the second half. Referee Des McEnery of Westmeath is more whistle-happy, and Cork's efficiency rate in front of the posts has severely dropped. Laura McMahon is straight through on goal but her left boot misfires a rasper over the bar and it's seventeen minutes now since Cork have given the umpires something to do.

A Tyrone goal brings the northerners back into it, and when McEnery sin-bins defender Bríd Stack for a high tackle and substitute Aisling Barrett for a dubious free less than a minute later, Cork's backs are against the wall, fighting fire with just thirteen players.

It's a tied game with five minutes left (1–10 to 0–13), and Cork have only scratched two points on the board for the entire half – a duo of frees.

There's a whiff of blood in the air and Tyrone go for the jugular.

With three minutes left, full-forward Sarah Connolly delivers the first punch when she slams the ball into the back of Elaine Harte's net (2–11 to 0–13).

Ryan is stunned on the sideline. He predicted it would happen, but not for a second did he think today would be the day.

'Well here we go, it's happening,' he says to himself as Sarah Donnelly surges past him up the field. With sixty seconds left, the result is inevitable now, but she's a woman on a mission, having made a bet during the week that she'd score the last goal, and she does (3–11 to 0–13).

Norma Kelly's eyes are glued to a television in an Irish

bar somewhere in Australia. Picking her jaw up off the floor, she scrambles through her handbag to find her phone to call Briege Corkery. The St Val's player took some time out and is now working on a dairy farm in New Zealand milking cows with her future husband, Diarmuid Scannell.

Corkery's convinced Kelly's taking the mick. It's one of Kelly's talents, but there's no doubt about the shock in her voice. Corkery can only imagine what her teammates, twelve thousand miles away, are going through.

Juliet Murphy is slumped in the middle of the pitch. Her head hangs. She's contemplating if this is the end of an era.

At the same time, Tyrone's Gemma Begley is running for Niall Colton's arms. Only they know what's gone into getting this win, and although Cork's bad luck all came at once, it doesn't take from Tyrone's unseen exertions to bridge the gap. Every other day Cork would have the answer, but their complacency, however brief, met head-on with Tyrone's newfound belief and work rate. Rena Buckley and her teammates must now pay the consequences.

Juliet Murphy makes a point of shaking hands with every Tyrone player and tells them to 'go on and win it now'. Eamonn Ryan heads for Tyrone's dressing room, and he too makes a point of staying longer than necessary. He doesn't want it to be a 'Mickey Mouse, three-cheers speech', he needs to let Tyrone know he respects their win.

Wedged into their own dressing room, Cork are devastated. The tears could fill the crates of water bottles they're forced to sit on. Bríd Stack is inconsolable, blaming herself for the loss because of her sin-binning. Geraldine O'Flynn is hopping on one leg trying to pack her gear bag, her tears as much as her injury hindering her. Her club teammate and good friend Norita Kelly is welling up too. Not so much because of the loss, but because she knows first-hand the hardship that awaits O'Flynn during recovery.

When the team are dressed, Ryan shuffles in, but he's not sure what to say, so he doesn't say much.

Some players return home on the bus, but others can't manage the magnitude of it all and filter off to be with their parents and partners. Tyrone head for a bar in Dromore, nine miles from Omagh. They don't do much celebrating despite the parish lauding them. To everyone else, today's victory was a surprise, but not to them.

The Cork players don't make contact with each other again until the week leading up to the All-Ireland final between Tyrone and Dublin, who dispatched Kerry and Laois respectively in the semis. It's only then the text messages start flying, with questions of what were people doing for the final. They were at a complete loss. It's the first time in five years that they're in limbo, and each of them is trying to gauge what's the right thing to do.

Mulcahy is asked to do radio commentary, but she can't bring herself to. She's torn; toying with the idea of going to Croker as some sort of punishment she could draw from. Instead, Elaine Harte represents the team and commentates on RTÉ Radio 1.

Bríd Stack can't even bring herself to watch the game,

and her father, Mick, breaks the result to her: Dublin 3–16 Tyrone 0–9. Juliet Murphy takes off to Cork city to be left alone walking the streets, listening to her iPod, but inside she's cracking up. She takes out her mobile and sends a text to Eamonn Ryan. He's watching the game in the sitting room when his phone beeps.

'We're feckin' eejits not to be there,' it reads.

Sick to his stomach, Ryan can't agree more.

'But if it hadn't happened, we wouldn't have gone on to win another few,' Ryan admits. 'Players can either offload the blame to someone, or they can face up to it and work. They never offloaded it. Even though there were two cruciates, two sin-binnings and some strange refereeing decisions, they never got cranky about it.

'It's just like a good student who does well for so long at a certain subject and then fails to study for a little bit and gets a poor result. That's what it boiled down to.'

Although the result still stings for some, Juliet Murphy points the finger at no one else but themselves.

'We got bloody well complacent. The summer training was poor and even though we were starting to get our act together, it was too late. If we'd got over Tyrone, I think we would've had enough time and a chance to reach another final. But when it started to crack on the pitch, we weren't able to pull it back.

'The injuries and sendings off were tough, but we still could've won. Had we prepared properly, we would have been capable of it, but that day we weren't. Tyrone had their homework done and they deserved it. I wouldn't for a second say that if we were right, we would have won. We were careless, lackadaisical and we deserved to be beaten.'

Elaine Harte agrees. 'That year in general, we took things for granted in ways that we wouldn't have any other year. I'd been in the Gaeltacht on teaching practice the week leading up to the game and I'd asked selector Noel O'Connor could I borrow an O'Neills ball and that I'd give it back to him in Banagher. But I forgot it and said I'd bring it the next night to training. I just presumed we'd have training again. I wasn't being cocky, because subconsciously you've to believe you're going to win. But maybe too, deep down, it was complacency. I was being presumptuous.

'Losing really instilled in us that we had to appreciate every game, enjoy it and do our very best to win. To feel what it's like to lose did us no harm at all.'

2010 was 'the year of the underdog', with Cork joining a line of reigning GAA champions to relinquish their titles. The Kilkenny hurlers lost their bid for five in a row, the Kerry footballers a bid for back-to-back titles, and the Cork camogie team failed to gather three in a row. But there was no solace in that.

For the next three months, the players hibernated. They didn't know if Ryan was coming back, and they didn't know either if they had it in themselves to come back. It had been a long slog, and they knew more than anyone the effort it took to get to the highest heights; hence some were slow to make their decisions.

On 3 November 2010, they gather upstairs in a city pub owned by former Cork All-Ireland-winning football captain Larry Tompkins. The mood is deflated, even after so many weeks of licking their wounds. Some players are only there out of respect. Some still don't know what they are going to do, and others are gung-ho to drive on again in 2011.

'It was a desperate mess really,' says Mulcahy. 'We were still in the same disarray that we had been in leaving the dressing room in Banagher. There was despair in the room. I think people thought it was the natural end. But there's no half-doing it. That was what was behind the indecisiveness for some because you knew if you were going again, you'd have to throw everything and more at it.'

Ryan wanted to have another crack at it too, but he didn't tell the players that. He needed them to decide for themselves. They needed to decide for themselves.

It's never an automatic outcome when they regroup in late winter. Ryan sees to it that they think long and hard about what lies ahead, and will let him know in early January where they stand. He knows they don't owe anything to anyone, but they do owe it to themselves.

•••

A week later, Bríd Stack, Geraldine O'Flynn, Nollaig Cleary, Rena Buckley, Juliet Murphy and Valerie Mulcahy attend the 2010 O'Neills/TG4 All-Star banquet at the Citywest Hotel. They're all nominated, but Stack is the only one to win a bronze statue.

During the ceremony, they can't help but notice the father of a Dublin player chanting all evening at the table beside them. The Dubs won their first senior All-Ireland title, tearing Tyrone to shreds in the process. They had a right to celebrate, but it ran deeper than that. The Cork contingent perceived he was making sure they were within earshot all night, and every now and then he would look over to see if they were taking notice. 'Weeeeee are the champions! No time for losers …' he'd gloat.

There was a sense of 'we've arrived, and Cork are finished' – and that grated. It hurt their pride more than anything, and there and then they made a promise to each other that they were coming back in 2011. Coming back for Brendan.

14

TURNING ON THE LIGHT

*'The willingness to experiment with change may be the
most essential ingredient to success at anything.'*
Pat Summitt

Driving home through Macroom late one Saturday night, two girls on rollerblades catch Rena Buckley's eye. It's close to midnight and they're whizzing along the footpath, down the hill at the far end of the town. It's steep, but they navigate expertly through the crowds emptying onto the streets after closing hours, and skate straight through the front door of the local nightclub. Fair play, Buckley thinks to herself. Fast, yet steady on their feet, their reaction skills impress the seven-time dual All-Star.

The following morning, she bumps into Briege Corkery and recounts the story of the talented duo from the night before.

'You should have seen them! 'Twas gas!'

'Oh yeah?' asks Briege. 'Sure, wasn't I one of them!'

They burst out laughing and realise it's moments like these they missed together the previous year in 2010 when Corkery was away travelling. Any chance to experience the world, and she's off – San Francisco, New Zealand, Vancouver, Las Vegas, Australia.

She didn't experience the nightmare that was Bana-gher, and her aptitude and attitude once she crosses the whitewash is the antidote Cork need to refocus in 2011. These are the characteristics that have helped her win sixteen All-Ireland medals alongside Rena Buckley (ten in football; six in camogie), thirteen All-Stars (eight in football; five in camogie), and Players' Player of the Year in both codes. Only the late Kathleen Mills, who won fifteen All-Irelands with Dublin camogie in the 1950s and 1960s, had come close.

The second youngest of ten growing up on a farm in Aghinagh, Corkery had no choice but to get stuck in. In the 2009 All-Ireland final against Dublin, she took a tumble, got up and played on. It wasn't until that night on the dance floor in the hotel that she realised her rib was fractured. But that's how she rolls.

'There will never be anyone like Briege in football again,' says Juliet Murphy. 'That combination of athleticism and determination. I've never seen a more fearless player. She trains hard and she plays hard, and she'll be the first one dancing on the bar without ever falling off, but her focus is just something else.'

Corkery's her own woman too. A leader, not a follower, she sees the bigger picture. Having once arrived late to underage training with Cork, a selector began to make an example of her, but he should have known her wit was too sharp.

'Briege, you're late!' he barked.

'You'd be too if you'd to milk two hundred cows!' she says flying past him, hardly up to his waist.

She loves football, but it's not her life. She knows there's much more to it and that's what makes Briege Corkery unique. For such a high-calibre athlete, she doesn't obsess about things. Performing is all that matters, and unless she gives 100 per cent on the pitch, she's not satisfied.

Off the field she's the life and soul of the party. On the 2012 All-Star trip to Toronto, for example, she had an entire Irish bar in awe of her while she sang a rebel song. But that's Corkery for you, uniting people wherever she goes.

A former stonemason, she lives in the moment, just as she does every day she puts on a Cork jersey. What she offers is priceless, and her return in 2011 is invaluable.

'Her get-it-the-feck-out-of-here mentality: you need that,' says 2011 Cork captain Amy O'Shea. 'Briege takes games by the scruff of the neck and we could have done with that in 2010. There's some Premiership soccer clubs that would pay millions to get what Briege has because she definitely has different batteries than the rest of us!'

If Corkery is the yang, then her dual teammate Rena Buckley is the yin. The quiet one. For years they've been one – two of a kind – playing, training and travelling to games in both codes since the age of fourteen. It's all they know.

Bar a two-month stint on a J1 visa to Hawaii in 2008, Buckley hasn't missed a beat. She's a home bird, and her close relationship with her twin sister, Mary, is precious. Establishing her own physiotherapy practice is a priority too, but she's relieved Corkery's back in the mix as they arrive for their first session of 2011.

With layers of coats on her, Corkery begins her quest to get fit again. She sweats out the fun of the last few months, and in turn her dedication to the cause inspires those around her. The intensity is back and no one dares miss a session. Just one absence from training and starting places are up for grabs.

The return of Corkery sees the departure of another dual star. Mary O'Connor calls it a day, aged thirty-three, with twenty-one All-Ireland medals between league, championship and club to her name. She celebrates retirement with a three-week holiday to America, but it's hard to let go. Her heart is telling her to stay for one more year, but her body is pleading with her to stop.

O'Connor doesn't want to be that older player who feeds off cameos. She's had a good innings, and now must live with her decision. But it's not easy. She misses the routine and so trains for and completes two marathons, but they don't give her anywhere near the same buzz.

O'Connor's contribution to the world of GAA doesn't go unnoticed, and she's awarded an honorary doctorate from UCC, on the same day as Irish rugby star Ronan O'Gara, former Ireland and Manchester United soccer player Denis Irwin, Kilkenny hurling manager Brian Cody, and Irish horse trainer Aidan O'Brien.

Eamonn Ryan had hoped O'Connor would return, but he'll just adapt. To him every player that walks away is a loss regardless of their stature, but it's just a matter of adjusting and moving on.

And 2011 is all about that: moving on.

In early spring, Cork are plagued with injuries and ten key players are on the physio table. Fifteen recruits are brought in on trial, but they're not there to fill in for those wounded. The likes of cross-country champion Orlagh Farmer and her cousin Emma Farmer, Orla Finn and Grace Kearney are bedding in, and Ryan uses thirty-six players in total during the league campaign.

In the fallout of losing to Tyrone in 2010, the depth of the bench came into question. So too did the management's belief in the players that sat on it, as the critics picked holes at Cork's most vulnerable time. In 2011, those critics would be answered.

•••

Six new names start in the 2011 national league final in Parnell Park, Dublin. Laois are tougher than they expect and their target woman, Tracey Lawlor, is dictating play. A natural talent with a sweet left foot, she's used to big days against Cork.

The third youngest of eight, Lawlor was born an hour before her twin brother, Paul – having a competitive streak even then. Growing up, they practised together for hours, and so good was Lawlor that she played on the boys' team up to minor level, before breaking her wrist in the first minor game put an end to it.

By fourteen, Lawlor had already made her adult inter-county debut – in the 1998 intermediate All-Ireland final against Cork. On the same day, 2011 Cork captain Amy O'Shea also made her debut, and thirteen years later, they're trying to outdo each other again in the league final.

The game is fifty–fifty up until the closing minutes and Ryan calls on five subs, including Geraldine O'Flynn and Ciara O'Sullivan. It's their first game back since limping off the field in Banagher ten months earlier against Tyrone in the All-Ireland quarter-final, and they combine to guide Cork to their fourth successive league title (4–15 to 3–9).

The depth of the bench has taken on a life of its own and a new era begins during Eamonn Ryan's reign. It's no longer expected that subs will change games, it's a given. There's a sense that those on the bench are empowered again, and the line between the starting fifteen and the rest of the squad has faded. Not that there was ever any divide, but things had become predictable. New faces brought a new fight, and competition was as fierce as it had ever been.

The work rate of the forward-line increased dramatically. Captain and corner-forward Amy O'Shea is named Player of the Match in the national league final, despite not having registered a single score. Valerie Mulcahy tallies 1–8, but O'Shea's persistence is what catches the eye.

She's a different captain. For a start, she has had to work twice as hard as any of her predecessors, coming back from injury. By the age of twenty-one she had suffered two cruciate knee injuries – one left, one right. The first she did aged nineteen; and while leaving Dr Tadhg O'Sullivan's office in Waterford on her last visit, she tripped on a step and damaged knee cartilage. O'Sullivan was walking her out as it happened; there and then he booked O'Shea back in for an appointment the following day.

During her second knee cruciate recovery, O'Shea's father, Dermot, would have to sit on his daughter's knee for ten minutes each night to help straighten it out. All in all, with eight knee operations during her career, injuries cost O'Shea four years, but she kept coming back for more.

In July 2011 she leads Cork out in the Munster final against William O'Sullivan's Kerry in front of a 1,200-strong crowd at Fitzgerald Stadium in Killarney. Kerry are hungry, but in the pre-game huddle Ryan reminds them of Arsenal FC's motto *Victoria concordia crescit* – 'Victory comes from harmony' – and they oblige, winning their eighth successive provincial title (2–15 to 0–11).

They get the 2011 division two league champions Dublin in the draw for the All-Ireland quarter-final, but the players are nervous. It's at this juncture twelve months previously that they imploded. In the dressing room in Birr beforehand, Eamonn Ryan tells another story that assures his players they're ready this time.

'I was listening to a woman on the radio the other day whose husband died,' he says. 'She was asked how she kept going. How was she able to see the light at the end of the tunnel? And, do you know what her answer was? She said she was able to keep going because she walked down that tunnel and turned on the feckin' light herself … Now, go out there and do the same!'

It's as simple as that, and the anecdote has pockets of adrenaline exploding in their muscles.

Cork are going well, but by half-time Dublin are still within a point (0–8 to 1–6). Like Tyrone a year earlier, Cork sense this one's here for the taking against the reigning champions.

The game restarts and Dublin captain Sinéad Goldrick's side bury two goals. Rhona Ní Bhuachalla responds with one for Cork, but the Dubs aren't fazed. They expected a response. They were warned it would happen, and when it did, they were told to keep driving on. They're coasting now, in front by six points (3–10 to 2–7) with sixteen minutes left on the clock. If they keep the engine running as well as it is, they'll become the second team to beat Cork in a championship game in six years.

For Cork, flashbacks to the devastation in the Banagher dressing room become vivid – and give them the jolt they need. Ryan knows it's time to make big calls. The substitutions will decide their fate. Three All-Stars and the Cork captain – Geraldine O'Flynn, Bríd Stack, Nollaig Cleary and Amy O'Shea – are whipped off; there's no time for loyalty.

Incredibly, Briege Corkery is still going at wing-back. There were doubts about her fitness given that she missed the Munster final due to viral meningitis. Uncharacteristic headaches and tiredness led to a trip to A&E, and she missed eight weeks of the championship. Today, you wouldn't know it; she's as energetic as ever.

So too is Rena Buckley. She's been flat out in midfield and her days of cross-country runs with Blarney-Inniscarra Athletics Club are standing to her. Substitute Orla Finn is another who likes to gallop, and on a national level too. In fact, prior to throw-in she was competing in the All-Ireland Athletics Championships in Tullamore, coming second in the 400m hurdles, competing in the triple jump, and finishing second in the team event. Two hours later in Birr, it's a team event of a different kind, and she fires over a point.

Dublin hearts sink a little as something clicks for Cork when Finn pulls the trigger. Up until now they've had thirteen wides, but up sprints Deirdre O'Reilly from corner-back to unleash a monstrous point. O'Reilly doesn't say much, but the look in her eye tells her teammates they're going to survive. They must survive.

Sticking to the basics, they begin to pass, move, pass, score. Repeat. The defensive unit keep Dublin scoreless for the next fifteen minutes – read, intercept, distribute. Repeat.

Cork gain a numerical advantage when Sinéad Goldrick is sin-binned for Dublin, and Rhona Ní Bhuachalla floats over the equalising point for Cork on the fifty-sixth minute. She's the biggest clutch player Ryan has got, and she delivers again.

A minute later, Juliet Murphy comes through from midfield to score the winning point. It's Cork's seventh unanswered point (2–14 to 3–10). Murphy turns and, with a smile on her face, points her finger to the sky – that's the one they needed.

Afraid to celebrate prematurely, the substitutes are bouncing on the line on the far side of the stand. Arms around shoulders, they try as best they can to keep each other calm, but it's nearly impossible.

With ninety seconds to go, Cork replicate what they did to the Dubs in the 2009 All-Ireland final. Keeping possession, they weave thirteen passes together before the hooter sounds: they're back into an All-Ireland semi-final. The celebrations are of epic proportions. They know how hard they've worked to get back there.

The first to hug Eamonn Ryan are captain Amy O'Shea and Nollaig Cleary, whom he called ashore with a quarter of an hour to go. The newfound belief in the bench has paid dividends and they all know it – *Victoria concordia crescit*.

'We threw caution to the wind and it worked,' admits Ryan. 'Players who would normally do well, weren't. They're all big names, but if time's running out, you've no choice. They all understood that too. But we were confident in the people we were bringing on – Aisling Hutchings, Norita Kelly, Orla Finn, Annie Walsh and Áine Sheehan. The mindset is different now than a few years ago. It's all about rotating players if things aren't going well.

'You'd be loyal to the older crew because they've done it so many times for you, but at the end of the day, it works on performance, regardless of who you are.'

In the All-Ireland semi-final against Laois in Cashel, Ryan takes the same stance and brings on five subs to get the win (4–10 to 1–6), and although the players are thrilled to be back in Croke Park, the facilities at the Tipperary venue are all they can talk about in the aftermath of the game.

'There was no running water in the toilets and no showers working after the match,' remembers Player of the Match Juliet Murphy. 'Not having running water to me is unforgivable. It's not a red carpet affair, but it's basic things we're talking about, and for me that was one of the lowest points of being involved in ladies football.

'I just thought it was very wrong. The same day, at the same venue, the bus of another inter-county team was broken into and their belongings taken. Where are you going like?

'I do acknowledge the leaps ladies football has made, but there are core issues that need to be addressed, like the standard of facilities and where we play. I would have gladly given up an All-Star trip to pump some money into better facilities because they're the main issues for players.'

The players' focus, however, soon returns to preparing for their first All-Ireland final appearance since 2009, and on the Wednesday night before the game, Ryan reveals that Mairéad Kelly, Anne-Marie Walsh and Grace Kearney are in the starting fifteen. For all three it will be their first start in Croke Park, but Kelly's inclusion stands out. She's waited seven years for this chance. The older sister of midfielder Norita Kelly made cameos in the 2005, 2006, 2007 and 2009 finals, but now her patience and commitment are being rewarded with the number 11 jersey.

Living in Harold's Cross in Dublin and working in the Irish Financial Services Centre, Kelly commutes up and down the M7 to Cork training two times a week, and has done so on and off for four years, while also taking in sessions with Ballyboden St Enda's ladies football team in Dublin. She departs the capital at 3.30 p.m. to be in Josephine's petrol station in Urlingford, Kilkenny, by 5 p.m. There she collects Geraldine O'Flynn, who's commuting from Portlaoise where she's worked as a PE teacher for five years, and Elaine Harte, who lives in Tipperary and travels from Thurles – and would do so for nine years in total until her retirement in 2013. By 6.40 p.m. they're at The Farm, with twenty minutes to spare before training, and it will be midnight by the time Kelly gets back home to Dublin.

In the summer evenings, she makes the commute solo because Elaine Harte and Geraldine O'Flynn are teachers and have summers off; she'll arrive at training, sometimes only having had a cup of tea beforehand courtesy of the groundsman at The Farm. She's doing that for years before Ryan latches onto it. Like him – who's travelled almost 72,000 miles just to Cork training over the years – she doesn't get travel expenses. They do it because they love it, and starting in an All-Ireland final is worth the wait for Kelly.

In the team meeting the night before the 2011 All-Ireland final, Ryan produces a good luck card from Mary O'Connor. Inside is a photocopy of a sheet of paper he gave the team many moons ago. On it, the flying V formation of geese is explained:

By flying in V formation, the whole flock adds at least 71% greater flying range than if each bird flew on its own. People who share a common direction and sense of community can get where they are going more quickly and easily because they are travelling on the trust of one another.

It is their season epitomised in one paragraph. From one to thirty-two, they all need each other if they're going to win their sixth All-Ireland title in seven years, but Monaghan are looking for retribution for the fourteen-point defeat in the 2008 final. They're the only team to beat Cork this year – a goal separated the sides in Emyvale in the second round of the league (2–7 to 1–13) – and they're more than capable of doing it again.

Therése McNally, Caoimhe Mohan and Ciara Mc-Anespie have scored twenty-seven goals and seventy-four points between them in their five championship games to date, and the bookies have Monaghan at 3/1 to win.

The Cork forwards are making hard work of things and full-back Sharon Courtney has Valerie Mulcahy in her pocket. But, with Monaghan goalkeeper Linda Martin gifting Nollaig Cleary a goal from a kickout midway through the first half, Cork lead 1–3 to 0–4 at half-time.

They've targeted the kickouts and won twenty to Monaghan's seven. Previously it had been their Achilles' heel, with Elaine Harte's distance somewhat limited. But working with one of the best goalkeeping coaches around, Kieran Dwyer, and a little advice from former Cork men's football goalkeeper Alan Quirke (Harte has being practising her kickouts with a size five men's ball instead of the ladies size four) has done wonders. The improvement is huge, and now she has the distance to match her accuracy.

In the second half, a cruel twist of fate befalls captain Amy O'Shea and seven minutes in she's carried off having suffered another knee injury.

While Cork's defence is keeping Monaghan's scoring threats at bay, with no one near getting past Player of the Match Angela Walsh, the forwards are squandering chances. So, just as he's done throughout the entire championship, Ryan turns to those at the back of the V formation and four of the starting forwards are replaced.

With a quarter of an hour remaining, wing-back Geraldine O'Flynn is playing the pantomime villain again, sneaking up the sideline to score the equaliser (1–5 to 0–8). Cork get a golden opportunity when substitute Orla Finn wins a penalty. Confusion sets in over who will take it, with Valerie Mulcahy having been taken off. Deirdre O'Reilly practised a few the previous week at training but as she's making her way up from the backline, Rhona Ní Bhuachalla is already placing the ball. In the stand, Mulcahy is praying that whoever takes it, makes it.

As twenty-year-old Ní Bhuachalla readies herself, Ciara O'Sullivan taps her on the shoulder and whispers in her ear. 'Just remember the penalties you scored underage with Cork,' she says with a wink. Ní Bhuachalla nods, grateful to O'Sullivan for the encouragement, and she sticks it.

Despite Monaghan's best efforts in the last fifteen minutes, Cork's rearguard isn't letting anyone through. As they did in the 2008 All-Ireland final, they keep the Farney side, who have now heartbreakingly lost their sixth

All-Ireland final in eight appearances since 1994, to eleven points (2–7 to 0–11).

Cork have come back from the darkest place they've ever known to win their sixth All-Ireland title. 2011 wasn't about redemption, although they have redeemed themselves; it was about the journey down a dark tunnel in the aftermath of their 2010 loss to Tyrone and turning back on the light.

Today it shone bright again.

15

FOR DONIE

'The strength of the team is each individual member.
The strength of each member is the team.'
Phil Jackson

Alone in the international departures lounge of Perth Airport, Angela Walsh's eyes are swollen from crying. Numb to everything and everyone, she's in a world of her own. Her limbs ache with weakness as she tries to comprehend the inevitable – saying goodbye.

The phone call came through that her father, Donie, wasn't doing well and she should get the first flight home. The summer before, he'd been diagnosed with an aggressive form of prostate cancer, but prior to Walsh's departure to Australia in June 2012 to visit her boyfriend, Kevin, there was no indication that her father would deteriorate. Treatment had gone well and things were looking up, so she headed away on her two-month travels, and her brother Andrew left for Saudi Arabia to work. Their father insisted they do so. Maybe he knew what was coming, but he didn't want to stop them from seeing the world.

'Go on away to Fiji and enjoy your holidays,' he'd say when Angela rang home.

'Dad, I'm not going to Fiji, I'm going to Bali.'

'Fiji, Bali, wherever you're going, just enjoy yourself!'

A gentleman, Donie Walsh was a home bird. Holidays

weren't his thing, and besides, an entire world could easily sweep through his kitchen any day of the week. There was never a dull moment, with visitors always calling to their home in Killeagh, and Donie enjoyed the constant stream of chats. He worked the farm all his life, with the help of his wife, Kathleen, who had taken a career break from nursing to rear their six children. Their second eldest, Angela was the best of the girls to tend to chores around the yard. She could put her hand to anything.

Sport was big in their lives too and Donie's claim to fame was that his father once marked the great Cork hurler Christy Ring. However, in his final months, it's his six-time All-Star-winning daughter and the Cork ladies footballers that Donie boasts about in his own quiet way. The previous September, when Angela was awarded Player of the Match in the 2011 All-Ireland final against Monaghan, he was the proudest man in Croke Park. Maybe it was fate, but it's fitting that it was the last time he watched his daughter play in a red jersey.

Visiting her father in hospital, Walsh would have to make a dash to get behind the curtain of his cubicle as fast as she could before her father announced to the ward that his daughter was 'the best full-back in Ireland'.

'Oh he'd mortify me, but he was so proud of me and the team,' Walsh smiles. 'It became such a big part of Dad and Mam's lives when my sister Ciara and I played. He worked so hard and made little time for himself, but he never enjoyed something so much as going to watch Cork play. The friendships my parents made along the way too, with the likes of Bríd Stack's parents, Liz and Mike, were just as special.'

In the week leading up to his passing, Donie Walsh's condition deteriorated and he requested to be brought home. Angela and her five siblings – Niamh, twins Ciara and Patrick, Andrew and Daniel – had a few special days with the man who had taught them so much about life. It was a difficult time, but a magical one too, as they sat in the kitchen recounting stories of how he was the best father in the world.

Every now and then Donie would speak out in his slumber, and almost every time he did, he mentioned the Cork ladies.

'What's the score in the match?' he'd murmur.

'How are the Cork girls doing now?'

'Angie, you'll go back playing for Cork won't you?' he'd ask.

Six days after she flew home from Australia, Angela Walsh's father passes away at 6 a.m. on Friday 3 August. His family are with him by his bedside.

The following evening, Walsh sits in Egan's Funeral Home in Youghal. Aged twenty-six, it's the first time she's been inside a funeral home. It's overwhelming, but she takes comfort in the mourners' warmth. There's no question how much her father is loved – the father who showed her the path of hard work and positivity, and held her hand every step of the way.

Donie's remains are carried into the Holy Family church in the town later that evening, and flanking either side of the doorway as he enters are Angela Walsh's teammates immaculately dressed in their Cork gear.

Donie, no doubt, was in his element.

'Angie was so strong,' remembers goalkeeper Elaine Harte. 'It was the first time a player on the team lost a parent and we needed to be there for her. We needed to give her something to pick her up, just to make her smile and help her get through it. We knew that Donie would have appreciated the gesture.'

A week after burying her father, Walsh packs her gear bag and lines out in a senior championship match with her club, Inch Rovers. It's been months since she's kicked a football, but it's her saving grace.

'Everyone was asking me if I was mad, but it was such a hard time at home trying to adjust to life without Dad,' Walsh admits. 'I just had to get out for an hour or two and get a bit of fresh air. Playing football helped me to forget about everything, if just for a little while. When you're chasing a ball around a pitch you're not thinking of anything else, and for those sixty minutes, you forget all your troubles.'

On summer holidays from work as a PE teacher at St Augustine's College in Dungarvan, Walsh is finding it hard to fill her time, but just three days after playing for Inch Rovers, Eamonn Ryan's name flashes across the screen of her mobile phone.

'It was about ten days after the funeral and I figured he was ringing to see how I was, which he was, but he also asked if I'd any interest in going back playing. It was about six weeks until the All-Ireland final and I hadn't played all year. I think he knew it would be good for me.

'But it was all my father. He was only up there a week or so and he already had Eamonn Ryan ringing me to try and get me to go back!' she grins. 'I didn't know what to do because there were girls training since January and here I am walking back in in August, but a few of the older girls said why not? But in a way I was going back for my father because it's what he would have wanted.'

•••

Earlier that spring, Cork lost their bid for five national league titles in a row when Monaghan outplayed them in Parnell Park (2–7 to 1–13) in the 2012 division one final. As disappointing as the defeat was, at no point was there a cause for concern. Cork prepared well, but their performance included twenty-four turnovers. Six balls were kicked short into Player of the Match, goalkeeper Linda Martin's hands, and five clear-cut goal chances were missed. It's a bad day at the office. Monaghan have less errors and it's as simple as that.

There have been some changes to the set-up at the start of the 2012 season, with James O'Callaghan – who himself played for Cork under Eamonn Ryan – replacing selector Noel O'Connor, while Amy O'Shea and Mairéad Kelly call time on their inter-county careers. Valerie Mulcahy opts out of the earlier league games to play on the left wing for Cork City Women's FC in the newly formed FAI domestic league and the one-time capped international finishes as their third highest scorer, before making her first start of the season for Eamonn Ryan in the Munster final against Kerry in July.

The break is Mulcahy's first from inter-county football since she was a teenager and she's embracing the challenge. Like most athletes, Mulcahy is quite self-critical and often goes in search of the littlest of margins to improve her kicking game.

In pursuit of perfection, she picks the brains of Kerry football legend Colm 'The Gooch' Cooper when they meet at an Adidas photo shoot, and within weeks the duo are comparing notes during a kicking session in Cooper's hometown of Killarney. Mulcahy's also pitted herself against some of the most physical defenders in Cork men's football, with one-on-one sessions against the likes of Eoin Cadogan and Paudie Kissane to improve her attacking moves.

But, despite taking years to perfect her free-taking skills – both off the ground and out of her hand, left leg and right – she's learned not to over-practice. Half an hour before training is as much as she'll do, concentrating 100 per cent on the mechanics of each individual kick. Quality over quantity wins every time.

In the Munster final against Kerry in Páirc Uí Rinn, Mulcahy scores 1–6 and Cork captain Rena Buckley lifts the Dairygold Cup for the county's ninth title in a row, despite having not played due to a broken toe. A week or two before the Munster championship began, however, it wasn't looking like Cork would be able to field a team, with the majority of the squad struck down by a tummy bug which had spread through the camp while on a training weekend in Ballyhass. There were fears it was going to be like Tunisia all over again and the curse of 2010 would return, but the squad recovered just in time.

In the seven-week gap between the provincial final and the All-Ireland quarter-final against Donegal, Ryan is fretting a little about Cork's play, but he doesn't let his concern show. Their last three games, the national league final, the opening round of the provincial championship against Clare, and against Kerry in the Munster final, have been mediocre. He's hoping it will come right, but in the meantime he calls on Jeff Gomez, an athlete performance manager at the UCC Mardyke Arena, to monitor the players' fitness levels.

French-born Gomez has worked with a number of top sports teams and Olympians, and the results open Ryan's eyes to the need for more cardio. They run faster and train harder. The true turning point in the season comes when Angela Walsh steps back through the doorway of the dressing rooms in The Farm in mid-August. The unity in the squad is lifted and gravitates towards her as she laces up her boots. She needs them, and they need her. It doesn't need to be said, but there is a realisation, in that refuge of theirs, that life is precious and that they are so lucky to be where they are.

Against Donegal in the quarter-final, Walsh wears number 30 and doesn't feature. She's happy not to either, taking it one day at a time. Unfortunately for the northerners, they're doing battle with a team that will stop at nothing now, and in a live television broadcast they suffer a forty-nine-point hammering in Dr Hyde Park, Roscommon. It's the second-biggest winning margin by a Cork senior team since the 1995 junior All-Ireland semi-final against the British champions, Lancashire, at the end of which the scoreboard read 15–30 to 0–0.

Michael Naughton's Donegal are depleted before the ball is even thrown in. Four of his starters – including prolific scorer Geraldine McLaughlin – are missing due to a family wedding, while the county was already trying to recover from losing fourteen players to emigration in the previous twenty-four months. At half-time, and trailing by twenty points (0–2 to 3–13), the four Donegal subs take turns doing the crossbar challenge to keep their spirits up.

At the final whistle the scoreboard reads 8–27 to 0–2 and Angela Walsh steps onto the field and begins to cry. All she can think about is her father's final days and his asking what the score in the match was. She can almost hear him.

Ryan sensed the players were on another level that day. It was written in their mindset. Not a single second was wasted and they played out of their skins to honour Walsh's father.

They did it for Angela, and they did it for Donie.

•••

In the All-Ireland semi-final Cork face Monaghan in a repeat of the league final, and Ryan is wound up long before they reach St Brendan's Park in Birr. He's not a fan of insinuations in the media that the Farney County has the upper hand because of their league final win, and the players assimilate his annoyance.

To counteract the pace of Monaghan's forwards, Ryan makes three changes to the forward-line, giving seventeen-year-old Doireann O'Sullivan her first senior championship start, but it's Player of the Match Briege Corkery who orchestrates the tempo. Her pace makes it look like her legs are constantly hovering over the turf as she takes off up the field from wing-back; she kicks two sublime points and the message is loud and clear: Cork aren't losing this one.

It's not just a victory, it's a performance. The nine-point margin (2–15 to 0–12) justifies the headline in the sports section of the *Evening Echo* the following day: 'The Hunger Game'.

Their blocking alone is a masterclass, and it's bordering on becoming a natural reflex after eight years of practice under Eamonn Ryan. It's a skill he focuses on in almost every training session, and on occasion when he doesn't include a blocking drill, there's genuine concern among the players. It's a mundane drill, but they understand the simplicity of it. They also understand that by doing the simple things right, they'll make life much easier for themselves.

'It's remarkable they get such a thrill out of something so basic,' says Ryan. 'There's times there that, let's say hypothetically, I headed off for a pint to the Bishopstown Bar down the road, and if I came back, they'd still be working away on the drill I left them doing – and they'd still be giving it 100 per cent too.

'Or, if I said to them, "Run into town there and get a cone for yerselves", they would. They wouldn't think twice about it! When they're focused, they're totally focused.'

It's that unwavering focus against Monaghan that leads them into their seventh All-Ireland final in eight years, and afterwards a few of the players venture across the road from the pitch in Birr to the County Arms Hotel for one celebratory beverage. Already sitting in the bar is Monaghan forward Niamh Kindlon and her sister Fiona, a member of the management team. It's not customary in GAA for opposing teams to socialise after games, but they signal to Valerie Mulcahy and Bríd Stack to join them. The gesture is not forgotten.

Niamh Kindlon is Monaghan ladies football. Aged just sixteen, she announced her arrival in the 1997 senior All-Ireland final against Waterford, scoring a cracking goal – the kind kids dream about scoring in Croke Park. It's a game remembered for the eleven minutes and fifty-two seconds of injury time played, during which Monaghan equalise on the sixty-sixth minute before adding two more points to retain their title. It's the only time, however, that Kindlon climbed the steps of the Hogan Stand, despite appearing in another five All-Ireland finals during her eighteen-year career, and her persistence commands the Cork players' respect.

On the bus home, however, celebrations are curtailed as concern mounts over a knee injury sustained by Ciara

O'Sullivan. Angela Walsh made her official comeback, replacing O'Sullivan eight minutes from time, and the swelling of the Mourneabbey woman's knee doesn't look good.

Preparations for the All-Ireland final against Kerry begin immediately, and while logistics are planned for Sunday 30 September, the squad take in a beach session at Inchydoney Strand in west Cork. It's the morning of the 2012 All-Ireland hurling final between defending thirty-five-time champions Kilkenny and four-time winners of the Liam McCarthy Cup Galway, and once showered the players reconvene for lunch to watch the hurling final.

As they chat amongst themselves, Ryan turns to those nearest him and asks a straightforward question.

'So, who are ye going for?' he enquires.

'Galway, of course, sure they're the underdogs,' comes the reply.

'God, I'm disappointed in ye now,' he says, shaking his head with legitimate disappointment. 'Yer the Kilkenny of ladies football. Yer the ones that everyone wants to see beaten. I thought now ye'd all be going for Kilkenny.'

And with that he takes his plate and walks off. With one elementary question he's gotten inside the players' heads and they don't even notice it happening.

The hurling final ends in a draw, with Galway's Joe Canning hitting a seventy-third minute equaliser from the forty-five-metre line, and that in itself sends its own message – reigning champions must always be watching over their shoulders.

Word has since come through that Ciara O'Sullivan has damaged her cruciate, and, as in 2010, it's her left one. It is among the fifteen or so cruciate injuries during Ryan's tenure, not to mention any other form of injury players suffered. It is akin to losing a full team in itself, but Ryan's ability to chisel versatility in his players stands to him when it comes to filling voids caused by injury.

The draw in the hurling final gives Ciara O'Sullivan a glimmer of hope for being fit for Cork's All-Ireland final. The ladies football final is rescheduled for 7 October because of the hurling replay and, even if Ryan is convinced that she won't make it back in time, there's no doubt in O'Sullivan's mind that she is going to give it her best shot. She has been thrown a lifeline; she quits her summer job and for the next fortnight is self-employed in the gym. Three times a day she climbs aboard the stationary bike and with every rotation of the pedals tries to build what strength she can in her knee. As her back aches and sweat drools from her face, a lady in her sixties on the opposite side of the gym is crushing her for pace. For O'Sullivan it's demoralising. 'This isn't going to work,' she thinks to herself. She fights with her inner self to get a grip on reality, but her stubbornness is slowly dragging her through her personal turmoil.

On nights when Cork training is on in the Mardyke, O'Sullivan arrives not in the best of form. As her teammates warm up for their first session of the day, she cuts across the pitch and into the gym for her third. It's going on two weeks now and although O'Sullivan has returned to light running, Ryan's still adamant she's not going to make the final. He's convinced of it and plans are afoot to find her replacement up front; O'Sullivan has different ideas.

It's now ten days before the All-Ireland final. The team's informed of an upcoming practice match, and O'Sullivan corners Ryan on his way out the gate after training.

'Eamonn, I'd like to play in the challenge match,' she says, and it's more of a statement than a request.

'You won't be able to, Ciara,' Ryan replies. It's only twenty days since she damaged her cruciate and he's understandably unconvinced.

'I can play for a half hour.'

'All right so, we'll see,' he concedes, not wanting to deprive O'Sullivan of at least a chance after she's worked so hard. He isn't one for playing God and starts her in the game; but what happens next Ryan can't explain to this day.

'It's the most amazing thing I've seen in all my years, maybe ever.

'She hadn't a hope of playing in the final, but who was I to stop her playing in the challenge match? She told me she'd be okay but I took it with two grains of salt. Honestly, I had her ruled out in my head. But she covered every blade of grass in that game. She hit every opponent deliberately too, just to prove she was ready. It was the bravery and the madness of it.

'I remember thinking to myself, "She's doing brilliant", but at the same time expecting her to collapse any second. After forty minutes I took her off and she wasn't impressed. But in the back of my mind I was saying, "Jesus, she might make the final." She actually beat the cruciate, if you can even say that!'

O'Sullivan takes part in two more training sessions before the showdown with the Kingdom, the first time the sides will meet in a senior All-Ireland final. Ryan calls out O'Sullivan's name in the starting fifteen and a smile shoots across her face. The agony of the past few weeks is all worth it just to hear her name. In a month's time she'll deal with the operation and the recovery, but for now she couldn't be happier.

Corner-back Deirdre O'Reilly is also cleared to start, despite having broken a bone in her hand in a club camogie game a few weeks before, but O'Reilly's a machine and a little strapping to conceal the injury from the old enemy is all that's required.

The same day that the team is announced, the mother of selector James O'Callaghan, Lily, passes away. But just forty-eight hours after she's buried, O'Callaghan stands on the sideline as the national anthem is played before the 2012 senior All-Ireland final and he looks to the sky above Croke Park. At the same time, Angela Walsh also looks to the heavens. Standing beside her, Bríd Stack is conscious of the moment and squeezes Walsh's shoulder in support. No matter what, they'll always be there for each other.

It's the Kingdom's first time in an All-Ireland final in nineteen years and the bookies have them at 6/1. Prior to the game, Kerry coach William O'Sullivan admits to the press that stage fright is a concern and he's recalled former captain Mags O'Donoghue from retirement to add some mental strength.

Ten minutes in, however, Kerry captain Bernie Breen suffers an injury to her shoulder AC joint. She plays through the pain but she's not going full tilt and she's a loss. Kerry are missing her vision in the creation of attacks. As a result their game turns too defensive and they concede thirty-two frees to Cork's eleven. They become the only team to keep Cork goalless in Croke Park, but Cork punish them nonetheless, kicking sixteen points (0–16 to 0–7) in front of a mediocre crowd of 16,998, and after eighty plus sessions, they're All-Ireland champions once again.

Rena Buckley makes her captain's speech ever so eloquently *as Gaeilge* and lifting the cup over her head declares, 'Brendan Martin, *tá fáilte romhat ar ais Cois Laoi!*'

The Kerry players respectfully stand in the middle of the pitch and listen to Buckley's words, but it's hurting. They're decent people and a decent side, and, try as she might, forward Louise Ní Mhuircheartaigh can't hold back the tears. This moment will stay with them and it'll stoke the fires of Kerry football as winter approaches.

16

THE INTERVENTION

*'What makes something special is not just what you
have to gain, but what you feel there is to lose.'*
Andre Agassi

Sitting next to President Michael D. Higgins in Áras an
Úachtaráin is a little surreal for Juliet Murphy. All winter
she has quarrelled with herself, and realises this could very
well be her last official function as a Cork footballer. The
reigning All-Ireland champions have been invited to the
president's residence in the capital to mark St Brigid's Day
2013 by Higgins' wife, Sabina, a first cousin of Nollaig
Cleary's father, Ned; but no one on the team knows of
Murphy's inner turmoil.

The president has extended the invite to the players'
families and partners, and when the formalities are over
Sabina quietly asks Nollaig Cleary for a list of singers in
the group. The usual suspects like Rena Buckley and Áine
Hayes take to the mic and, with the help of the resident
piano player, entertain the guests in the very venue where
President of the United States Barack Obama and Queen
Elizabeth were given State welcomes.

Unknown to Murphy she's on the list and when she
hears her name called out at the top of the room, the
ground can't swallow her up fast enough. Not once, in all
her years with Cork, has she sung solo in front of the group,

nor Ryan, never mind the President. She scans the room trying to find the culprit; the girls are already cheering her on and she can't refuse the President a note or two. With sweaty palms, she holds the microphone and sings 'Annie's Song' by John Denver. Murphy sings ever so sweetly, and it's a new sight for her teammates to behold; but, when the afternoon comes to a close, they're quick off the mark for a spot of banter – 'Juliet, do you remember the time you sang for the President?' they ask intermittently all the way back to Cork.

Murphy's thinking to herself that she'll miss this, but after fifteen years of playing inter-county football, things aren't how they used to be. Over the winter, the thirty-three-year-old has struggled with motivation. She's never agonised as deeply as this, but as winter rolls into spring, the idea of retirement becomes more embedded. This feeling of flatness is new to her. It makes her agitated and she doesn't have the resilience to fight it.

Last October she hung her 2012 All-Ireland medal from a picture frame in her room smothered in victorious pictures from Croke Park over the years, but she's not sure where her other six medals are. Perhaps they're at home in Donoughmore, but she can't bring herself to check. Her mother, Mary, will know for certain where they are, while her father, Michael, can sense something is on the cards. They have lived all the highs and the lows on their daughter's journey. Murphy knows her decision will affect them as much as it will her, but she's got to do this for herself.

Eamonn Ryan knows it too, and when they meet for a coffee near Murphy's gym at the start of the 2013 league campaign, he doesn't try to sway her either way. Another coach might, but not Ryan. Murphy tells him she's unsure of her future with Cork, and the father in him advises her to take her time.

They've had a special bond over the years, but he treats her no differently to anyone else. They share similar personality traits and their mannerisms combine to mould a culture of modesty and work ethic.

'The consistency of Juliet's play over the years was incredible,' says Ryan. 'She was either good, very good or excellent. She was never poor. You could depend on her to reach a certain level all the time, which is very hard for a player to do, but she always seemed to be consistently good, which is a difficult thing to do.

'But it was in the way she trained and the way she lived her life, her diet, her performances, it was a package which was invaluable to the whole thing.'

There was no better candidate to be captain when Ryan first arrived in 2004, and he knows she's not like any other player. She's one of the best the sport has ever seen, but it's not in his nature to force players to stay. It's a choice, not a sacrifice – and it's a choice she has to make for herself.

Angela Walsh, Deirdre O'Reilly and Nollaig Cleary return in the latter stages of the league, and it's hoped their decisions will encourage Murphy to do the same. However, in a second meeting with Ryan, it's obvious she's still as torn as she was the first day they met. In truth her confidence has taken a knock. She's always been intense about her sport, but doubts about whether she still has the ability to compete at the highest level have corroded her confidence. It's ironic though, because it's that exact vulnerability that's seen her win numerous Player of the Match awards, albeit never in an All-Ireland final.

'Those overconfident might have played bad and still thought they did good, but Juliet was tough on herself and never settled. I think that helped her in a perverse way,' says Ryan. 'She doubted herself to a small extent the whole time, but that was one of her strengths because she had to overcome that. That fear of failure drove her on, and you'd find that with a number of very good players. It's almost that fear of failure, rather than reaching for the stars, that made her so good. Fear aversion I think they call it.'

Failing is exactly what Murphy's afraid of, but with Cleary, Walsh and O'Reilly having returned to the squad, she's content she can walk away knowing that things are solid. She knows life will go on without her and gradually comes around to her decision.

She watches the 2013 league final between Cork and Mayo in the conservatory of her parents' home during her niece's Holy Communion celebrations. It's a milestone she'd have missed had she been playing in Parnell Park. Watching Anne-Marie Walsh lift the cup, she doesn't feel resentment or frustration not being there, she's just happy her friends have won (0–14 to 0–7).

The following week she informs Nollaig Cleary and Rena Buckley of her decision, but delays contacting

Eamonn Ryan. It's a phone call she doesn't want to make. When she comes around to it, she's sick to her stomach and for the first time the reality of retirement is staring her in the face. She's having second thoughts. Maybe she should have tried going back to feel what it was like again. Maybe she should have had a little more faith in herself, but it's a week before the opening round of the 2013 Munster senior championship and it's too late to turn back.

The phone call is short and Ryan is polite. When Murphy hangs up, she begins to cry. Ryan means so much to her. The team means so much, and the perceived guilt that she's letting them down is overwhelming.

Now that the words have been spoken, it's official in her world, but not yet to the public. She meets with this author in The Bodega restaurant in Cork city and, uncharacteristically, she's visibly nervous. It's not like any other interview she's done before and she's finding it difficult. After ninety minutes of reeling in the years, she bows her head and says, 'Sin é.'

On Friday 14 June, the announcement is made and other counties breathe a sigh of relief. With Murphy out of the equation, there's a chance Cork might not be as good as they once were. In fact, Cork are struggling. In part it's due to the absence of their midfield unit of almost a decade, Juliet Murphy and Norita Kelly, with the latter away travelling. But it runs a little deeper than that.

On the surface they're training hard, but there's a hint of intolerance in some departments, primarily in attack. There's no verbal arguments, but just like a family that has spent too much time together, there's a slight undercurrent of annoyance with one another. It's not as cohesive as in other years, but perhaps it's stemming from the fact that they're not playing well. The uncertainty over the last few months about whether Murphy would return or not has affected them. So too has the positional change of five-time-All-Star full-back Angela Walsh to centre-forward, and the lack of a consistent pairing in midfield.

In the opening round of the championship, Cork travel to Cahersiveen, where nine years earlier Ryan lost his very first game at the helm in 2004. They lose there again (3–8 to 3–10). Kerry are mentally stronger and growing in confidence, with a division two league title win under their belt and an unbeaten run so far in 2013. It's the Kingdom's first championship win over Cork in almost a decade, and the 2012 All-Ireland final loss incubated a new hunger.

In the second round, Cork deny Clare (0–21 to 0–8) to set up another clash with Kerry, this time in the Munster final. In Castletownroche, on a day when 1,100 supporters crackle in twenty-five-degree heat, Cork go in search of their tenth successive provincial title. Should they win, they'll match Kerry's record.

Eleven times the sides are level. The pace of the game is ferocious and water is carried on and guzzled at every chance. Kerry lead by a point (1–16 to 1–15) in the final minute, but Cork's Geraldine O'Flynn has a chance to level it, forty metres out on the stand side. With Murphy retired, O'Flynn has taken up the right-legged kicking duties and the ball looks to have the distance, but as it begins its descent, it hits the crossbar and falls into the hands of a Kerry defender.

Referee Mike Duffy calls time and Kerry's Bernie Breen lifts the Dairygold Cup for the first time since 2003. Their winter slog has paid off.

On the bank in Castletownroche, Juliet Murphy has been looking on covertly, sunglasses acting as a buffer between her and a former world. She can't stand to watch her friends looking lost and bewildered, and signals to her parents that it's time to leave. She doesn't know how she should act in her new world, and the impulse is to vanish.

Ryan isn't too unhappy with the performance given that it's centimetres that have denied them a draw. He knows he must take the good days with the bad. He's gracious in defeat, but in truth he is relieved Cork will have another chance through the back door with the qualifiers. It's the first time in their history that they've had to go that route, and for the older players it hurts their pride.

In the aftermath of the defeat, Murphy's uncle-in-law, selector Frankie Honohan, has been in contact with her. Angela Walsh has texted, Briege Corkery has rung, and Nollaig Cleary meets her to ask her face-to-face to reconsider coming back.

'Look Juls, we need you, just come and try one session,' Cleary pleads. 'We're not doing any more hard running, you wouldn't believe it. I'll collect you and we'll go together, and just see how you get on.'

Murphy agrees to at least give it a chance. For forty days she's been retired. It must be a new record for the shortest time in retirement, but the regret of not giving things another chance earlier on in the year has been eating away at her. She declines Cleary's offer of a lift and opts to make her own way instead.

Driving up the winding avenue of The Farm, she's as nervous as the day she walked out under the Hogan Stand in her first All-Ireland final in 2005. Her gear is already on and, bar putting on her boots, she's ready to go. But it's not in an eager way. It's a defence mechanism to avoid the dressing room altogether. She's feeling awkward about the situation, and getting out on the field where she's most comfortable can't come quick enough.

The players notice her but make no fuss of her arrival. They know that's what Murphy would appreciate. Instead they give subtle winks and thumbs up to acknowledge her presence.

She hasn't said a word to Ryan that she'll be attending. Not one. They spot each other from across the car park but don't acknowledge one another. It's a conversation neither wants to have, and instead they go to work.

To this day they've never spoken about that night, or Murphy's return in general.

Cleary was wrong about one thing, however, because Ryan runs them into the ground with his dreaded three-track runs. She whispers an apology to Murphy during the cool-down, but the three-time captain had survived, just about. After nine months out, her football is certainly rusty, but fitness-wise she's not too far off the pace and is content that she has done the right thing by the team coming back.

In a challenge match against Mayo before the qualifier, Murphy features briefly and takes a hit from Claire Egan when bending down to get the ball. Egan is the most physical midfielder there is and Murphy expects the knock, but not the extent of its force. It winds her, but she doesn't let on she's hurt. In the past she wouldn't have thought twice about such a hit, but it's a reminder of how much catching up she has to do.

Against division three league champions Armagh in the qualifier, Cork lead comfortably by seven points at half-time (0–10 to 0–3), but when Murphy makes her first official appearance of 2013 in the second half, it all falls apart. Armagh drive on and take the lead in the closing minutes, but Cork hold on with an equalising and then a winning point from soon-to-be Players' Player of the Year Geraldine O'Flynn from wing-back. The Orchard County have a chance at parity and captain Caroline O'Hanlon stands over a kickable free. But thinking there's two points separating the sides, she drops the ball high into the square to no avail, not realising that if she puts it over the bar, they'd have pushed it to a replay. Instead the game ends 0–16 to 2–9.

It's a lucky escape in Birr and, despite the opening loss to Kerry in the Munster championship and again in the provincial final, it's the first time Ryan's concerned. 'I was as worried as I was in 2010. I thought the balloon had burst. There was no spirit in the team that day. We went completely out of the game and the bite we'd normally have in getting over the line wasn't there.'

Murphy is just as perturbed. That night she lies on her couch for hours staring at the ceiling with just her thoughts and a glass of wine. The team had been doing well until she came on, and in her mind it all imploded with her arrival. She knows she didn't play well by her own standards, but since her return she has sensed the dynamic of the squad has shifted from the previous autumn. There isn't the same unity.

She phones captain Anne-Marie Walsh and asks for permission to hold a team meeting the next night before training. With Walsh's blessing, she contacts key players in the squad to each write a few paragraphs about what it is to be a Cork senior ladies footballer. They need to get back to what it all means to them and, more importantly, to each other.

'I felt it needed to be done,' confides Murphy. 'I was nervous about doing it because I felt who am I to come back here and instigate a meeting, but I just had to do something. If people thought I was doing it for another reason bar the good of the team, then they don't know me at all. A grounding was needed, or at least the realisation that we all needed to be one again.'

Crammed into a Portakabin, baking in the summer sun on the fringes of The Farm, they sit shoulder to shoulder. Captain Anne-Marie Walsh explains why they're there and why it's the first time in ten years the squad need an intervention. They've drifted ever so slightly away from one another. There's a hint of agitation. They're not the unit they once were, and no one bar themselves can fix it.

Elaine Harte and Bríd Stack take to the floor and read out the words they've penned at Murphy's request. Harte is one of the vocal elders, while Stack has a way with words, and they reel off what playing with Cork means to them, and what's made them seven-time All-Ireland champions.

Honesty. Hard work. Unity.

Angela Walsh is up next, and after just a handful of words, there's not a dry eye in the room. Football was there for her in her darkest hour as she came to terms with the loss of her father the summer before. Those seated in front of her had been there when she needed them most, and it meant the world. But, from here on in, they don't get second chances. They have to bring a halt to their downward spiral.

'I spent hours thinking about what I was going to say,' Walsh remembers. 'I felt it was a good time to put everything down on paper about Dad passing and what the girls and football meant to me during that time, and how if Dad was still around he'd be telling us how good we were.

'I began to read, but I was bawling. I knew what was coming so Juliet had to finish reading it for me. It meant more to me than anybody, but it opened all our eyes and we realised in that room what we all meant to each other. It showed how close we actually were if we could lay everything out on the table.'

As tears are wiped away, Murphy switches on the CD player she's brought with her. Al Pacino's famous, inspirational speech from the movie *Any Given Sunday* plays through the speakers.

The words resonate so much, that when they walk through the doorway, they're new people, new players and a new team:

Either we heal as a team or we are going to crumble.
Inch by inch, play by play, till we're finished.
We are in hell right now, gentlemen believe me,
and we can stay here and get the shit kicked out of us
or we can fight our way back into the light.
We can climb out of hell.
One inch at a time.

17

UNDER SIEGE

'The most difficult thing is the decision to act, the rest is merely tenacity.'
Amelia Earhart

That night Cork step onto the field and train like demons. The meeting sparks the revival, but an exercise carried out by captain Anne-Marie Walsh with the help of her cousin, Angela, adds even more weight to it. Every player on the thirty-five-member squad writes one positive thing about each of their teammates on a page, and painstakingly the cousins cut out each comment and sort them into envelopes to present to every player the next night at training.

In essence, it's an envelope of positivity. It's to rebuild each individual's confidence, but more importantly their confidence in each other.

'It just lifted all of us,' says Briege Corkery. 'In hindsight, we had become too hard on each other, cranky even. We just needed to remember that we could play football. It was all in our heads, it was all about attitude. I know I sometimes would doubt myself even if I was working hard enough, but when I saw that sheet it gave me huge confidence, that people still had confidence in me.'

Against Dublin in the All-Ireland quarter-final their faith in one another is truly put to the test. At half-time they trail 0–7 to 1–8, and Ryan is animated in the dressing room in St Brendan's Park in Birr.

'We're like Michael Collins and the lads under siege,' he says, 'we're at war!'

And he's right, Dublin are gunning for it.

Juliet Murphy started, partnering Angela Walsh in midfield, but when Walsh reverts to full-back for the first time all season in a direct swap with Bríd Stack in the second half, Dublin's Lindsay Peat burns her and finds the back of Martina O'Brien's net. The fist pump by the former Irish international basketballer signals to the Dubs to get the job done, and with forty-one minutes gone they've carved out a nine-point lead (2–12 to 0–9).

Ryan shuffles his deck again, ordering Bríd Stack to return to defence and up he sends Deirdre O'Reilly to midfield. During a stoppage in play while substitute Rhona Ní Bhuachalla is sent in, Briege Corkery and Geraldine O'Flynn concur and get word to the forward-line not to panic and to pick off their points.

Immediately O'Reilly's aggression turns the game. She's loving the challenge that playing in midfield presents, and the stamina she has built up in her day job as a gym owner has caused all hell to break loose. Juliet Murphy, Nollaig Cleary and Valerie Mulcahy feed off O'Reilly's assists and fire over three successive points, before Rhona Ní Bhuachalla delivers a trademark goal just minutes after coming off the bench on the forty-third minute.

Cork's dominance in the last ten minutes has hit Dublin on the blind side and when Cleary's left boot restores parity

(1–15 to 2–12) the minimal Cork support that's in the stand are leaping from their seats. There's eleven minutes remaining and Valerie Mulcahy registers what will be the winning point. In the final twenty minutes Cork scored an incredible 1–10 without reply (1–19 to 2–12).

Just as they had done in the 2011 All-Ireland quarter-final against Dublin, they came back from the dead to not only outscore their opponents but hold them scoreless for the final third of the game. The intervention was the reason they pulled together when it looked like all was lost, and the win sets up a third championship meeting of the year with Kerry in the All-Ireland semi-final.

A week out from the game in Semple Stadium, Thurles, Ryan knows Cork are going to win. He senses it in the players' body language, their communication, and in how fast they're rotating between drills. They've turned a corner mentally, and the resolve dredged from the close victories against Armagh and Dublin stands to them as they end Kerry's unbeaten run (2–9 to 0–11).

It's three weeks until Cork face Monaghan in a repeat of the 2008 and 2011 All-Ireland finals, and they happily take in their first ever session at the home of Cork GAA, Páirc Uí Chaoimh, but Eamonn Ryan isn't himself. Goalkeeper Martina O'Brien has featured in four championship matches in this, her first year playing senior, but he's unsure if she's ready for the big stage that is Croker. His number one goalkeeper since 2004, Elaine Harte, missed much of the league due to an Achilles injury, and played just the opening round of the championship due to holidays in Australia. If he's to go on this year's service, hands down O'Brien deserves to start. But this isn't just another game – it's Cork's eighth All-Ireland final in nine years. Management have debated the dilemma over the last few training sessions and the consensus is to go with Harte's experience.

Ryan doesn't do confrontation and on the one-hour drive from his home in Ballingeary to the Mardyke for their last training session, he's gearing himself up to announce the starting fifteen. Tonight he'll break his own rules and tell O'Brien she hasn't made the cut. He's never once told a player they've been dropped, but feels he owes it to the twenty-three-year-old in this, her first season with the squad.

During the cool-down he gestures to O'Brien to join him on the sideline. 'Look Martina, this is the hardest decision I've had to make but I just feel in my gut that I should go with Elaine,' he says.

The shock is obvious on O'Brien's face, but she holds it together.

'I know it's hard for you to make sense of that and there's no logic to it from your point of view, and I'm sorry,' Ryan adds, before making his way to the dressing room to officially announce the team.

He hasn't mentioned to Elaine Harte that she'll be given the number 1 jersey, and won't do so either, but by the time he makes it to the changing room, O'Brien's already sat next to her mentor in a show of solidarity.

'Traumatic would be dramatising it, but it was the

toughest decision I've had to make over the ten years,' Ryan admits. 'I'm not very good at confrontation. I'd react to something all right, but I find it very hard to commence proceedings. It might be from a lack of confidence, I don't know, maybe some other mental defect, but I don't tell players they're dropped. It's better to announce it and leave it at that because otherwise you'd be tying yourself up in knots trying to give everyone a reason. But Martina deserved one because it was such a specialist position.

'When I saw her sitting next to Elaine and supporting her, and her demeanour was like, "This is just life and get on with it", I was hugely impressed. I wouldn't be as magnanimous if it was my position. It must have been tough, not only for her, but her family too, yet she handled it brilliantly.'

Getting on the bus heading to Dublin the day before the All-Ireland final is a proud moment nonetheless for Martina O'Brien. She has vowed to do everything in her power to use the weekend to learn everything she can. She is grateful to be the pupil of one of the greatest keepers in the history of the sport, and she will absorb every move Elaine Harte makes in her preparations.

Logistically, however, things aren't going to plan. For the first time ever, the management team have decided not to stay in the Red Cow Moran Hotel so as to avoid the supporters attending the 2013 All-Ireland hurling final replay between Cork and Clare. Instead they'll have a kickaround in Kilmacud Crokes at 4 p.m. and continue on to their hotel in Leopardstown to watch the replay. But when they hit Portlaoise, traffic is at a standstill. Cormac O'Connor quietly informs Ryan that they won't make Crokes by 6 p.m., and that if he wants to get the routine kicking session in, he'd want to concoct a plan B.

Within seconds Ryan whips out his phone and dials the number of an old friend – John Divilly, the former Galway footballer now residing in Kildare.

'There's a pitch in the Curragh,' Divilly tells Ryan, 'it belongs to the Army and you've no permission to use it, but I'll work on that.'

And with that, Ryan turns to the players and announces there's a change to the schedule. The kickaround the day before the All-Ireland has been part of their routine since their first final in 2005 and Ryan is stubborn in his own little way, and if it meant setting up goalposts in a local farmer's field, so be it.

The pitch in the Curragh is encircled by wire fencing and within minutes of their arrival the military police descend on the scene to question what's going on. Ryan explains the situation and, satisfied there's no espionage at play, they take off.

As management contend with fencing, the players change into their gear on the bus and on the side of the road. They're met with beeping horns from the nearby motorway and a cyclist keen to give them a wave for their impromptu strip show, but the players take no notice.

'Here they were, modern women changing on the side of a road and not a bother on them,' says Ryan. 'In they hopped over the fence and did their twenty-minute kickaround, and not a word out of any of them. There was no one saying we weren't professional, whatever that means, and they just got on with it.'

A total of ten players – Bríd Stack, Rena Buckley, Deirdre O'Reilly, Nollaig Cleary, Angela Walsh, Juliet Murphy, Elaine Harte, Geraldine O'Flynn, Valerie Mulcahy and Briege Corkery – with seventy Celtic crosses between them, still remain on the squad since Ryan first introduced himself in the spring of 2004, and they have yet to pick holes in his preparations. It is what it is; and, just like if things aren't going right in a game, they adapt and find a solution.

The bookies have Monaghan at 13/10 to win their first title since 1997, and although Cork have registered four losses all season (against Laois and Monaghan in the league, and Kerry twice in the championship) compared to the northerners' one, the reigning champions are still surprisingly favourites at 8/11.

The addition of former Meath senior football manager Séamus 'Banty' McEnaney – whose daughter Laura plays wing-back – to the Monaghan back-room team has paid off. Although they trail 0–6 to 1–6 at half-time, they kept their composure with two monstrous points from Caoimhe Mohan before the turnaround.

On the thirty-third minute Monaghan are awarded a penalty and goalkeeper Linda Martin sprints the length of the pitch to put the ball into the back of Elaine Harte's net. Harte had earlier justified her selection with a superb save against Cathriona McConnell.

Cork are winning possession, but eight wides have been detrimental. As she has done so many times over the years, Geraldine O'Flynn slithers her way forward for a point, before Nollaig Cleary adds another to make it 1–8 apiece.

Niamh Kindlon – owner of the only senior All-Ireland medal in the Monaghan squad – is flitting around on the sideline, itching to come on; but there appears to be a delay. Things go from bad to worse as Eileen McKenna is sent to the sin bin with eleven minutes remaining for a body-check on Deirdre O'Reilly.

Defensively, Cork have held firm and at the sight of Caoimhe Mohan breaking through for a potential winner with seven minutes left on the clock, five Cork defenders converge and throw themselves at her feet. It's a snapshot of their desire to win, and, with four minutes to go, Juliet Murphy sends over another equaliser.

Rhona Ní Bhuachalla, who was subbed off at half-time has been brought back on to see if she can score a winner, but Valerie Mulcahy holds her nerve and kicks over a free at the Davin Stand end to take the lead (1–10 to 1–9) with 2.50 remaining.

Monaghan instigate another attack, but Angela Walsh wins possession and dances out of defence, soloing the ball awkwardly as she goes, keeping possession no matter what the cost. Cork string twelve passes together with Walsh at the crux of it all, before Briege Corkery uncharacteristically loses the ball in a tackle with fifteen seconds reading high up on the screen to the left of the Hill 16 end.

Monaghan break again and advance to within forty metres of the Cork goal line.

'Don't foul! Don't foul!' Murphy screams. But no sooner have the words left her mouth than Rena Buckley illegally tackles Monaghan captain Therése McNally to the ground.

Murphy throws her hands in the air with disgust, but Buckley argues to this day it was the right thing to do. She figured it was too far out and not on the most favourable side for Monaghan's primary free-taker Cathriona McConnell.

With three seconds left, the hooter prematurely sounds. McConnell still has the right to take the free kick. If it goes over she'll send the game to a replay, but it's at an awkward angle and into the wind.

Looking forward, the twenty-three-year-old All-Star gauges the distance and the elements as Cork stack the goalmouth. McConnell swings the ball round in her hands, and connects her foot with the ball, but long before it makes the distance, the Cork players can tell it doesn't have the accuracy it needs and sprint out from Elaine Harte's domain, cheering as they go.

It's Harte's last time playing in Croker and when she finds Juliet Murphy to hug, they don't have to say a word. The power of the embrace alone acknowledges that this is their final victory on the hallowed turf, and they'll savour this moment together forever.

They're two of four players to have now played every minute in all of Cork's eight All-Ireland final wins, with Bríd Stack and Briege Corkery the other two. But they're all oblivious to that fact until journalists point it out to them and photographers happily snap their personal milestone.

Monaghan are inconsolable.

Therése McNally is face down, her tears staining the grass, while full-back Sharon Courtney falls to her knees. First over to put an arm around her is Briege Corkery. She's lost camogie All-Ireland finals in Croke Park and knows exactly the isolation Courtney is feeling. Bar the dual stars, the Cork players don't know what it's like to lose in Croke Park; and maintaining their 100 per cent winning record in All-Ireland football finals is what drives them on. Ryan, however, has instilled in them a grateful-ness for their privileged position and an acceptance that the journey isn't going to last forever. They know how lucky they are, and visiting the Temple Street Children's Hospital, and Our Lady's Children's Hospital in Crumlin with the Brendan Martin Cup the morning after the final solidifies that fact.

'It just hits you how lucky we are that we can get up and play football,' says Valerie Mulcahy. 'Maybe it wouldn't be a bad idea for the losing team to visit the hospitals the morning after too. I'm sure you'd be down, but you wouldn't be long realising how lucky you are when you see those kids and how strong their parents are.'

For Bríd Stack, a visit after the 2008 All-Ireland final to see baby Laura Mai Cahill from her home parish of Rockchapel in north Cork really struck a chord.

'Myself and Angela were allowed in to see her. She

was in a special incubator but we got to hold Laura Mai for a little while. She was so small and I could feel her breathing against me. But that day her parents, Marguerite and Donal, were so upbeat despite what they were going through. They were just incredible. Sadly, Laura Mai passed away in Crumlin a couple of months later.'

After the 2011 All-Ireland win, Stack also visited a boy from Carrigaline, where she teaches, by the name of Danny Crowley. 'He was a gorgeous young man who was very involved in sport. He didn't go to my school, but a lot of his friends were in second year where I teach. After he passed, the students and some of his close friends organised a sponsored fun walk in aid of The Kids and Teens Appeal at the Mercy University Hospital in Cork. They raised €5,385, and there's now an underage soccer trophy named after Danny, which is a lovely tribute to him.

'I just love going in to see the kids. In the build-up to us calling, they make posters all morning and it's such a big distraction for them, and it means so much to their families. One year we sellotaped all of the posters the kids made for us to the windows on the side of the bus on the way back to Cork because it really did make us realise how lucky we were.'

•••

The year ends as it began – with a knees-up with President Michael D. Higgins and his wife Sabina.

They're attending the December wedding of Nollaig

Cleary and former Cork footballer Micheál Ó Crónín, and although the weather's chilly, the banter between her teammates warms up proceedings fairly lively. The novelty of attending a wedding with the President of Ireland has them excited, but so too does news that RTÉ are to do a live broadcast from the afters of the wedding during the airing of the 2013 RTÉ Sports Star Awards later that night.

Cork are up for the Team of the Year award once again, alongside eight other nominees – the All-Ireland-winning Clare hurlers, the Dublin footballers, the Galway camogie team, the Ireland men's boxing team, the first-time Grand-Slam-winning Irish women's rugby team, Rabo Pro 12 winners Leinster, the Paralympic swimming team and Airtricity League winners St Patrick's Athletic.

Eamonn Ryan is also in the running for Manager of the Year, and RTÉ manage to coax both him and Cleary to say a few words during the live broadcast at 10.30 p.m.

The winners are due to be announced at 11.30 p.m., and the anticipation among the guests in the function room at the Rochestown Park Hotel is mounting. Cork have been nominated for the award a number of times since their first win in 2005, and the hope is that the public will acknowledge their impressive achievement of eight All-Irelands in nine years.

As soon as they see the RTÉ crew dismantling the cameras in the corner of the room, however, they realise they haven't won. The Clare hurlers have won and so has their manager, Davy Fitzgerald. It doesn't bother Cork too much; they know deep down that it would take something extraordinary for the public to ever vote them as Team of the Year. For now, they'll dance the night away with Sabina Higgins.

18

A CHANGE OF GUARD

'The best way to improve the team,
is to improve yourself.'
John Wooden

Elaine Harte is as anxious as hell. It's a fourteen-hour flight to Hong Kong for the 2014 All-Star trip, and she's frantically scribbling on a notepad before take-off.

Her brain is totting up numbers. Her jittery hands jotting down figures, $14 \times 14 + 7 + 22 - 31 = 194$; $10 \times 20 / 9 = 22.2$, etc. For take-off, the mathematician in her goes into overdrive. It's a coping mechanism she's learned on a fear-of-flying course, and multiplication and long division is taking the edge off.

The part of the brain that deals with maths is close to the fear section, Harte explains to Derek Kinnevey, the press officer of the LGFA, who is sitting next to her. 'By doing maths it halts the anxiety process, because the brain prioritises the higher task of doing math,' the two-time All-Star reveals, before burying her head back in the notebook as the plane revs its engines for take-off. Ten minutes later, and by the time the landing gear is tucked away, Harte's pulse has returned to normal and she's back to her bubbly self.

She wants this to be a trip remembered for all the right reasons, given that eight weeks ago at the start of January she announced her retirement from inter-county football. At thirty-three, injury forced her to call time on her eleven-year career. Protruding bones in both ankles have been painfully rubbing off her Achilles for some time, and there's nothing left to do but sign off in style.

This will be her last adventure with eleven of her teammates as they take part in an exhibition game at Hong Kong Football Club, with Harte and Juliet Murphy the respective captains of the 2012 and 2013 All-Star team selections. It's a nice gesture by managers Eamonn Ryan and Kerry's William O'Sullivan as it's Harte and Murphy's last game as inter-county footballers, both bowing out with eight All-Ireland medals and having played every minute in every final.

Harte's record stands at an incredible average of 0.9 goals conceded in 110 league and championship appearances, but her real contribution was off the field. In 2003, mentally bruised from years of defeat in a Cork jersey, she was the only senior player at the county board AGM when the reformation began in the back function room of Murray's Bar in Macroom. Standing up for what she believed in, Harte changed the course of Cork ladies football. That will be her true legacy.

Eamonn Ryan knows Harte's decision is final and talks of any mid-season comebacks are instantly dispelled. However, the conversation with wing-forward Nollaig Cleary is a little different. In the moments after the All-Star game in Hong Kong, Cleary was hoisted into the air alongside the retired Juliet Murphy, and the travelling photographer mistakenly captioned the photograph as a gesture by Cleary's teammates to recognise her 'last football match before retirement'. The following day the image adorned the back page of Irish national papers, yet Cleary hasn't said, officially or otherwise, what her future plans are.

Aged thirty-three, the Castlehaven woman has been having her doubts. Like Murphy the previous winter, she's lacking motivation, but comes to an agreement with Eamonn Ryan that she'll take time out during the league to nurse a hamstring injury and come back to him before the championship with her decision.

In Cleary's absence, there's been a change of guard in the back-room team and an initial bedding-in period may be the explanation for Cork's mediocre league performances in 2014. Selectors Justin McCarthy and James O'Callaghan have moved on with eight years of service between them, and two new mentors – Pat O'Leary and Shane Ronayne – join the management team.

Ryan still has the loyalty of the long-serving Frankie Honohan, his son Don and liaison officer Bridget O'Brien to rely on. However, as to how O'Leary and Ronayne were appointed, he's still not sure. It was a Monday evening in January 2014 when Ryan answered his phone to a number he didn't recognise.

'Hi Eamonn, this is Shane here. I'm just ringing to say I'm looking forward to working with you during the year,' says the voice on the other end.

Ryan is confused and doesn't know who this Shane fella is, thinking momentarily that it's an electrician by the same name that his wife, Pat, has called on to do some work. But, as the conversation continues, Ryan realises it's Shane Ronayne, the 2013 Cork U16 ladies football coach. A secondary school teacher in his thirties, Ronayne is steeped in GAA and makes no bones about his ambitions to make it as a top coach.

Two days later, Ryan opens the sports section of the *Irish Examiner* to find that Pat O'Leary – a member of the management team for the 2013 county senior club champions, St Val's – is to be the second addition to his back-room team. Ryan was never officially informed by the county board of Ronayne's or O'Leary's appointment, nor was he asked to contribute in any way to the decision. It's hard to imagine that happening to someone like Kilkenny hurling boss Brian Cody, but that is how it transpired with Cork ladies football.

Luckily for Ryan, Ronayne and O'Leary work out brilliantly, and the slagging between them is as sharp as their footballing intellect. More importantly, Ronayne and O'Leary's knowledge of the underage inter-county and club scenes is the ideal combination in spreading the net to find rising talent. For a start, Eimear Scally is on their list. Small and slight, she registered 2–7 in the 2013 U16 All-Ireland final, and, although young, she has a confident head on her shoulders. The plan is to gradually introduce her to the physicality of the game at the top, but Scally isn't overawed. She was born to do this.

In the fifth round of the league against Dublin in Parnell Park, it's all on the line and Eamonn Ryan throws Scally to the lions on her debut. It's sink or swim for them both now. Having already lost to Monaghan (0–14 to 2–13) and Kerry (1–7 to 1–8), if Cork are to lose again it'll be the first time since 2002 that they'll have lost three games in a row. But a whippet-like dash by Scally in the final minute creates an opening for Ciara O'Sullivan, who does the smart thing and fists the ball over the bar to draw (2–10 apiece). As it transpires, that score is the lifeline Cork need to qualify for the league semi-finals.

A fusing of new and old is gradually taking place among the panel of thirty-eight, but Scally isn't the only one to make a household name for herself. Nineteen-year-old dentistry student Róisín Phelan has also had a baptism of fire, man-marking three of the country's top footballers in her first few games – Mayo's Cora Staunton, Kerry's Louise Ní Mhuircheartaigh and Monaghan's Caoimhe Mohan – but she's done well. Her demeanour fits the exact mould of a Cork defender. A mould that's been shaped by the likes of Bríd Stack, Angela Walsh and Rena Buckley, and involves clean, honest football. As a defensive unit, they have never lost their way. Consistency has helped with that, but so too has the culture they've promoted within themselves. If they're to ever lose that honesty, they'd lose their way, Bríd Stack would say.

Like Phelan, Vera Foley is another who's impressed her way onto the starting fifteen. She has big boots to fill, taking the number 5 jersey from her club teammate Briege Corkery. For years, the number 5 was like a GPS coordinate to locate exactly where Corkery was furrowing away on the pitch, and now it's Foley's time to defend and let fly.

As legendary as her own jersey has become, Corkery now wears an even more powerful number on her back – Juliet Murphy's number 9. Historically, Corkery's the joker in the pack, but as the new Cork captain she knows she must morph into a stronger leader. Having almost single-handedly won the 2013 Cork senior club championship for her club St Val's, the first in their history – kicking the winning point against former All-Ireland champions Inch Rovers, with her weaker left leg, forty metres out, two minutes into injury time – there was never any doubt she was going to be the next captain of Cork; but she'll have to work on her timekeeping!

En route to the 2014 division one league semi-final against Kerry, Corkery's newfound logistic skills are tested. Travelling from the middle of Cork to Dromcollogher/Broadford, near the Limerick border, Corkery acts as navigator for Vera Foley. It's her protégé's turn to drive the St Val's cohort, with Corkery's younger sister, Mairéad, and Marie Ambrose in the back.

Driving through the remote boreens of north Cork, Foley senses that her 2001 Volkswagen has the shakes but continues to motor on knowing that the timely arrival of Corkery is important. The car's been spluttering for the last ten minutes and now smoke is bellowing from the exhaust pipe in the rear-view mirror.

'Oh shit!' Corkery laughs, looking out the back window. 'I'd say it's the head gasket Vera.'

They spot a laneway into a farmyard just a few metres up the road and manoeuvre the car in to inspect it.

'Are ye all right girls?' an elderly farmer with dung-splattered wellies and a cap asks.

Corkery takes control of the situation and explains that they're fine, that the head gasket is gone, and asks would it be okay if they left the car in the yard until someone collected it tomorrow.

'Not a bother,' he says, offering to drop them wherever needs be.

But Foley's already on the case, ringing Geraldine O'Flynn, who's just minutes behind. Conscious of time, Foley, Ambrose and the Corkerys thank him and head off back down the lane to the main road to await O'Flynn's chariot.

'Sure lads, I'll never find this place again,' says Foley. 'How will we know where to come back to?'

They stop in the laneway for a mini confab. Should they go back and get the farmer's number? Or should they leave one of their mobile numbers with him?

The decision is no. They don't have time and O'Flynn will be on the lookout for them any minute, but Corkery has an idea. She rummages through her gear bag and finds an old Laois jersey. It's seen better days and she agrees to part ways with it.

They're now at the top of the laneway and Corkery climbs up onto the ditch by the entrance. Keeping her balance, she grabs hold of a branch, and ties the jersey to it. It'll be their marker in finding their way back.

Corkery's quick thinking gets them to the game on time and she scores two points from midfield for good measure, beating Kerry (3–13 to 3–8) to secure a place in their tenth league final in eleven years. The same afternoon, Dublin beat Monaghan in their semi-final to reach the county's first division one league final. The addition of Monaghan's previous coach, Gregory McGonigle, to the Dubs' back-room team has paid off.

In the lead-up to the final, however, Corkery must balance bridesmaid duties with that of being captain. Her older sister, Katherine, is to wed the day before the league final, and as the celebrations continue long into the night, Corkery sneaks off to bed at midnight ahead of an early morning departure for Parnell Park in Dublin. It's not ideal, but she's had her few hours of fun, and besides, if Cork do win, it'll be the first time she'll lift silverware as captain of a Cork senior team, despite already being the owner of twelve senior All-Ireland medals, between both football and camogie.

The return of Deirdre O'Reilly and Norita Kelly at the latter stages of the league adds to the intensity at Cork training; but Dublin haven't lost a game yet in 2014, and their supporters live in hope that today is their day. Even though Cork are the reigning league and All-Ireland champions, they're still intimidated by the Dubs. It's their presence. There's an aura about Dublin that Cork have never come across with any other team. Individually, they're all nice, but collectively Dublin emanate a confidence that surpasses that of any other county.

Cork trail by two points (1–2 to 2–1) at half-time, and just after the restart the gap widens to four. But inside the whitewash they're not fazed. If the turbulence of last season taught them anything, it's how to turn things around.

McGonigle is roaring instructions to the Dublin players from the sideline. He's been here before with Monaghan, outsmarting Ryan in 2012 – but Dublin have been left defenceless in the face of Cork comebacks before.

The introduction of Deirdre O'Reilly on the thirty-sixth minute instigates the comeback charge for Eamonn Ryan, just as it did in the 2013 All-Ireland quarter-final the summer before. On her first touch, she drives forward. The ball is lost mid-tackle, but O'Reilly somehow wins it back. Before she even has time to think, her foot connects ever so sweetly with the ball, despite the difficult angle, and her point puts Cork back on par with seventeen minutes left. It's that ability of O'Reilly's to overlook the errors and persist when the pressure's on that makes her, what Ryan calls, 'a warrior'.

In the stand, Dublin fans realise it's happening all over again – that inexplicable implosion in the closing quarter. Their players know it too, and as fast as you can say 'comeback', Cork kick six unanswered points to win by two (1–9 to 2–4).

It's been a hectic thirty-six hours for Corkery and getting her hands on the silverware comes as a relief. As she tells the waiting media, all she wants now is a cup of Ovaltine and the couch.

•••

'And one, and two, and three …' Deirdre O'Reilly instructs. In the far corner of the field in Mourneabbey, thirty-eight bodies circle her as she puts the players through almost one hundred abdominal exercises. Not a word is spoken as the management look on.

Cork have just beaten Clare by thirty-six points in the first round of the Munster championship (7–23 to 1–5), but even at that there's no time for pats on the back. They worked hard during their training weekend at the University of Limerick in the interim since the league final, and the official return of three-time All-Star Nollaig Cleary is a huge boost. The primary school teacher spent the Easter holidays honeymooning on the Amalfi coast and the possibility of returning was discussed many a night over dinner with her husband, Micheál Ó Crónín.

'I didn't think I would be returning. You need hunger and enthusiasm for it. I didn't have that over the winter,' said Cleary. 'When I stopped for the spring and Micheál was out training three nights a week with Naomh Abán, if anything it half encouraged me to go back. Sitting at home as a housewife drinking tea wasn't for me. Even making tea wasn't for me!'

At thirty-three, she's sixteen years older than Eimear Scally, and both come off the bench against Clare. With Scally's first touch she scores her first goal at senior level, and two minutes later adds a second just for fun. Against Kerry in round two, she does the same. Coming off the bench in Páirc Uí Rinn when the Kingdom are kicking on to draw level in the closing minutes, she helps herself to 1–1 to ensure the win (3–11 to 2–10).

Cork and Kerry must do it all over again in the Munster final. It's the seventh time in fifteen months that the sides will square up to each other. The rivalry is strong, but at the same time there's huge respect. Many of the players have lined out shoulder to shoulder for Munster in the Interprovincial series and with UCC in the O'Connor Cup, and they know each other's pre-game rituals and mannerisms inside out. But, on a misty afternoon in Rathmore on the border, Cork are in the mood for a performance to win back the Dairygold Cup.

Kerry boss William O'Sullivan changes his entire half-forward-line and it throws his system out of sync. His players can't get into their stride and Cork take advantage of the chaos. Player of the Match Ciara O'Sullivan is like a Pac-man, gobbling her way through Kerry defenders, and Cork's efficiency in front of goal is through the roof: inside the first five minutes of the second half they hit the Kingdom for four goals – Emma Farmer getting a hat-trick. The victory restores some of the pride they lost in the 2013 Munster final defeat.

Mayo are next, in the All-Ireland quarter-final, and despite initially finding it hard to break them down, they're seen off 1–15 to 0–9. Full-back Angela Walsh puts the matter to bed when she wins the ball in front of her own goal and runs the length of the field, exchanging passes as she goes, before fisting the ball over Yvonne Byrne's crossbar. Walsh is having the best season of her career and will soon be nominated by her inter-county peers for the Players' Player of the Year award.

The win sets up an All-Ireland semi-final clash with Armagh in a repeat of the 2013 qualifier, and Eamonn Ryan is nervous sitting on the bus to Pearse Park in Longford. Armagh are the division three league champions and they're capable of throwing anything at Cork, and having shocked Monaghan in the Ulster final, winning by nine points in Clones, he knows they'll be prepared. But the Orchard County have another motivation, the type that cuts into the core of a team and manifests in powerful ways.

Armagh manager James Daly lost his wife, Ann, and goalkeeper Katie Daly lost her mother, just a week after winning the Ulster championship in July. The week before, Ann was collating information for the Ulster final match programme, but after bravely battling cancer for eight years, the mother-of-three's fight comes to an end. Eight days later, James Daly's father also passes away.

Football becomes his refuge, and that of his daughter Katie also. The Armagh team have journeyed with the Daly family over the past few weeks, just as Cork had united following the death of Angela Walsh's father, Donie, in 2012.

In his pre-game speech in Longford, Eamonn Ryan reminds the Cork players of their own unity, and its power. Standing with his back to the door of the dressing room he holds a small bundle of kindling. From it, he pulls a medium-sized twig and begins to apply pressure to it. Instantly it snaps in two, the shards flying across the floor. Handing the bundle to his right-hand man, selector Frankie Honohan, he asks him to try to break the moss-covered kindling in two. Try as he might with bended knee, Honohan's efforts are in vain.

It's an 'agricultural' analogy, by Ryan's own admission, but it's a compelling one. The older players have taken the younger ones under their wing, and when united, the old guard with the new, no one will break their spirit.

Cork explode from the first whistle and Angela Walsh is at the heart of it all. The post-match analysis reveals she has the second highest possession rate, with an incredible twenty-seven possessions at full-back. Armagh captain Caroline O'Hanlon – who just weeks before competed at the Commonwealth Games in Glasgow with the Northern Ireland netball team – is trying her best to instigate attacks, but there's just no getting past Walsh.

At the other end of the pitch, Nollaig Cleary enters the arena. She has ten minutes to prove herself worthy of a starting place in the 2014 All-Ireland final. She makes her point, scoring 1–3; but Eamonn Ryan has bigger plans for her against Dublin in three weeks' time.

19

THE COMEBACK

'It's hard to beat a person who never gives up.'
Babe Ruth

There's ten more sleeps until the 2014 All-Ireland final and the cameraman shadowing Deirdre O'Reilly at the Cork press night in Erin's Own GAA Club asks his final question.

'If you had a message for Dublin, what would you say?'

The reply is immediate.

'I'd say, we won't lie down. We'll play to the bitter end and I hope they're prepared for that.'

It's an indication that Cork are aware of how close the fight will be, but also that no matter what Dublin throw at them on 28 September, Cork will be relentless in their response.

The night is a success for the Cork county board, as a hundred or so GAA fans immerse themselves in watching Eamonn Ryan and his players during the open training session. New sponsors SuperValu are on site selling jerseys and training tops, and the players are enjoying the professionalism of the set-up. They sign autographs, but it's the chance to interact with young fans that makes the occasion so special.

The local media are happy to wait their turn, and when it does arrive, they're free to talk to whomever they choose. Ryan has never put an embargo on players doing interviews. Both he and they know that they're representing something much bigger than themselves, and for seasoned sports journalists it's refreshing. Every player is willing to speak and no one is shirking that responsibility.

Training in the lead-up to the final has gone well with the exception of an injury to Elaine Scally – Eimear's older sister – who broke her jaw in an A versus B game a few days earlier. The games are as intense as championship mauls, with thirty-eight players battling to make it onto the first thirty and the match-day programme. To do so in itself is an honour; and Doireann O'Sullivan has timed her recovery from a leg injury to perfection to claim the number 27 jersey.

Ryan has scheduled a session at Páirc Uí Chaoimh for the second year running and the Cork men's GAA county board can't be more accommodating. Under Ryan's reign, however, the Cork ladies footballers had won sixteen national titles between league and championship at that point, yet had never played in their home county's GAA ground, and to some it's not good enough. But Ryan doesn't agree.

'I couldn't care less if they played there or not. I'd be way more interested in seeing a big crowd coming to see them play first.

'This is what bugs me about women's sport. Like, where are all the matches played? On GAA pitches. They might be played out of the way all right where no one might come to see them, but they're still played on GAA pitches.

'We've played in a 53,000-seater stadium in Thurles and there was no one there; only the usual suspects and a couple of jackdaws – and they only stayed for a bit of the first half before fecking off because we were so far ahead!'

Twenty-nine years earlier, the 1985 ladies football All-Ireland final between Kerry and Laois was in fact played in Páirc Uí Chaoimh with five thousand supporters in the stands. It was the last venue to host the ladies finals before they were transferred to Croke Park, and on Sunday 28 September 27,374 fans will be there to watch the forty-first instalment between Cork and Dublin.

For the second year running, Cork change their accommodation and stay at Bewleys Hotel near Dublin Airport. Ryan's concerned the players may not get a good night's sleep with aircraft flying overhead, but staff reassure him they won't hear a thing.

Prior to dinner at 6.45 p.m., he takes an amble out the front gate to carry out a reconnaissance of where he'll take the squad in the morning for their ritual 11 a.m. walk. Turning left at the busy junction, he spots a footpath a couple of metres up leading to a quiet country road. 'That'll do grand' he thinks to himself and heads back for grub.

In the team meeting at 9.30 p.m., the players are relaxed. The vibe is good. Corkery, Buckley and Walsh won the senior All-Ireland camogie final two weeks before and their triumphant energy at training in the last fortnight has roused the others. In this, their ninth football All-Ireland final in ten years, they've never once lost in Croke Park and their intention is to keep it that way.

Ryan keeps the meeting short and sweet. Addressing scepticism about Cork's longevity and doubt from some quarters about whether they still have the legs to stay with Dublin, he has just one thing to say: 'We've been up one side of the mountain, lads, but just remember this: when you're coming down the other side, you're going to gain momentum!'

The following morning, the squad head for the country road that Ryan had scouted the evening before, with Honohan, O'Leary and Ronayne shepherding the players along. After 500 yards, they turn the first corner and are met with the first obstacle of the day. The footpath has disappeared and they're at the mercy of the traffic. Ryan's up front and cursing himself. He didn't do his homework as thoroughly as he should have.

Across the road he spots a gap in a ditch. It's the entrance to a ploughed field, and as luck would have it there's no gate. There are flashbacks to climbing over the fence in the Curragh in 2013, but they're easily herded in. Bright new runners are getting muddied, but there's not a peep out of the players as they tiptoe their way through the whipped-up earth. Ryan's trying to alleviate the situation and directs them into a second field, but that too is ploughed. It makes no odds to the players: if Ryan says jump, they'll jump; if he says follow, they'll follow.

Back at the hotel, Cormac O'Connor has their gear bags loaded onto the bus, and after lunch the players scamper on with muddied soles, but O'Connor doesn't bat an eyelid. All he wants is to see them win, and to have the Brendan

Martin Cup strapped into the front passenger seat later that evening.

All aboard, he pulls off with the Garda escort waiting at the gate to chaperone them through lunchtime traffic to Croke Park. But the car park barrier is jammed for some reason and they're trapped. The Gardaí dismount their bikes and come to O'Connor's assistance, but they're at the mercy of the hotel security man.

Twelve minutes pass before the barrier raises, and Ryan is flustered. Everything on All-Ireland final day is timed to the second and this has thrown him.

•••

High up in the wilderness of the press box in Croke Park, Armagh's Caroline O'Hanlon and Monaghan's Niamh Kindlon are shivering. They've agreed to do the match commentary with RTÉ Radio 1's Jacqui Hurley, and neither know how to call it. The bookies have Cork 4/7 odds-on to win, Dublin are 13/8 and it's 10/1 for a draw. It has been sixteen years since there has been a drawn game in the senior ladies football final – the last being in 1998 when Waterford and Monaghan forced a replay in what was the first ever televised ladies football final.

O'Hanlon and Kindlon know how good the Dubs are, but they've both been on the end of one-point defeats to Cork in All-Ireland finals, in 2006 and 2013 respectively. Their verdicts hinge on who wants it most. Former Cork captain Juliet Murphy is also doing punditry, sitting pitchside with TG4. The fact that she is no longer playing for Cork is the least of her concerns. Her nerves are consumed with doing commentary *as Gaeilge*, despite getting grinds from Eamonn Ryan in the past.

Dublin are first onto the field, with Cork following them out the tunnel two minutes later at 3.26 p.m. The breakdown for the warm-up is eleven minutes, and Cork have rehearsed every move to the second, but six minutes in an official informs Ryan that time is up. The President of Ireland, Michael D. Higgins, is on his way to greet the teams and the players must line up, no buts.

Ryan is raging. 'It's one of the most important parts of the entire day, mentally and physically, and the next thing we're told stop. After six minutes?

'It all just added to the incident earlier in the car park. I got very uptight about it, but that communicated itself to the players, and I don't think it helped. The last drill we did, which would have been the fourth last if we'd enough time, went very badly as a consequence. People were dropping the ball and running at the wrong time. It was a complete disaster.'

The lack of kicking practice shows in the opening half, and Cork register eleven wides; wides so bad they're spirit breaking. Twelve minutes in and already Lindsay Peat has Martina O'Brien picking the ball out of the back of the Cork net. Peat, Sinéad Aherne and Lyndsey Davey are soaking up the energy in the stadium, and the performance they're scripting in the full-forward line is electrifying, scoring 1–5 without reply.

Cork are playing their worst football all season, and

there's no glimmer of inspiration coming anytime soon. Household names are producing uncharacteristic turnovers by the handful. Errors pot-mark every advance, and Dublin look fitter, faster and hungrier.

The first thirty minutes are a blur, and when the half-time whistle sounds, Cork lethargically retreat to Dressing Room One under the Hogan Stand. They trail by six points (0–4 to 1–7) and despite it being just four scores in the difference, they're downhearted. Their eyes are glued to the ground, almost ashamed to look at each other. The silence of it all isn't helping.

Ryan is conversing with Honohan, Ronayne and O'Leary in a separate side room, giving the players a little breathing space, but stats man Don Ryan sticks his head in. His duty is to hand over the stats to the selectors and move on, but today he can't let it go. 'Girls, for all yer wasted chances, ye're actually beating them when it comes to territorial possession. If ye just put the ball over the bar, ye'll be fine. I'm telling ye now, ye'll be fine.'

It's comforting to hear, and the information he imparts surprises them. Maybe it's not as bad as they think. Don Ryan steps back outside to present the stats to the selectors and as he does Angela Walsh stands up. Two weeks previously, she stood in the exact same spot, when the Cork camogie team trailed Kilkenny at half-time in their All-Ireland final (0–4 to 1–6).

'Girls, we've thirty minutes left. We either lie down and go to sleep, or we can get up and fight.' Her plea is impassioned, but she holds her composure. Looking across the room, she can see substitute Rhona Ní Bhuachalla hanging on her every word. Walsh can tell Ní Bhuachalla would go through the wall there and then just to get onto the pitch, but management call on veteran Nollaig Cleary instead.

At TG4's pitchside punditry table, Juliet Murphy can't find the words in her Irish vocabulary to criticise her former teammates. In her head she's wondering what the hell is going on. Cork have barely made a correct decision all day, she tells presenter Gráinne McElwain, but the pace at which Dublin are going will eventually begin to wane, or at least she hopes it will.

As Cork return to the field, the noise seems to have multiplied. The stadium feels like it's closing in on them, and so too is the pressure. They've never trailed by as much in Croke Park, and they know that communicating in such a noisy vacuum will make it even more difficult.

On the restart, they register another three wides into the Hill 16 end, and Ryan sends word to forwards Rhona Ní Bhuachalla, Doireann O'Sullivan and Eimear Scally to warm up. But as they stretch on the sideline, a huge roar from the crowd signals another goal for Dublin – Peat has penetrated for her second.

The gap is now ten points (0–6 to 2–10), and O'Sullivan and Scally turn and look at each other. Ní Bhuachalla sees a glimmer of doubt in their faces and pulls them in. 'Girls, cop the fuck on! Ye know what job ye have to do – so just go out there and do it!'

She's the first of them to enter the fray. As the assistant

referee processes her arrival, selector Shane Ronayne sprints onto the field towards full-back Angela Walsh. 'You're going out midfield Angie. Send Rena to centre-back and Bríd in full-back,' he tells her.

Walsh looks at the time counting down on the giant TV screen in the far corner of the field – sixteen minutes left, ten points the difference.

As she makes her way outfield, she spots Deirdre O'Reilly and captain Briege Corkery. They can't hear anything through the noise of the crowd, but the whites of their eyes double in size. They needn't say a word. The time is now. They can't go out like this because to do so would wipe away in a heartbeat the other eight All-Irelands they've fought so hard for.

Underneath the stadium screen, Juliet Murphy sits with her TG4 headset on. Despite the void on the scoreboard, her faith is intact – there's always a chance!

A TG4 cameraman zooms in on Eamonn Ryan and, watching at home in Rockchapel, former team manager Mary Collins senses that he thinks it's gone. And he does. For three minutes at least, Ryan thinks this is the end of the road, but he just hopes the players will do themselves justice and not bow out like this.

In the press box, Paudie Palmer of Cork's C103FM is already broadcasting the eight-time champions' epitaph, but he stops mid-sentence as Valerie Mulcahy latches onto the ball; Orlagh Farmer has taken a quick free and pumped it in to her on the edge of the semi-circle. Mulcahy takes one hop to her left, and out of the corner of her eye sees

Ní Bhuachalla sneaking in behind the Dublin defence and nods to tell her to go back door.

Angela Walsh spots the run too. She also spots the run of a Dublin defender, which she cleverly cuts off, leaving a clear path for Ní Bhuachalla – who scoops up Mulcahy's fisted assist and blows the ball past Dublin goalkeeper Cliodhna O'Connor.

Ní Bhuachalla swivels around and punches the air. It's the injection they need, and in that moment they know they can catch Dublin. Although still seven points adrift, their self-belief has skyrocketed.

Nollaig Cleary is now subtly dictating everything up front. Winning ball, laying it off, running and creating space, and Dublin are failing to pick up on the threat she's posing. Mulcahy, Orla Finn, Ní Bhuachalla and Geraldine O'Flynn feel the tremors under the Dublin defence too, adding a stream of points to narrow the deficit further.

The crowd are already reminiscing about the great Cork comebacks: from six points down to win the 2011 All-Ireland quarter-final; and from nine points down in the 2013 All-Ireland quarter-final. Those games are being replayed in the Dublin players' heads too, and they struggle to find the mental strength to change the pattern of history.

Ryan's heartbeat isn't fluctuating. His vitals remain static. Time may still not be on their side.

Seven minutes are left and three points separate the sides. Cleary wins a free close to the halfway line and steadies herself, before spotting Ciara O'Sullivan inside. Her left leg floats the ball in, and O'Sullivan manages to knock it down to herself, before handpassing the ball over the top to substitute Eimear Scally.

A minute earlier Scally had been sent on. Ronayne instructed her to go on at wing-forward and to send Cleary into the corner. But Scally naively asked to be put in corner-forward instead. She knew the damage Cleary was doing on the wing and said to Ronayne, 'If you put me inside, I'll get ye a goal.' He agreed. Now Scally is stuttering her run: she takes two Dublin defenders out of it, before squeezing the ball between them and goalkeeper Cliodhna O'Connor to score the most important goal of her career on her Croke Park debut. And it's a tie game (2–11 apiece).

But again the Cork forwards' radar goes askew and they miss three easy point-scoring chances, including two by Geraldine O'Flynn. They are two chances she'd usually put over with her eyes closed. Dublin hang on, with substitute Siobhán Woods pointing to put them one point ahead again. But Ciara O'Sullivan equalises at the Hill 16 end for Cork with three minutes on the clock.

Paudie Palmer is now on his feet in the press box. Over the airwaves he tells of the best comeback he's ever witnessed in thirty-odd years of broadcasting, and apologises for ever doubting a side that has never lost in Croker. The game is not yet won, but the emotion of it all has already sent tears streaming down his face.

The ensuing Dublin kickout is gloriously snatched out of the air by Deirdre O'Reilly, who lays the ball off to Cleary on the right wing. Cleary shuffles across the pitch, indicating for someone to come to her to receive the pass. Doireann

O'Sullivan obliges and she too works her way towards the left wing, where Geraldine O'Flynn is arriving from wing-back and takes the assist thirty yards out. Planting her left foot, O'Flynn dummies and sells her defender. Arriving back onto her stronger side, she fires over a point – splitting the posts, it signals a one-point lead for Cork.

The greatest players have an in-built sense of space – and O'Flynn is one of them. She has done this before – in the 2006 final against Armagh – and her bravery to have a pot, despite having missed chances earlier in the game, sees Cork win their ninth All-Ireland title in ten years (2–13 to 2–12).

The hooter sounds and the substitutes go crazy. The players on the pitch, however, stand still: shell-shocked and too tired to even react, until their teammates arrive and submerge them in euphoria.

Juliet Murphy is jumping in the air, trying to hang on to her headset. She beams with pride at the manner in which her friends have pulled themselves back from the very edge of defeat.

'It was the most incredible game. There was a young girl next to me and she asked me for my autograph at the final whistle and I started talking to her as if she was my neighbour,' Murphy recalls. 'I told her I'd love to go out there and congratulate them, and she said, "Go on!" I figured she was right and I thought my job on TG4 was done so I threw off the headset and took off to hug the girls! It was just instinct.

'It turned out I wasn't finished on air at all! So, when I got back, Valerie had been presented with the Player of the Match award and when I saw her on the TV screen, I waved at her as if I was on Bosco! I was just so delighted to see her. I asked her how she felt and she literally couldn't even speak with the shock of it all.'

Briege Corkery is still stunned when handed the Brendan Martin Cup on the Hogan Stand. Not only is it her first time captaining Cork to a senior All-Ireland title, she now owns fourteen All-Ireland medals between football and camogie, alongside Rena Buckley. And, there, hidden in the crowd, watching Corkery lift the cup, is her older brother Jeremiah. She doesn't know it yet, but he's flown in from Canada to see his baby sister go down in history as one of four dual players to captain Cork to a senior All-Ireland football title.

As Eamonn Ryan makes his way down from the stand, Dublin manager Gregory McGonigle asks if Kilkenny hurling coach Brian Cody and himself would consider retiring so as to give other counties a chance. This is the seventeenth national title win for Cork that Ryan has overseen since 2005. Ryan can barely answer, after witnessing what is arguably the greatest quarter-hour of football his players have produced during what has been the most remarkable decade.

•••

The following week, ten Cork players are named on the forty-five-nominee shortlist for the TG4 All-Star awards, which takes place in November at the Citywest Hotel in Dublin.

On the night, captain Briege Corkery wins an incredible eighth bronze statuette to become the most successful All-Star winner in the history of Cork ladies football. Players' Player of the Year nominee, Angela Walsh, and Bríd Stack collect their sixth All-Star awards, Geraldine O'Flynn her fifth, Ciara O'Sullivan her second and Vera Foley her first.

However, the most obvious omission is full-forward Valerie Mulcahy – the Player of the Match winner in both the 2014 division one national league final and the All-Ireland final. In the foyer after the team is announced, players and officials from every county discuss the shock snub. It doesn't make sense that the top player in the LGFA's top two showcase games has been overlooked. Even social media gets in on the act, with Premier League soccer star David Meyler of Hull City FC tweeting that 'it's completely wrong' that Mulcahy didn't get selected.

But Mulcahy isn't bothered. There was a time when she would have been, but as people come up and almost sympathise with her, she just smiles and says, 'I have an All-Ireland medal and I'm happy with that.'

All-Stars are nice individual awards, but for Cork it has always been about the team. Winning the 2014 RTÉ Sports Team of the Year award was the best feeling, because, finally, after a decade of dominating their sport, the Irish sporting public saluted their collective achievements. The team award means much more to them than the fifty-six All-Stars they have won individually since Eamonn Ryan's reign began.

20

BASICS AND BABY BUMPS

'Whether you're shuffling a deck of cards or holding your breath, magic is pretty simple: it comes down to training, practice, and experimentation, followed by ridiculous pursuit and relentless perseverance.'
David Blaine

Sunday, 11 January 2015
The Farm, Bishopstown

It's 105 days since Cork became the 2014 All-Ireland champions. Today, though, they're just like any other team, starting out on a nine-month journey to be the best. Back to business; back to basics.

Nine years at the top could make your head swell, but come the first session of the year, they're nobodies. They each have to work as hard as every other inter-county player, if not harder because they have to fend off the chasing pack. This is how they have done it for the last decade: every January is treated like the first.

It's 9.40 a.m. on 11 January 2015, and cars are already whizzing through the winding entrance of The Farm. Most are purring diesel engines, heavily splattered with mud, a contrast to the flashier cars the UCC Fitzgibbon hurlers drive in minutes later.

The O'Sullivan sisters, Ciara and Roisín, are greeted by

Emma Farmer outside the green-painted dressing room, their inner sanctuary for close to a decade. It's smiles all the way, but it's brief: they're here to work. Ciara O'Sullivan doesn't know it yet, but she'll soon become the eighth captain during Ryan's reign.

Orlagh Farmer gives selector Frankie Honohan a hug as he shuffles across the car park with loaded water bottles in this, his twelfth season with the Cork ladies.

Eamonn Ryan, nearing seventy-four years of age, is sitting on the boot of his silver Toyota Yaris putting on heavy-duty boots, chatting to a young hurler in a Tipperary jersey who has gone out of his way to say hello. Five cars up, and former Cork hurling goalkeeper Ger Cunningham is doing the same.

More hurlers filter past Ryan and say 'how ya', 'congrats' and 'well done'. The Master just nods and smiles, a little embarrassed. He knows the days of celebrations are long gone. No need to mention them any more. Cunningham heads in his direction and the two legendary Cork GAA men shake hands and exchange greetings.

It's 9.50 a.m., ten minutes before training is due to start, and the ladies footballers are already trotting over to the pitch right of The Farm entrance. Its rugby posts will do for now.

A batch of soccer players stroll by, gear bags thrown over their shoulders, but a handful are aware of who just passed them – 'That's the Cork ladies footballers, lads!'

Ryan follows the squad to the pitch and the players are already jumping, twisting, kicking balls, anything to stay warm. It's bitterly cold but there's nothing fancy about their gear. A fraction are wearing Skins compared to the UCC hurlers who are now sprinting past, already late for their own session.

It's bang on 10 a.m. but selector Shane Ronayne has long counted the numbers and kicking commences. There's a lot of hopping from one foot to the other – either from the cold or nerves. It's time to impress, show you've maintained a respectable level of fitness during hibernation.

This is Ronayne's second season and he has learned to keep it simple.

Jogging. Butt kicks. Lunges. They're all done in harmony.

Ryan and Honohan watch on, leaning against the rugby posts.

Reverse lunges.

A number of familiar faces are missing, but word of retirements won't filter out of the camp until before their opening game against Mayo in Swinford in three weeks' time. It's not intentional, but the media don't care for now.

Full-back All-Star Angela Walsh is expecting her first child, legendary midfielder Norita Kelly and former captain Anne-Marie Walsh have retired, and Nollaig Cleary won't announce her status officially until the summer rolls in.

A handful of new bodies have joined the squad. It's difficult coming into a team of multiple All-Ireland-winning players and All-Star winners, but they're made to feel part of the set-up from day one. The veterans make sure of it.

Skipping. Hopping. Jumping.

Selector Pat O'Leary runs an errand for Ronayne, who's in his element. This is where he's meant to be. 'Jump and land into it girls, jump and land into it!' he shouts, demonstrating the move himself.

Another late batch of hurlers run by. It's 10.07 a.m. and already Cork limbs are sweating. 'Be aggressive about it,' Ronayne shouts.

This doesn't look like a fluffy pre-season session for one second. The diligence and focus of the players is akin to that prior to a league final, a Munster championship opener with Kerry even. The operation is so smooth that it's baffling to think that this is their first session in nearly four months.

Winter, and winning, didn't distract them. This is a well-oiled machine.

Core exercises. High knees and sprints. High heels and sprints.

'Some of us aren't changing correctly. Press go when you get to the green cone!' Ronayne instructs.

10.15 a.m. The warm-up ends. United, they walk to Honohan's water bottles. Ryan has yet to officially welcome them as a group. He still stands under the posts, but Bríd Stack, the eldest present, approaches him. They smile and share a joke.

Ryan thanks the players for being there and then reads from a piece of paper in his right hand, explaining the next drill. There's no dilly-dallying or 'fannying about' – as they'd say in Cork. As he speaks, ponytails are fixed and stretches are completed. The girls are utilising their time efficiently, just like The Master.

He points to his head. All eyes are on him and they know they need to maintain 100 per cent focus. It's ball work straight off. Running at full tilt, handpassing. It's freezing and the wind is picking up. Limbs are red and blue beneath the overcast Sunday morning sky, but it's high pace, high intensity. Short and snappy.

Ryan constantly encourages, his desire for the game keeping him warm, and he follows with whistle in hand. The intensity has gone up another notch.

Liaison officer Bridget O'Brien and Frank Honohan huddle in the distance, and join Ronayne and O'Leary in a chorus of constant encouragement.

No one is hiding, new or old, and there's communication and movement in bucketloads – surprisingly so for January.

'A minute and a half left,' Ryan calls out.

Everything is timed. To the second. But it's not all perfection. Mistakes are made and a few of the fresher faces lose possession and fail to get back and defend, but that'll soon be knocked out of them. The whistle sounds and they instantly jog it in, forming a semi-circle around their general with military precision.

It's time for a possession game. Instantly things get faster and more physical, and blocking comes into play.

The players are happy to be back. Happy to have a routine again and happy that a new year brings a new challenge. The duration of the drills is neither too long nor too short and everything is perfectly balanced to their satisfaction.

This is how Ryan has kept their attention for eleven years – by making them central in every session.

Ryan looks to be in his element too. He loves this and he feeds off their energy. His son Don, the team's statistician, arrives a little late, but that's no surprise given the arrival of his first child, Doireann, just a few months earlier. There's no physio on site: Brian O'Connell is only twenty-four hours back in the country after his honeymoon, so he too is excused. They all have lives outside of this.

Ryan checks his watch. They're an hour in and the drills have flown by. It's match situation now: game on. 110 per cent, no less – and this is just day one.

At 11.18 a.m. the game finishes and selector Pat O'Leary brings in the water bottles. Press-ups are done. Roll over: abs. Jumping jacks. Burpees. It's old school – simple, but effective.

No one is slacking, even now when shadow punches are thrown. They will be hit; as reigning champions, it comes with the territory. But they're not done yet. Ryan issues instructions, so sprints it is. Sixty legs turn and pump.

Now, in twos, it's a tug of war for the ball.

'Don't let them take it off you,' Ryan instructs. 'Brilliant, well done. You've had to work hard to get to where you are so don't give it up easy!' he says, referring to the task at hand, but it could just as well be meant for the last decade.

'That's it so lads, see ye Wednesday night,' he adds, and instinctively the players huddle together. Arms around each other's waists as if to say this is where it starts, the first of ninety sessions in 2015.

Another year, another chapter.

•••

Ryan lands in Knock Airport and Don collects him to take him to Swinford for the opening league game against Mayo. He's returning from Liverpool where he has been presenting GAA medals, but the journey is cut short to return for Cork's first game of 2015.

Mayo offer to clap Cork, as reigning champions, onto the frost-hardened pitch, but Ryan respectfully declines the gesture as Clare Clarke of the LGFA had passed away that morning following a five-year battle with breast cancer. A mum of two, Clarke was aged just thirty-five.

Cork come away with the win, despite having trailed. They would do the same against Kerry in the second round – Geraldine O'Flynn kicking a point in injury time to win it, just as she had done in the All-Ireland final the previous September. Talks of that comeback have been put to bed long before heading on their team holiday in March to celebrate their ninth All-Ireland title win. For months, Bríd Stack has worked tirelessly in helping to coordinate the trip, which includes time in New York, Miami and a cruise. But things don't exactly go to plan.

Arriving at Dublin Airport, the travelling party of forty-five are informed that their flight to London is delayed by two hours, and as a consequence they miss their flight from Heathrow to the States. The plan is shuffled and a flight to Boston with a connecting flight on to Miami is organised. Although there are three hours until boarding, the queue isn't moving. Annie Walsh is using her imposing stature to fend off queue rule breakers, but with the clock counting down, panic sets in as they realise they may miss this flight too. A sprint to the boarding gate pays off and when, finally, they are all aboard, the party commences.

However, on arriving in Miami, after thousands of air miles, thirty-six hours of travelling, six bus transfers and a train ride, there's no sign of their luggage. Just a handful of bags filter around the carousel, and they're told to return tomorrow. When they do, there are still no bags.

Goalkeeping coach Kieran Dwyer has done well to keep the positivity levels up, but on day three his spirit breaks and he rings American Airlines. WhatsApp messages begin to fly and fifteen bodies surface from bed to beat rush-hour traffic in a hail of taxis to the airport. Still wearing the same clothes they departed Ireland in, they finally gather their luggage. Dwyer's bag happens to be the first to surface; however, unfortunately for his pupil, Martina O'Brien, hers hasn't made it and she's forced to borrow clothes for the remainder of the trip.

Two training sessions are held, but other than that it's cocktail o'clock. A pool party somehow evolves into an impromptu hen party for Valerie Mulcahy ahead of her wedding in June.

Upon their return home, they lose by sixteen points to Dublin in the last round of the league; it's the biggest league defeat during Eamonn Ryan's tenure. In the semifinal, mistakes have been rectified and they dispatch Kerry before a mighty tussle with Galway in the division one league final in Parnell Park. Tracey Leonard in maroon is exceptional and hits eight points, while Lorna Joyce scores an equalising point to force a replay (3–8 to 1–14).

There's an unnecessary worry for Eamonn Ryan, however, in the week leading up to the replay. It is scheduled to be played in Portlaoise at 7.30 p.m., but the Cork camogie team are due to play the Munster camogie final the same day in Cashel at 4.30 p.m. There's uncertainty as to what the dual players should do. Briege Corkery and Rena Buckley opt to go with the footballers, while Meabh Cahalane – the younger sister of Cork footballer Damien Cahalane – heads with Paudie Murray and the camogie squad to Tipperary. Both coaches have been in contact briefly, and the players are left to decide what's best for themselves, but it's a curveball Ryan could do without.

In Portlaoise, Cork are better prepared for Galway. Ryan asks Geraldine O'Flynn to sacrifice her own attacking game at wing-back to shackle Leonard at full-forward, and it works. Entering the last two minutes, it's level again (0–13 to 1–10). Storming through from midfield, Rena Buckley fires over the winning point and Cork claim their ninth league title since 2005.

A week's leave is granted and Valerie Mulcahy finalises her wedding plans. The wedding takes place two weeks before the Munster final. Having spent many evenings in the spring canvassing for a yes vote in the Same-sex Marriage Referendum, the day is especially poignant for Mulcahy. Her teammates join in the wedding celebrations at the Royal Cork Yacht Club in Crosshaven, but no alcohol is consumed.

A fortnight later, in the Munster final against Kerry, there may as well have been. The issue of dual player fixture clashes has arisen again, for the third time this season, and Cork's focus isn't where it should be. Corkery and Buckley are now expected to play a senior camogie championship match against Offaly in Páirc Uí Rinn at 2 p.m. before getting in the car and driving forty minutes to Mallow to play the Munster football final at 6 p.m.

Eamonn Ryan mentions the debacle to the media at the launch of the TG4 Football Championship in Croke Park, and Corkery's phone begins to buzz with interview requests. It's out of her comfort zone; conflict is the one thing her repertoire doesn't include. She confides in Ryan and they agree it's time to speak out if things are to change. Never in their eleven seasons working together have either made an issue of the clashes that occur during the league, nor has Corkery ever voiced her own opinion in public. But there's no excuse for clashes occurring during championship and a decade of discord has taken its toll.

'Maybe we're just being paranoid, but we're wondering if they're trying to squash out the dual players,' Corkery tells a local Cork radio station prior to the games. 'Are they trying to force us into making a decision so one team will be at a disadvantage? I don't know. Maybe it's just paranoia, but it's unfair.

'I don't want to put the blame on one organisation over the other, because in my eyes they're both to blame because they don't sit down and talk to each other. They talk about women in sport growing in strength, but there's no way it's going to grow in strength if our games are being fixed for the same day. This happened back in 2012 and we were assured it wouldn't happen again, but already this year we have had a clash of fixtures on three occasions.'

Kerry have never been more prepared for a Munster final, but Cork are sidetracked by the dual-star crisis, as is Ryan. Physically, training is good, but mentally it's crumbling all around them and they don't even know it. The talk among the players is coated in frustration and anger, and Kerry aren't on their radar as much as they should be.

Corkery and Buckley help the camogie team defeat Offaly, and then drive to Mallow to tog out again. Kerry lead by two points at half-time, but in the second half it all caves in as the dual stars fade and no one else steps forth. For the first time ever, Cork give up with ten minutes to go. They'd rather be anywhere else but soaked on a soggy, overcast night, humiliated to the core. They lose 2–13 to 2–4 and the nine-point defeat is the biggest championship defeat ever under Ryan.

'We had been going well in training, but the dual star thing did affect us,' says forward Aisling Hutchings. 'The rest of us needed to step up to cover Rena and Briege, but we didn't. The girls would go out and play three games in the same day if you asked them, but that's not the point. The rest of us didn't stand up, and that was a big realisation that day.'

The fallout would change Cork's entire season.

21

THE PERFECT TEN

'Perfection is not attainable, but if we chase perfection,
we can catch excellence.'
Vince Lombardi

In the aftermath of the Munster final, Cork are in disarray. They lost to Kerry in 2013, but it didn't feel like this. There's an emptiness, and the dread is that Ryan will run them into the ground at the upcoming annual training weekend at the University of Limerick, but Ryan's smarter than that. He knows the group needs to pick each other up and get their focus back. After the first day of training, they head to Flannery's Bar in Limerick city. It's the first time in almost a decade of training weekends that Ryan has prescribed a meal and a few drinks, and it reignites the bond that slightly dissolved the same night their pride did against Kerry in Mallow.

Try as they might to focus on themselves, they're hit once again by circumstances outside their own control. Another dual clash is on the cards, with the All-Ireland camogie semi-final against Kilkenny and the All-Ireland football quarter-final against Galway pencilled in for the same day.

Meath have to be devoured first in the All-Ireland qualifier, but, in a pre-emptive strike, a meeting with the older players, Eamonn Ryan and selector Frankie Honohan is

called. Rena Buckley hosts the gathering at her physiotherapy practice in Macroom a week before the Meath
game. Options are discussed, debated and dissected, but at
the crux of it is whether to pull out of the 2015 championship. They contemplate making a stand once and for all
for their teammates, the two players who have given the
most to both codes for more than a decade. Throughout
the discussion there is no mention of titles or records; it
simply boils down to player welfare. A statement is drafted
regarding their disappointment over yet another clash, and
it's agreed that if they beat Meath, Ryan will put the options to the team collectively.

They annihilate Jenny Rispin's side by forty points in
Semple Stadium (7–22 to 0–3). Beara's Áine O'Sullivan
has bagged 3–5 on her senior championship debut, but
as she carries her Player of the Match award back to the
cool-down at the far corner of the pitch, Ryan huddles the
players together. There's an emotional surge going through
them. Something isn't quite sitting right with the younger
members. They know this is serious. Ryan puts the options
to them – do they want to stay in the championship or pull
out?

Briege Corkery immediately raises her hand. 'I want to
stay in. If we're going to go out, we'll do it on our own
terms, with dignity, and no other way.'

The rest nod in agreement. What Corkery says goes
and Ryan instructs that there be no more talk of clashes if
they're to arise again. He let the issue get to him before the
Munster final and he isn't going to make the same mistake

twice, and certainly not during knockout. They're all in it together and, regardless of what others impose on them, they're going to stick to the task set on 11 January and get back to Croke Park.

The statement regarding the upcoming clash on 15 August will still be sent out, but just minutes before the Cork county board is to release it, word comes through in Semple Stadium that the Camogie Association has moved back the All-Ireland semi-final between Cork and Kilkenny to Sunday 16 August, to facilitate the dual players.

It's a relief to Ryan and his management team. The quarter-final against Galway was tipped by many at the start of the season to be the eventual All-Ireland final pairing. But they've reined themselves in. At a training session in the Mardyke before the game, Ryan speaks after the warm-up, and what he says changes the players' perspective.

'We had to get back to basics. I just asked them a few simple questions. What did we want to get out of it, and that the reason we were all there was because we enjoyed it. We all liked being part of the gang, we were good at it and we had success at it, but they weren't doing it for Cork, or me, or the jersey, they were doing it for themselves. It's not being selfish, it's more self-interest, and there is a distinction.

'I just knew that night by their demeanour that they got what I was saying.'

Their renewed focus on themselves is unyielding against the side that tested them to their limits in the league final replay. After just twenty seconds and five passes, Ciara

O'Sullivan has the umpires raising a green flag. Cork are in control and they lead Kevin Reidy's side in the Gaelic Grounds by seven points at half-time. But they lose their grip in the second as Geraldine Conneally drags Galway back to within two points. Superb defending by Vera Foley, Deirdre O'Reilly, Marie Ambrose, Aisling Barrett and a Player of the Match performance by Briege Corkery keeps the Tribeswomen at bay and Cork win (1–12 to 1–10).

Twenty-four hours later, Corkery and Buckley are back out on the field helping the camogie team to an All-Ireland final, defeating Kilkenny and ensuring themselves a chance to at least match Dublin camogie player Kathleen Mills' fifty-four-year-old record of fifteen senior All-Ireland medals.

Kerry are next in the semi-final of the football championship. After beating Galway, Cork's confidence is back. Valerie Mulcahy's confidence, however, isn't as high. Since the Meath game she's been uncharacteristically scuffing easy frees and it's eating away at her. Against Galway, Ryan called her ashore after forty-one minutes, but this evening against Kerry in the Gaelic Grounds she's out to prove a point.

She's not the only one, though, as possible starting places in an All-Ireland final are up for grabs and semi-final debutantes Marie Ambrose, Aisling Barrett, Áine O'Sullivan and Aisling Hutchings are also looking to impress; Barrett more than anyone, as she has been in the side since 2009 and has yet to start in an All-Ireland final.

Cork lead Kerry by four points at half-time. Upon the

restart, substitute Eimear Scally adds 1–2 in a twenty-minute cameo. Mulcahy finishes with 2–2, while Ciara O'Sullivan and Áine O'Sullivan get a goal each, to win 4–14 to 0–13. The recalibration launches Cork into their fifth successive All-Ireland final and a bid for a second five in a row.

•••

Before boarding the bus to Croke Park for the tenth time in eleven years, Briege Corkery and Geraldine O'Flynn make a pact. They take a moment before leaving the foyer at the Clayton Hotel in Leopardstown to remind themselves of what they've been through this season. From the outside, many aren't surprised to see Cork back in Croker; they're the bookies' favourites, but it's not as straightforward as it seems.

They were defeated three times this season: by their opponents today, Dublin, and Monaghan in the league, before letting themselves down against Kerry in the Munster final. That defeat to Kerry turned their season on its head, and after it Corkery and O'Flynn spent hours on the phone trying to figure things out. Their pact was that, given all they'd been through together, win, lose or draw today, they would be the first to hug each other.

Corkery and Rena Buckley had collected their fifteenth senior All-Ireland medal when the camogie crew defeated Galway the previous fortnight, and their victory brought a buzz to the football camp. But there's no guarantee they'll win. Dublin are a different outfit to the side that Cork faced twelve months ago. Eight of their starters are no more, but Gregory McGonigle's side has a new air of belief.

In the past they brought over New-York-born motivational speaker Gian Paul Gonzalez. Gonzalez was a high-school teacher but found fame when his friend, a chaplain to the New York Giants, asked him to speak to the team during their 2011/2012 season. Things hadn't been going well, but a pep talk from Gonzalez turned men into Giants and they went on to win the Super Bowl. He gave each member of the team a poker chip to carry with them; on the back, each player wrote 'All In', as a reminder that when the chips are down, they had to be 'All In'. For Dublin, the message was the same.

Eamonn Ryan keeps faith with the same fifteen he started in the semi-final against Kerry, giving Aisling Barrett her debut start in an All-Ireland final, having been in the squad for six years. Barrett was the substitute goalkeeper for Elaine Harte in 2011, prior to becoming corner-back. But hers isn't the only role that has changed. Twelve months earlier, when Cork made their ten-point comeback against Dublin, Áine O'Sullivan was a watergirl; today, however, she's making her debut on Jones' Road at full-forward, and marking her is Muireann Ní Scanaill, herself a watergirl in 2014.

As the Dublin starting team huddle after the parade, Cork captain Ciara O'Sullivan rallies every player from one to thirty-six into their huddle. It's a subtle reminder that they're all in this together. Defensively, the game is cagey. Both sets of backs are applying serious pressure, but fifteen minutes in Geraldine O'Flynn's knee buckles as she follows Dublin captain Lyndsey Davey out for a ball. She tries to walk it off, but, having done her cruciate in 2010, she knows it's not good. Physio Brian O'Connell goes to her aid, but when O'Flynn pulls up for a second time, she knows she can't continue.

It's a psychological blow for Cork, who trail by a point. But Róisín Phelan, who lost out on a starting place earlier in the championship, seamlessly slots in next to Bríd Stack and Deirdre O'Reilly. It isn't an aesthetic first-half, but a monstrous point by Rena Buckley just before half-time brings them level (0–5 apiece) at the turnaround.

As they enter the dressing room, players are quiet – downbeat, even. Not because of their performance, but because they know that Geraldine O'Flynn is hurting.

'Ger came in and she was emotional, and that set us all off,' says Briege Corkery. 'She said a few words. That it was up to us and we were the players on the pitch that could make it happen. We were the ones in trouble, and we were the ones who had to get ourselves out of it. All of us welled up, and there was no more to be said after that. We knew what we had to do.'

Cork go out and kick four unanswered points, three frees from Mulcahy and a thumper of a point from Doireann O'Sullivan. Dublin continue to drive on in the final quarter, but Corkery is a woman on a mission now, cleaning up what she can around the backline.

By now, Eimear Scally is on the pitch and Cork's momentum up front has lifted. She kicks a beauty of a point off her left and, more importantly, tracks back to intercept a ball in her own backline, where she has no business being. She's in survival mode – they all are.

Mulcahy kicks her sixth free of the day to put two points between the sides as the clock counts down. But, uncharacteristically, Cork are giving away possession and Dublin are handed lifelines for free.

With a minute and a half left, Dublin advance into enemy territory. Doireann O'Sullivan has no other option but to take one for the team, getting sin-binned and delaying the clock.

Eventually, the ball finds its way into the square in front of Martina O'Brien, but red jerseys swarm Sinéad Goldrick as she tries to sneak through. As the adrenaline pumps, they have the composure not to give away a penalty. Goldrick releases her shot, but standing in the way is Bríd Stack, who – like Corkery – has played every minute of Cork's ten All-Ireland finals when the hooter sounds. Corkery and Buckley officially become the greatest GAA players of all time, each winning their sixteenth senior All-Ireland medal and surpassing Kathleen Mills' record.

As her teammates throw their hands in the air, Corkery whizzes across the field to the subs' bench. There, waiting for her with a smile and tears in her eyes, is Geraldine O'Flynn.

'I had to make sure that she was the first person I saw and hugged,' says Corkery. 'We'd made the pact and it made it worse then when she went off injured.'

Corkery knows that without O'Flynn, Cork would

never have achieved the 'Perfect Ten', having kicked the winning points in the 2006 and 2014 All-Ireland finals. Corkery wins the Player of the Match award for good measure. In that moment, however, it isn't about her. It isn't about records. It's about being there for O'Flynn – and that's what sums them up. Good players, but great people.

That night, as they return to the Clayton Hotel, Eamonn Ryan has a word with Rena Buckley. 'I'd love to organise an ol' singsong, just the team, later tonight – like what happened in Lanzarote years ago,' he says.

'Ah that'd be mighty, yeah,' Buckley replies.

'Right so, you'll organise it! At midnight, we'll all go into a room and just have an ol' singsong!'

And with that, Buckley quietly spreads the word among the players during the meal. She doesn't know how many will be willing to drag themselves away from the celebrations – but she needn't have worried.

Bang on midnight, the entire team and management assemble, making their way downstairs to a meeting room. For the next hour and a half, they belt out songs just as they did that night in the restaurant in Lanzarote many moons ago. Together, in harmony, they couldn't be happier.

Don't give up 'til it's over, don't quit if you can,
The weight on your shoulder will make you a stronger man,
Grasp your nettle tightly, though it will burn,
Treat your failures lightly, your luck is bound to turn,
Don't give up 'til it's over, don't quit if you can,
The weight on your shoulder will make you a stronger man.

22

RIVAL RESPECT AND LEGACIES

*'You can have a certain arrogance, and I think that's
fine, but what you should never lose is the respect
for others.'*
Steffi Graf

On a fourteen-hour flight to Singapore for the 2006 All-Star trip, Cork's Angela Walsh and Mayo's Cora Staunton didn't utter a single word to one another. The greatest defender and forward in the history of ladies football couldn't even muster a hello, such was the rivalry between the sides at the beginning of Cork's rise.

Staunton's shyness held her back from breaking the ice with Walsh. She hardly spoke, either, to Michaela Downey of Down on the other side of her during the flight. Her Mayo teammate Claire Egan happened to be put sitting between two of her biggest opponents, Galway's Annette Clarke and Lisa Cohill, and this situation kept Staunton entertained all the way to Changi Airport.

The relationship between the Connacht sides has always been turbulent, but this, surprisingly, is not the case with Mayo and Cork. The 2007 All-Star trip opened the Mayo and Cork players' eyes to each other, and the opponents bonded. Soon Martha Carter, Fiona McHale, Yvonne Byrne and Staunton were hanging out with Elaine Harte, Nollaig Cleary, Juliet Murphy and Valerie Mulcahy.

Having the craic and slagging each other too – some more than others.

'We know each other well enough now to be able to wind each other up. But we'd always be very respectful,' says Staunton. 'Val takes the brunt of it, but she's well able to handle it. The Mayo gang might be having a go at her about her white boots – all in fun – but the Cork girls would be rowing in with us, and you can see just how much they enjoy each other's company.'

But, for Staunton, the respect that Mayo and other teams have developed for Cork has stemmed from how Eamonn Ryan and his players have carried themselves throughout their decade of dominance.

'It's the way they conduct themselves. That's a huge thing. There's not that arrogance or cockiness about Cork. They've won so many medals, they've a right to be cocky, but it's another All-Ireland, they've won it and that's it. They'll go celebrate for the week and that's the end of it. They were never in your face about it and were always so respectful of others.

'We offered to give them a guard of honour in their first league game in 2015 away to us in Swinford as All-Ireland champions, but they didn't want it. Eamonn thought it was inappropriate given that Clare Clarke of the Ladies Gaelic Football Association had passed away from cancer that morning, but either way, they wouldn't have wanted it.

'It says a lot about them as individuals, but it probably comes down to Eamonn, the back-room team and their influence. It's what's made them the team they are.

'They're just so grounded, after all they've won. Winning has become a habit, and it would have been easy after the 2010 All-Ireland quarter-final loss to Tyrone to just sail off into the sunset and say, "We've won what we've won", but they wanted more.'

To offer such generous praise about the team that's quenched Mayo's dreams so often says a lot about Staunton herself too. Aged fifteen, her mother passed away and three days after the funeral she played in a minor Connacht final. Ladies football came to her rescue, but not initially. In grief, she rebelled against football, against everything. But, gradually, Staunton's resolve saw her transformed into the most skilful player the game has ever seen. When Cork were coasting in their first league final against Mayo in 2004, six points up at half-time, they got what *Irish Times* sports writer Malachy Clerkin coined 'Cora Stauntoned'. Scoring 1–9, the Carnacon woman ended Eamonn Ryan and Cork's hopes of a title in his first year in charge.

'They should have beaten us that day,' Staunton admits. 'We didn't know much about them at senior level, but that day you could see they had it in them. I remember thinking these are a serious outfit. I went home and looked at the match programme and went through the team's average age. Bar a couple of players, they were all still very young, but at the same time they were all physically able to compete at that level. I knew then they were going places.'

Cora Staunton is the most marked woman in the history of ladies football, but for all of Cork's physical prowess, she says they never went about it the wrong way.

'They're probably one of the most physical teams you'll come up against, but they were never dirty,' says Staunton. 'They're well able to mix it, and they're cute, but in no way would I class them as a dirty team. Okay, they know tactically when to foul or slow the game down, but that's the sign of a good team. I don't ever remember coming off the pitch and raging about Cork, or saying, "I can't believe they've done that."

'Eamonn just has it drilled into them that if you lose the ball, then everyone's working back, then they're breaking forward. They all know their jobs on the pitch.'

At a bar in San Francisco in 2010, Staunton spoke to Eamonn Ryan for the first time, and their friendship grew from there, with each learning from the other. She, perhaps, learning more than he.

'You could listen to him all day. His mindset on sport is amazing. You could ask him anything about the game and he'd be very open about everything.

'He's like Mick O'Dwyer in that he's won so much. But in my eyes he wasn't always respected by ladies Gaelic as much as he should have been. That's just my opinion, but you can't argue with what he's done for the sport.'

What Staunton learned from Ryan in the bar that day, however, is just a fraction of what she'd take from his training sessions on the All-Star tour. 'It's the way he explains things. He's a real thinker. An out-and-out coach.

'It's what he does, and how he does it. He's demonstrating things the whole time, explaining why things are done. Skills are huge and everything is done with a ball in hand. Just even watching how the Cork girls respond to him you'd learn a lot.

'You can manage a team and possibly get away with winning an All-Ireland, but for a player to improve, that boils down to their skills and how they're taught. You can see that improvement in all the Cork girls from 2004 right up to now, and that's because of Eamonn's coaching. He's not managing, he's coaching.

'But he's not afraid to clip players' wings either. Not that their heads were ever getting big, but he wasn't afraid to rein players in if they needed a kick up the arse. Ten minutes to go he could whip off a top player and it would make you think. It's the subtle psychology of it.

'There's no one ever allowed get above themselves because of that. Okay, you could nearly name twelve out of the starting fifteen, and his teams down the years have been consistent, but within the girls' heads themselves, they're always wondering, "If I'm not performing now, am I going to be dropped, or is someone going to take my place?" That's the mark of a good coach.

'I don't think too many other teams, if any, could do that. There's no one indispensable, no matter who they are.'

As to the legacy her biggest rivals will leave behind, Staunton's in no doubt.

'I've heard things being said like there needs to be a new winner for the health of the sport, but in my eyes that's rubbish. Cork's legacy is that they've lifted the standard of ladies football and made it better from a skills point of view. You only need to look at some of the finals they've been involved in over the years.

'That way of thinking was probably more so at the start when they'd won three or four titles. People were saying, "Oh it would be good for a change", but they now respect what Cork have achieved and how hard it is to stay at the top. They appreciate that. The same players are around since 2004 and they're still putting in the hard work and still competing at the top.

'Winning the 2014 RTÉ Sports Team of the Year said it all. To them that meant something. It was them being recognised on a national level outside of the GAA, and recognised as a team that has really done something in a whole sporting context.

'That to them was more important than getting six All-Stars the month before. You could see that, and that comes down to the fact that there's a massive team ethic there. You can't ever really know that unless you're in the dressing room, but you can tell they're all one. Everyone is there for each other, and that's it.'

A Simple Legacy

Bruce Lee once said that simplicity was the key to brilliance, and the simplicity of it all will be Cork's legacy.

From 2004 to 2015 under Eamonn Ryan, they won twenty-nine titles – ten All-Ireland titles, nine division one national league titles and ten Munster titles – and not once has he spoken of systems or tactics. In his eyes, putting the player and fundamental skills at the centre of the entire process is how Cork have achieved all they have.

'A fella rang me one day and he'd seen us playing, and he was gushing in his praise of my system,' says Ryan. 'I told him I'd no system, and he said, "It was brilliant the way ye had the blanket defence and how ye'd break then" and I didn't have a clue what he was on about! Some people might criticise you for not having a system, but generally the players appreciate that there's no codology.

'It's all about them, and then it's all about technique. Everything else is subsidiary. Psychology, nutrition, rest, they all have their place, but basic skill is at the centre of it all. You could make it all up and have all the tactics in the world, but you can never foresee what's going to happen in a football match. The players must be able to think for themselves.

'We're realistic enough to know it's not an exact science. Players need to concentrate more on the performance than on the outcome, but if your head is full of information overload, then it's very hard to go out gung-ho because you're analysing while you're doing it. The modern player might be more in tune with dealing with that than someone of my vintage, but it must be an awful encumbrance.'

It's such clarity that's allowed his players to think for themselves, fend for themselves and win for themselves. They bought into Ryan's method of hard work and high expectations, and that too is the essence of their success.

'Our legacy was the ability to get pleasure out of the simplest of things,' says eight-time All-Ireland winner

Juliet Murphy. 'Eamonn always made reference to working hard on the same drills over and over, and we never raised an eyebrow. We got massive satisfaction by doing so-called monotonous drills and trying to get them as near to perfect as we could, but always feeling like we never got it perfect at the same time. There was never a sense of "Oh yeah, we nailed that now." Simply put, we were a group of like-minded people who were always looking to improve themselves.

'It's a culture that's been created and Eamonn is like the queen bee. This is what ladies football in Cork looks like now. It means you work hard and be modest. It's not just luck, it's what's been formed. I imagine he moulded us unintentionally. His own way led us. We had high expectations of one another and you'd be foolish to think you'd get away with anything other than absolute commitment.'

For Bríd Stack, the secret to their level heads is in the friendships they formed early on, when graft dissolved the abrasive rivalries. 'We would be nowhere only for us all being friends. Not a prayer!

'Once the rivalry thing sorted itself out, there was never any bitching or moaning, hatred or cliques, and by being such good friends, it allowed us to stay level-headed throughout it all. We all started at the same level, not having won anything at senior level. There was [*sic*] enough of us that if someone was to derail, they'd be brought back down to earth fairly lively. But that never happened.

'We spent so much time together, and the fun and craic we have off the field just makes us try so much harder on the field. You're going out there, and you realise you're not doing it for yourself.'

Their modesty stemmed from how Eamonn Ryan and his back-room team carried themselves too.

'I'm sure all the adoration for Eamonn would make him crawl, but his contribution can't be underestimated,' adds Murphy. 'It is what it is, and I've no doubt in my mind that the team would have one, maybe two All-Irelands, but the impact he's had has ensured all the success happened, and the manner in which it was done. But the contribution of all the selectors certainly can't go unnoticed in the entire thing either. They were all so brilliant at what they did.'

Ryan believes there will be no legacy when all is said and done. New winners will come along and life will move on, but one thing that he will never forget is the loyalty every member of his back-room team showed.

'A lot of the success is attributed to them. This is going to sound clichéd, but genuinely I couldn't have asked for more supportive people over the ten years. I just couldn't. None of them ever tried to undermine me, or blame me when things went wrong, and that meant I could follow my gut quite a bit.

'When they backed me when I made stupid or dopey decisions, that was a huge help. You might have an idea and you wouldn't have total conviction about it, but they were all willing to go along and try things with you. You weren't doing it out of arrogance, you were doing it because you thought it was the right thing to do and they understood that. We all knew the other was just trying to do their best.'

There's no underestimating how much respect the players have for Ryan, and for a lot of the older players who were there since 2004, he's like a second father.

'I get emotional talking about him now,' says Murphy. 'Our lives are completely different because of him. He's changed our lives. You could say the same thing about teachers who leave a mark on students, but you'd generally have students for one or two years, but Eamonn's had us for over a decade. It's magnified, and we can never thank him enough for what he's done for us.'

Ryan, however, deserves the last say on this incredible journey.

'It's not about fame or medals, but being with like-minded people is a huge part of all of this, because when they come out on the field before training they're like Labrador puppies with each other.

'They don't moan and they don't look for excuses. They're good footballers that work very hard at their game. They will extract the best from themselves and they won't look to offload the blame. They cut you a bit of slack if you make a balls of it, and not every team does that – and that's the extraordinary thing about them.

'I'm grateful for their cooperation. I'm grateful for no recriminations when I made a mess of things, and I'm grateful for their patience when things didn't go well.

'They did their best, I did my best, and we all had a great time.'

AFTERWORD

On 17 December 2015, news bubbled out into the public sphere that Eamonn Ryan's twelve-year reign with the Cork ladies footballers was coming to an end. An article in *The Irish Examiner* alluded to discussions that had taken place with Ryan and the new Cork senior men's football coach, Peadar Healy. 'No final agreement' had been made, but it dawned on those reading the newspaper over a cup of tea that morning that the end was likely nigh. Two days later, Healy confirmed the appointment of his new selector. For the Cork ladies, it was the end of an era.

Ryan had come to a decision. It wasn't easy to walk away. He had overseen 165 games and masterminded twenty-nine titles out of a possible thirty-six, including ten senior All-Irelands and nine Division 1 NFL titles. Prior to his arrival in 2004, Cork had never won a Munster Senior Football Championship title. Now, they had ten.

Aged 74, it was time for another challenge. The players that Eamonn Ryan left behind wished him well. To them, he was a genius, and a gent. He was also a father figure, and his departure would never dilute the great memories he had given them, or Cork ladies football.

As a new year unfolded, speculation grew with every dark evening of winter as to who would replace Ryan. Among the media, the open role was referred to as a 'poisoned chalice', but for one man it was anything but.

Ephie Fitzgerald was his own man. As a player he had in fact played under Ryan for Cork in the 1983 Munster

Senior Football Championship. He had coached Bally-landers of Limerick to county success, as well as his own club, Nemo Rangers of Cork. As well as managing the Cork minor men's team, he had coached the senior men's Limerick football team, was involved with Clare too, and as of January 2016, was coaching the Waterford men's footballers.

On 18 January of that year, however, the Cork Ladies Football Board ratified Fitzgerald as their new head man. He had just a few weeks to re-adjust. Given that he's a man of his word, however, he followed through with his commitment to stick with the Déise men ahead of their Division 4 National Football League opener away to Wicklow. After that game, his involvement would cease. On that same day as Waterford faced Wicklow, the Cork ladies had their first outing in the Division 1 National Ladies Football League in Mallow, and Frank Honohan and Pat O'Leary, selectors for the ladies team, took charge in Fitzgerald's absence. In the previous weeks, as the team waited to hear of Ryan's replacement, Honohan and O'Leary had taken charge of training. And when they heard that Fitzgerald was the man, they first met him a week out from their opening league game in Whitechurch GAA Club.

On his first night, Fitzgerald stood on the sidelines and watched, but he wasn't afraid to call things as he saw them or give encouragement. He had huge admiration for all that the players before him had achieved. However, this was a new beginning too, and it would take time for everyone to adjust.

His honesty during his first meeting with the team impressed the players. Fitzgerald wanted effort and commitment. After that, everything else would fit into place – and it did. Despite losing their first three league games, Fitzgerald and Cork went on to win every other game in the National League, including their fourth successive Division 1 title. That May in Parnell Park in the league decider they denied a feisty Mayo side, with veteran Deirdre O'Reilly stepping up to lift the trophy in the absence of her concussed captain, Ciara O'Sullivan.

During the league, Cork lost the services of several stalwarts, such as Valerie Mulcahy and Geraldine O'Flynn, but Fitzgerald was unperturbed. He knew that was the life cycle awaiting him when he took the job. The greats would go, but he would help create the next generation.

Come the 2016 TG4 Championship, Kinsale's Orla Finn was Cork's newest star. She had won Player of the Match in the National League final and would do so again in the 2016 All-Ireland final against Dublin in Croke Park. It was Fitzgerald's biggest test to date, and many questioned whether the Dubs could overcome their mental block of having lost the previous two finals. With Ryan gone, it was one less cog in an incredible machine for Dublin to worry about.

Cork passed the test with flying colours, however, using their relentless knack for grinding out games, beating Dublin by a stinging, solitary point (1-7 to 1-6).

Over the course of the next twelve months, Fitzgerald lost the services of dual stars Briege Corkery and Rena

Buckley, Deirdre O'Reilly and eventually Bríd Stack and Annie Walsh. Despite that, Cork retained the 2017 Division 1 National League title, only to bow out of the All-Ireland to Mayo at the semi-final stage.

Fitzgerald was faced with a complete rebuild and to his credit he instilled a new self-belief in the 2018 squad. Players like Emma Spillane, Eimear Meaney, Melissa Duggan, Libby Coppinger, Hannah Looney and Saoirse Noonan all made a name for themselves, and through sheer determination they reached the 2018 All-Ireland final, only to face the reigning champions Dublin – who had yet to beat Cork in a championship match.

Regardless of history, Fitzgerald's Cork side were the underdogs, no question, but no one wanted to write them off. With a quarter of an hour remaining, Cork were still in the game. It was Dublin's dogged desire to beat the old enemy that proved decisive, however, and on All-Ireland final day in Croke Park, Mick Bohan's players banished the ghosts of Septembers past.

At the final whistle, Fitzgerald and his players stood shoulder to shoulder in the middle of the hallowed turf and watched Dublin captain Sinead Aherne lift the Brendan Martin Cup over her head in the Hogan Stand. It was the first time Cork had lost an All-Ireland final in Croke Park, and they vowed to themselves that they would be back.

Relentless, there and then, they decided to go again in 2019.

APPENDICES

CORK SENIOR PLAYERS UNDER EAMONN RYAN (2004–2015)

Emma Farmer, Róisín Phelan (Aghada), Blathnáid Wiseman, Karen Con O'Sullivan, Laura Power, Amanda Murphy, Claire O'Donoughue, Áine T. O'Sullivan (Beara), Anita Thompson (Ballingeary/Inchigeela), Shauna Kelly (Boherbue), Eleanor Ahern, Grace Kearney, Jennifer Barry (Bride Rovers), Áine Cott (Castlemagner), Martina O'Brien (Clonakilty), Hanora Kelleher, Louise Murphy, Emer Walsh, Sarah O'Connell, Aisling O'Connor, Linda Barrett, Rosie O'Mahony, Juliet Murphy, Aisling Barrett, Rena Buckley (Donoughmore), Elaine Scally, Eimear Scally, Maebh Cahalane (Éire Óg), Niamh O'Keeffe (Erin's Own), Aisling Hutchings (Fermoy), Nollaig Cleary (Gabriel Rangers), Áine Sheehan (Glanworth), Ciara Walsh, Mary O'Connor, Amy O'Shea, Claire Keohane, Angela Walsh, Anne-Marie Walsh, Sarah Harrington, Annie Walsh, Jessica O'Shea (Inch Rovers), Elaine O'Riordan, Mairéad Kelly, Norita Kelly, Lisa Crowley (Liscarroll), Orla Finn (Kinsale), Orlagh Farmer (Midleton), Síle O'Callaghan, Jenny Luddy, Roisín O'Sullivan, Ciara O'Sullivan, Máire O'Callaghan, Bríd O'Sullivan, Doireann O'Sullivan, Maeve O'Sullivan, Eimear Meaney, Laura Fitzgerald (Mourneabbey), Siobhán Buckley, Fiona O'Sullivan (Naomh Abán), Carmel McCarthy, Rhona Ní Bhuachalla (Naomh Fionnbarra), Deirdre O'Sullivan, Marie O'Connor, Regina Curtin, Norma Kelly, Sinéad O'Reilly (Rockchapel),

Deirdre Foley, Niamh Keohane, Cathriona Foley, Elaine Harte, Valerie Mulcahy, Laura Crowley (Rockbán), Laura MacMahon, Áine Hayes (Rosscarbery), Bríd Stack, Deirdre O'Reilly, Geraldine O'Flynn (St Mary's), Kate Leneghan (St Michael's), Jean Lucey, Fiona Crowley, Louise Cohalan, Caoimhe Creedon, Jean O'Sullivan, Marie Ambrose, Vera Foley, Mairéad Corkery, Briege Corkery, Sinéad Cotter (St Val's), Síle Johnson, Ann O'Donovan (Valley Rovers), Laura Cronin (Watergrasshill).

CORK'S RECORD UNDER EAMONN RYAN (2004–2015)

2004 (7W–6L–0D) (25G–145P)

Captain: Juliet Murphy, Donoughmore

Management Team: Mary Collins, Eamonn Ryan, Frankie Honohan, Ger Twomey, Timmy O'Callaghan, Eileen O'Brien-Collins (liaison officer)

League

Rd 1: Kerry 2–13, Cork 2–6, Cahersiveen

Rd 2: Cork 3–9, Monaghan 0–7, Mountmellick

Rd 3: Mayo 2–13, Cork 1–8, Ballyline

Rd 4: Cork 5–24, Longford 1–5, Donoughmore

Rd 5: Galway 0–10, Cork 0–8, Donoughmore

QF: Cork 3–13, Meath 0–13, Portarlington

SF: Cork 0–8, Galway 0–6, Corofin

Final: Mayo 1–13, Cork 1–11, Pearse Stadium (POM: Cora Staunton, Mayo)

Championship

Munster Rd 1: Kerry 3–11, Cork 1–11, JP O'Sullivan Park, Killorglin

Munster Rd 2: Cork 3–16, Clare 1–6, Doonbeg

Munster SF: Cork 1–11, Waterford 0–10, Dungarvan

Munster final: Cork 4–13, Kerry 1–9, Páirc Uí Rinn (POM: Geraldine O'Flynn, Cork)

All-Ireland QF: Mayo 1–11, Cork 1–7, Tullamore

2005 (14W–1L–0D) (37G–211P)

Captain: Juliet Murphy, Donoughmore

Management Team: Mary Collins, Eamonn Ryan, Frankie Honohan, Ger Twomey, Jim McEvoy, Eileen O'Brien-Collins (liaison officer)

League

Rd 1: Cork 5–9, Kerry 2–5, Dromtarriffe

Rd 2: Cork 3–14, Kildare 1–3, Glanworth

Rd 3: Cork 2–18, Monaghan 2–3, Mountmellick

Rd 4: Galway 0–11, Cork 0–7, Donoughmore

Rd 5: Cork 2–10, Mayo 2–9, Rosnevin

Rd 6: Cork 5–13, Roscommon 0–7, Nenagh

SF: Cork 6–11, Waterford 2–6, Dungarvan

Final: Cork 2–13, Galway 0–6, Gaelic Grounds (POM: Valerie Mulcahy, Cork)

Championship

Munster Rd 1: Cork 2–14, Kerry 2–7, Killorglin

Munster Rd 2: Cork 5–28, Clare 1–2, Donoughmore

Munster Rd 3: Cork 0–16, Waterford 1–8, Páirc Uí Rinn

Munster final: Cork 2–15, Kerry 1–8, Killarney (POM: Juliet Murphy, Cork)

All-Ireland QF: Cork 2–19, Meath 3–10, Portlaoise (POM: Briege Corkery, Cork)

All-Ireland SF: Cork 0–13, Mayo 1–9, Portlaoise (POM: Claire Egan, Mayo)

All-Ireland final: Cork 1–11, Galway 0–8, Croke Park (POM: Valerie Mulcahy, Cork)

2006 (14W–0L–0D) (19G–184P)

Captain: Juliet Murphy, Donoughmore

Management Team: Mary Collins, Eamonn Ryan, Frankie Honohan, Ger Twomey, Jim McEvoy, Eileen O'Brien-Collins (liaison officer)

League

Rd 1: Cork 0–10, Galway 0–9, Tuam Stadium

Rd 2: Cork 0–21, Roscommon 0–4, Templederry

Rd 3: Cork 2–12, Meath 1–10, Mountmellick

Rd 4: Cork 0–12, Monaghan 0–7, Abbeyleix

Rd 5: Cork 4–14, Donegal 2–11, Keenagh

QF: Cork 2–12, Armagh 0–10, Ratheniska

SF: Cork 2–14, Galway 2–9, Galway

Final: Cork 0–14, Meath 0–12, Parnell Park (POM: Gráinne Nulty, Meath)

Championship

Munster Rd 1: Cork 3–15, Waterford 1–11, Dungarvan

Munster Rd 2: Cork 1–12, Kerry 0–7, Donoughmore

Munster final: Cork 1–17, Waterford 1–6, Gaelic Grounds

All-Ireland QF: Cork 2–12, Mayo 1–11, Portlaoise

All-Ireland SF: Cork 1–12, Laois 0–8, Tullamore

All-Ireland final: Cork 1–7, Armagh 1–6, Croke Park (POM: Nollaig Cleary, Cork)

2007 (14W–1L–0D) (36G–198P)

Captain: Juliet Murphy, Donoughmore

Management Team: Mary Collins, Eamonn Ryan, Frankie

Honohan, Ger Twomey, Jim McEvoy, Eileen O'Brien-Collins (liaison officer)

League
Rd 1: Cork 0–14, Galway 3–4, Tuam
Rd 2: Cork 3–12, Meath 1–5, Mountmellick
Rd 3: Cork 3–22, Donegal 1–6, Cong
Rd 4: Cork 0–14, Monaghan 0–2, Ferbane
Rd 5: Cork 3–7, Kildare 0–8, Clonoulty
QF: Cork 2–11, Armagh 0–8, Ratheniska
SF: Mayo 4–12, Cork 2–12, Banagher

Championship
Munster SF: Cork 3–12, Kerry 1–13, Beaufort
Munster final: Cork 3–7, Waterford 1–6, Fitzgerald Park
All-Ireland qualifier, Rd 1: Cork 2–13, Galway 1–11, Gaelic Grounds
All-Ireland Rd 2: Cork 4–11, Monaghan 0–11, Crettyard
All-Ireland Rd 3: Cork 2–21, Roscommon 0–2, Claughaun
All-Ireland QF: Cork 3–17, Dublin 1–4, Wexford Park
All-Ireland SF: Cork 4–14, Laois 0–6, Portlaoise
All-Ireland final: Cork 2–11, Mayo 2–6 (POM: Bríd Stack, Cork)

2008 (10W–1L–0D) (34G–141P)
Captain: Angela Walsh, Inch Rovers
Management Team: Eamonn Ryan, Frankie Honohan, Jim McEvoy, Justin McCarthy, Noel O'Connor

League

Rd 1: Cork 3–9, Kildare 1–6, Narraghmore

Rd 2: Cork 1–10, Galway 1–6, Mallow

Rd 3: Cork 4–8, Meath 0–3, Mallow

Rd 4: Dublin 2–11, Cork 2–8, Mallow

Rd 5: Cork 3–16, Monaghan 0–6, Aughnamullen

SF: Cork 4–12, Armagh 0–5, Crettyard

Final: Cork 6–13, Kerry 2–10, Ennis (POM: Amy O'Shea, Cork)

Championship

Munster final: Cork 1–23, Kerry 2–7, Páirc Uí Rinn

All-Ireland QF: Cork 2–11, Galway 1–7, Dr Hyde Park

All-Ireland SF: Cork 4–18, Tyrone 0–11, Tullamore (POM: Nollaig Cleary, Cork)

All-Ireland final: Cork 4–13, Monaghan 0–11, Croke Park (POM: Valerie Mulcahy, Cork)

2009 (10W–2L–0D) (30G–163P)

Captain: Mary O'Connor, Inch Rovers

Management Team: Eamonn Ryan, Frankie Honohan, Justin McCarthy, Noel O'Connor

League

Rd 1: Cork 2–12, Kildare 0–4, CIT

Rd 2: Cork 3–16, Galway 2–3, Cregg

Rd 3: Cork 3–11, Clare 1–5, Cooraclare

Rd 4: Dublin 1–10, Cork 1–9, Naomh Mearnóg

Rd 5: Monaghan 2–8, Cork 0–13, CIT

QF: Cork 2–14, Kerry 1–7, Killarney

SF: Cork 4–11, Dublin 0–8, Semple Stadium (POM: Deirdre O'Reilly, Cork)

Final: Cork 1–20, Mayo 0–11, Kiltoom, Roscommon (POM: Emma Mullins, Mayo)

Championship

Munster final: Cork 6–15, Kerry 0–9, Bruff (POM: Norita Kelly, Cork)

All-Ireland QF: Cork 4–23, Kildare 0–6, Nenagh (POM: Juliet Murphy, Cork)

All-Ireland SF: Cork 3–10, Mayo 1–9, Nenagh (POM: Briege Corkery, Cork)

All-Ireland final: Cork 1–9, Dublin 0–11, Croke Park (POM: Mary Nevin, Dublin)

2010 (8W–2L–1D) (26G–144P)

Captain: Rena Buckley, Donoughmore

Management Team: Eamonn Ryan, Frankie Honohan, Justin McCarthy, Noel O'Connor

League

Rd 1: Dublin 1–12, Cork 3–3, Fermoy

Rd 2: Cork 1–16, Kerry 1–9, CIT

Rd 3: Cork 4–7, Galway 2–13, Buttevant

Rd 4: Cork 3–13, Tyrone 0–4, Augher

Rd 5: Cork 4–18, Laois 1–11, CIT

Rd 6: Cork 1–22, Mayo 0–6, Ballinrobe

SF: Cork 1–21, Monaghan 0–11, Banagher (POM: Mary

O'Connor, Cork)

Final: Cork 2–10, Galway 1–9, Parnell Park (POM: Cathriona Cormican, Galway)

Championship

Munster SF: Cork 2–8, Kerry 1–6, CIT

Munster final: Cork 5–13, Clare 2–9, Castletownroche (POM: Valerie Mulcahy, Cork)

All-Ireland QF: Tyrone 3–11, Cork 0–13, Banagher (POM: Maura Kelly, Tyrone)

2011 (13W–1L–0D) (47G–178P)

Captain: Amy O'Shea, Inch Rovers

Management Team: Eamonn Ryan, Frankie Honohan, Justin McCarthy, Noel O'Connor, Bridget O'Brien (liaison officer)

League

Rd 1: Cork 4–11, Kildare 0–15, Ballykelly

Rd 2: Monaghan 1–13, Cork 2–7, Emyvale

Rd 3: Cork 2–17, Mayo 2–7, Mallow

Rd 4: Cork 5–17, Donegal 0–7, CIT

Rd 5: Cork 3–7, Laois 0–12, Portlaoise

Rd 6: Cork 4–12, Galway 0–9, Mountbellew

Rd 7: Cork 3–11, Tyrone 1–9, CIT

SF: Cork 7–16, Donegal 1–10, Tuam

Final: Cork 4–15 Laois 3–9, Parnell Park (POM: Amy O'Shea, Cork)

Championship

Munster SF: Cork 3–19, Clare 1–2, Clarecastle

Munster final: Cork 2–15, Kerry 0–11, Dr Crokes (POM: Bríd Stack, Cork)

All-Ireland QF: Cork 2–14, Dublin 3–10, Birr

All-Ireland SF: Cork 4–10, Laois 1–6, Cashel (POM: Juliet Murphy, Cork)

All-Ireland final: Cork 2–7, Monaghan 0–11, Croke Park (POM: Angela Walsh, Cork)

2012 (13W–1L–0D) (34G–189P)

Captain: Rena Buckley, Donoughmore

Management Team: Eamonn Ryan, Frankie Honohan, Justin McCarthy, James O'Callaghan, Bridget O'Brien (liaison officer)

League

Rd 1: Cork 4–9, Donegal 1–7, Ballyshannon

Rd 2: Cork 3–11, Monaghan 1–13, Páirc Uí Rinn

Rd 3: Cork 1–8, Dublin 0–8, Ballyboden St Enda's

Rd 4: Cork 3–8, Meath 2–8, Ashbourne

Rd 5: Cork 2–15, Laois 2–6, Fermoy

Rd 6: Cork 0–22, Kildare 0–3, Rathcormac

Rd 7: Cork 2–10, Tyrone 0–11, Killyclogher

SF: Cork 3–10, Meath 0–10, Crettyard

Final: Monaghan 1–13, Cork 2–7, Parnell Park (POM: Linda Martin, Monaghan)

Championship

Munster SF: Cork 1–19, Clare 0–11, Doneraile

Munster final: Cork 3–12, Kerry 2–9, Páirc Uí Rinn (POM: Annie Walsh, Cork)

All-Ireland QF: Cork 8–27, Donegal 0–2, Dr Hyde Park (POM: Nollaig Cleary, Cork)

All-Ireland SF: Cork 2–15, Monaghan 0–12, Birr (POM: Briege Corkery, Cork)

All-Ireland final: Cork 0–16, Kerry 0–7, Croke Park (POM: Geraldine O'Flynn, Cork)

2013 (12W–4L–0D) (33G–222P)

Captain: Anne-Marie Walsh, Inch Rovers

Management Team: Eamonn Ryan, Frankie Honohan, Justin McCarthy, James O'Callaghan, Bridget O'Brien (liaison officer)

League

Rd 1: Monaghan 1–12, Cork 0–11, Inniskeen

Rd 2: Cork 3–15, Meath 4–4, Mourneabbey

Rd 3: Cork 3–15, Tyrone 0–13, Killeagh

Rd 4: Cork 6–13, Dublin 2–8, Fermoy

Rd 5: Cork 2–10, Mayo 1–11, Claremorris

Rd 6: Laois 1–9, Cork 0–11, Stradbally

Rd 7: Cork 7–23, Donegal 0–3, CIT

SF: Cork 4–12, Laois 2–8, Tipperary Town

Final: Cork 0–14, Mayo 0–7, Parnell Park (POM: Yvonne Byrne, Mayo)

Championship

Rd 1: Kerry 3–10, Cork 3–8, Cahersiveen

Rd 2: Cork 0–21, Clare 0–8, Shannon

Munster final: Kerry 1–16, Cork 1–15, Castletownroche, (POM: Louise Galvin, Kerry)

All-Ireland qualifier, Rd 2: Cork 0–16, Armagh 2–9, Birr (POM: Geraldine O'Flynn, Cork)

All-Ireland QF: Cork 1–19, Dublin 2–12, Birr (POM: Juliet Murphy, Cork)

All-Ireland SF: Cork 2–9, Kerry 0–11, Semple Stadium (POM: Valerie Mulcahy, Cork)

All-Ireland final: Cork 1–10, Monaghan 1–9, Croke Park (POM: Bríd Stack, Cork)

2014 (12W–2L–1D) (42G–207P)

Captain: Briege Corkery, St Val's

Management Team: Eamonn Ryan, Frankie Honohan, Shane Ronayne, Pat O'Leary, Bridget O'Brien (liaison officer)

League

Rd 1: Cork 1–10, Mayo 1–8, Mallow

Rd 2: Cork 3–13, Donegal 2–10, Castlefin

Rd 3: Monaghan 2–13, Cork 0–14, Mallow

Rd 4: Kerry 1–8, Cork 1–7, Dingle

Rd 5: Cork 2–10, Dublin 2–10, Parnell Park

Rd 6: Cork 3–19, Laois 0–4, CIT

Rd 7: Cork 4–20, Tyrone 2–8, Tattyreagh

SF: Cork 3–13, Kerry 3–8, Dromcollogher/Broadford

Final: Cork 1–9, Dublin 2–4, Parnell Park (POM: Valerie Mulcahy, Cork)

Championship

Munster Rd 1: Cork 7–23, Clare 1–5, Mourneabbey

Munster Rd 2: Cork 3–11, Kerry 2–10, Páirc Uí Rinn

Munster final: Cork 6–14, Kerry 2–11, Rathmore (POM: Ciara O'Sullivan, Cork)

All-Ireland QF: Cork 1–15, Mayo 0–9, Tullamore (POM: Rena Buckley, Cork)

All-Ireland SF: Cork 5–16, Armagh 2–11, Pearse Park, Longford (POM: Ciara O'Sullivan, Cork)

All-Ireland final: Cork 2–13, Dublin 2–12, Croke Park (POM: Valerie Mulcahy, Cork)

2015 (11W–3L–1D) (33G–186P)

Captain: Ciara O'Sullivan, Mourneabbey

Management Team: Eamonn Ryan, Frankie Honohan, Shane Ronayne, Pat O'Leary, Bridget O'Brien (liaison officer)

League

Rd 1: Cork 2–13, Mayo 1–8, Swinford

Rd 2: Cork 1–13, Kerry 1–12, Cloughduv

Rd 3: Monaghan 2–11, Cork 2–10, Blackhill

Rd 4: Cork 1–14, Galway 3–7, Mourneabbey

Rd 5: Cork 3–12, Tyrone 0–7, Fermoy

Rd 6: Cork 5–18, Laois 1–4, Mountmellick

Rd 7: Dublin 5–13, Cork 2–7, CIT

SF: Cork 0–13, Kerry 0–10, Dromcollogher/Broadford

Final: Cork 3–8, Galway 1–14, Parnell Park (POM: Tracey Leonard, Galway)

Replay: Cork 0–14, Galway 1–10, Portlaoise (POM: Bríd Stack, Cork)

Championship

Munster final: Kerry 2–13, Cork 2–4, Mallow (POM: Louise Ní Mhuircheartaigh, Kerry)

All-Ireland qualifier: Cork 7–22, Meath 0–3, Semple Stadium (POM: Áine T. O'Sullivan, Cork)

All-Ireland QF: Cork 1–12, Galway 1–10, Gaelic Grounds (POM: Briege Corkery, Cork)

All-Ireland SF: Cork 4–14, Kerry 0–13 (POM: Valerie Mulcahy, Cork)

All-Ireland final: Cork 0–12, Dublin 0–10 (POM: Briege Corkery, Cork)

CORK'S RECORD UNDER EPHIE FITZGERALD (2016–2018)

2016 (10W–5L–0D) (32G–190P)

Captain: Ciara O'Sullivan, Mourneabbey

Management team: Ephie Fitzgerald, Pat O'Leary, Frank Honohan, James Masters, Con O'Sullivan, Bridget O'Brien (liaison officer)

League

Rd 1: Mayo 2–8, Cork 0–7, Mallow

Rd 2: Kerry 0–12, Cork 2–5, Brosna

Rd 3: Cork 2–21, Tyrone 1–3, Mallow

Rd 4: Dublin 3–10, Cork 1–13, Parnell Park

Rd 5: Cork 5–17, Monaghan 1–3, Mourneabbey

Rd 6: Cork 6–16, Galway 1–11, Tuam Stadium

Rd 7: Armagh 4–12, Cork 2–16, Abbotstown

SF: Cork 1–15, Dublin 0–11, Birr

Final: Cork 1–10, Mayo 0–10, Parnell Park (POM: Orla Finn, Cork)

Championship

Munster Rd 1: Cork 1–10, Waterford 0–7, Fermoy

Munster Rd 2: Kerry 2–14, Cork 2–9, Macroom

Munster final: Cork 3–17, Kerry 1–3, Killarney (POM: Orla Finn, Cork)

All–Ireland QF: Cork 3–17, Cavan 1–3, Birr

All–Ireland SF: Cork 2–10, Monaghan, 1–10, Gaelic Grounds

All–Ireland final: Cork 1–7, Dublin 1–6, Croke Park
  (POM: Rena Buckley, Cork)

2017 (9W–5L–0D) (25G–189P)
Captain: Ciara O'Sullivan, Mourneabbey
Management team: Ephie Fitzgerald, Pat O'Leary, Frank
  Honohan, James Masters, Con O'Sullivan, Bridget
  O'Brien (liaison officer)

League
Rd 1: Cork 5–17, Kerry 1–11, Mallow
Rd 2: Cork 2–11, Dublin 1–8, Mallow
Rd 3: Armagh 0–12, Cork 0–9, Clonmore
Rd 4: Cork 3–9, Mayo 1–8, Swinford
Rd 5: Cork 2–14, Monaghan 1–12, Clones
Rd 6: Cork 1–11, Galway 2–5, Mallow
Rd 7: Donegal 3–16, Cork 0–12, Mallow
SF: Cork 1–16, Dublin 0–13, Nowlan Park
Final: Cork 2–15, Donegal 2–14, Parnell Park (POM: Orla
  Finn, Cork)

Championship
Munster Rd 1: Waterford 3–11, Cork 1–11, Dungarvan
Munster Rd 2: Kerry 2–15, Cork 2–13, Fitzgerald Stadium
All–Ireland qualifier: Cork 0–14, Monaghan 1–10,
  Tullamore
All–Ireland QF: Cork 6–19, Galway, 1–10, Cusack Park
All–Ireland SF: Mayo 3–11, Cork 0–18, Kingspan Breffni
  (POM: Cora Staunton, Mayo)

2018 (11W–4L–0D) (44–189)
Captain: Ciara O'Sullivan, Mourneabbey
Management team: Ephie Fitzgerald, James Masters, Diarmuid Vaughan, Con O'Sullivan and Jo Shirkie

League
Rd 1: Cork 2–17, Kerry 0–9, Knocknagoshel
Rd 2: Cork 2–13, Westmeath 1–6, Mallow
Rd 3: Dublin 3–9, Cork 1–14, Croke Park
Rd 4: Cork 4–14, Monaghan 1–7, Mallow
Rd 5: Donegal 4–11, Cork 2–3, Letterkenny
Rd 6: Cork 1–12, Mayo 2–8, Mallow
Rd 7: Cork 3–12, Galway 1–11, Clonberne
SF: Mayo 1–20, Cork 3–12, Birr

Championship
Munster SF: Cork 2–12, Tipperary 1–10, Ardfinnan
Munster final: Cork 5–13, Kerry 2–10, CIT
All-Ireland qualifier, Rd 2: Cork 7–7, Monaghan 1–9, Birr
All-Ireland, Rd 3: Cork 1–19, Armagh 1–7, Ballinasloe
All-Ireland QF: Cork 8–18, Westmeath 1–6, Gaelic Grounds
All-Ireland SF: Cork 2–11, Donegal 0–11, Dr Hyde Park
All-Ireland final: Dublin 3–11, Cork 1–12, Croke Park
   (POM: Carla Rowe, Dublin)

CORK'S ALL-IRELAND FINAL LINE-OUTS (2005–2018)

2005

Cork 1–11, Galway 0–8, Croke Park

Scorers for Cork: V. Mulcahy 1–5 (1–0 pen, 0–3 f), N. Cleary 0–3, D. O'Reilly 0–2, B. Corkery 0–1.

Scorers for Galway: N. Fahy 0–3, P. Ní Fhlatharta, N. Duggan 0–2 (f) each.

CORK: E. Harte; B. Stack, A. Walsh, R. Buckley; B. Corkery, C. Walsh, S. O'Reilly; J. Murphy, N. Kelly; A. Murphy, R. Curtain, N. Cleary; V. Mulcahy, C. Creedon, G. O'Flynn.

Subs: M. O'Connor for G. O'Flynn, D. O'Reilly for C. Creedon, A. O'Connor for R. Curtin, N. Keohane for A. Murphy.

GALWAY: U. Carroll; M. Glynn, R. Stephens, A. McDonough; M. O'Connell, A. Daly, E. Flaherty; A. Clarke, E. Concannon; G. Conneely, N. Duggan, P. Ní Fhlatharta; R. McPhilbin, N. Fahy, L. Joyce.

Subs: C. Molloy for A. McDonough, L. Cohill for R. McPhilbin, P. Gleeson (0–1) for L. Joyce.

Referee: T. Clarke (Dublin).

Player of the Match: Valerie Mulcahy (Cork).

2006

Cork 1–7, Armagh 1–6, Croke Park

Scorers for Cork: N. Cleary 1–2, G. O'Flynn, A. Murphy, M. O'Connor, C. Creedon, J. Murphy 0–1.

Scorers for Armagh: M. Tennyson 1–1, C. O'Hanlon and M. McAlingden 0–2 each, A. Matthews 0–1.

CORK: E. Harte; B. Corkery, A. Walsh, R. Buckley; G. O'Flynn, B. Stack, S. O'Reilly; J. Murphy, N. Kelly; N. Cleary, D. O'Reilly, A. Murphy; V. Mulcahy, M. O'Connor, C. Creedon.

Subs: M. Kelly for V. Mulcahy (43), C. Walsh for A. Murphy (48), A. Murphy for C. Creedon (51).

ARMAGH: F. McAtamney; C. Marley, F. Quinn, A. Murphy; R. O'Mahony, B. O'Donnell, S. McCleary; A. O'Donnell, C. O'Hanlon; M. Tennyson, S. Duncan, S. O'Hagan; M. O'Donnell, M. McAlinden, A. Matthews.

Subs: P. McEvoy for A. Matthews (38), O. Murtagh for A. Murphy (45), D. Toal for M. O'Donnell, M. Moriarty for S. Duncan (54).

Referee: D. Corcoran (Mayo).

Player of the Match: Nollaig Cleary (Cork).

2007

Cork 2–11, Mayo 2–6, Croke Park

Scorers for Cork: V. Mulcahy 2–1, A. Murphy, G. O'Flynn, 0–3 each, N. Cleary 0–2, D. O'Reilly, J. Murphy 0–1 each.

Scorers for Mayo: C. Staunton 1–2, F. McHale 1–0, D. O'Hora 0–2, C. McGing, L. Cafferkey 0–1 each.

CORK: E. Harte; C. Walsh, A. Walsh, R. Buckley; L. Barrett, B. Stack, B. Corkery; J. Murphy, N. Kelly; G. O'Flynn, L. MacMahon, N. Cleary; V. Mulcahy, A. Murphy, D. O'Reilly.

Subs: C. Foley for C. Walsh, S. O'Reilly for L. Barrett, R. Buckley for N. Kelly, M. Kelly for L. McMahon and A. O'Shea for N. Cleary.

MAYO: Y. Byrne; S. McGing, H. Lohan, N. O'Shea; M. Heffernan, M. Carter, C. McGing; C. Egan, C. O'Hara; F. McHale, C. Staunton, C. McDermott; A. Herbert, C. Heffernan, D. O'Hora.

Subs: M. Kelly for N. O'Shea, L. Cafferkey for A. Herbert, J. Moran for C. McDermott.

Referee: E. O'Hare (Down).

Player of the Match: Bríd Stack (Cork).

2008
Cork 4–13, Monaghan 0–11, Croke Park

Scorers for Cork: V. Mulcahy 3–2 (2–0 pen, 0–1 f), C. O'Sullivan 1–0, J. Murphy 0–3 (f), N. Cleary, M. O'Connor, R. Buckley 0–2 each, A. Murphy, A. O'Shea 0–1 each.

Scorers for Monaghan: E. Byrne 0–3, C. McConnell 0–3 (0–1 f), T. McNally 0–2, N. Kindlon 0–1 (f), I. Kierans, C. McAnespie 0–1 each.

CORK: E. Harte; C. Walsh, A. Walsh, L. Barrett; B. Corkery, B. Stack, G. O'Flynn; J. Murphy, N. Kelly; N. Cleary, M. O'Connor, A. Murphy; V. Mulcahy, A. O'Shea, D. O'Reilly.

Subs: R. Buckley for C. Walsh (29), C. O'Sullivan for D. O'Reilly (41), R. Ní Bhuachalla for A. Murphy (48), R. O'Sullivan for A. O'Shea (54), S. O'Reilly for N. Cleary (55).

MONAGHAN: L. Martin; G. McNally, S. Courtney, C. Reilly; A. McAnespie, A. Lennon, F. Courtney; A. Casey, I. Kierans; C. McConnell, N. Kindlon, T. McNally; C. McAnespie, E. Byrne, N. Fahy.

Subs: L. Connolly for A. Lennon (44), C. Courtney for C. McConnell (48), E. McCarron for N. Fahy (51), U. McNally for C. Reilly (54).

Referee: K. Tighe (Dublin).

Player of the Match: Valerie Mulcahy (Cork).

2009

Cork 1–9, Dublin 0–11, Croke Park

Scorers for Cork: V. Mulcahy 0–5 (0–3 f), N. Cleary 1–1, J. Murphy 0–2 (f), M. Kelly 0–1.

Scorers for Dublin: S. Aherne 0–3 (0–1 f), M. Nevin, A. McGuinness 0–2 each, S. McGrath, E. Kelly, L. Davey, L. Peat 0–1 each.

CORK: E. Harte; R. Buckley, A. Walsh, G. O'Flynn; C. O'Sullivan, B. Stack, B. Corkery; J. Murphy, N. Kelly; N. Cleary, D. O'Reilly, A. O'Shea; M. O'Connor, V. Mulcahy, R. Ní Bhuachalla.

Subs: L. McMahon for A. O'Shea (39 inj), L. Barrett for R. Ní Bhuachalla (42), M. Kelly for M. O'Connor (50).

DUBLIN: C. O'Connor; A. Cluxton, N. Comyn, M. Kavanagh; C. Barrett, S. Furlong, S. McGrath; D. Masterson, N. McEvoy; M. Nevin, A. McGuinness, E. Kelly; L. Davey, S. Aherne, L. Peat.

Subs: L. Kidd for A. Cluxton (26), N. Hurley for E. Kelly (39), E. Travers for C. Barrett (54), K. Flood for N.

McEvoy (56), R. Byrne for M. Nevin (57).

Referee: D. Corcoran (Mayo).

Player of the Match: Mary Nevin (Dublin).

2011

Cork 2–7, Monaghan 0–11, Croke Park

Scorers for Cork: N. Cleary, R. Ní Bhuachalla (pen) 1–0 each, J. Murphy 0–3 (0–2 f), G. O'Flynn, R. Buckley, G. Kearney, V. Mulcahy 0–1 each.

Scorers for Monaghan: C. McConnell, N. Kindlon 0–3 each (0–2 f each), E. McCarron 0–2, C. McAnespie, C. Mohan, L. McEnaney 0–1 each.

CORK: E. Harte; A. M. Walsh, A. Walsh, D. O'Reilly; B. Corkery, B. Stack, G. O'Flynn; J. Murphy, R. Buckley; N. Cleary, M. Kelly, G. Kearney; V. Mulcahy, R. Ní Bhuachalla, A. O'Shea.

Subs: C. O'Sullivan for A. O'Shea (38 inj), O. Finn for V. Mulcahy (39), N. Kelly for N. Cleary (46), A. Sheehan for R. Ní Bhuachalla (53), Annie Walsh for R. Buckley (55).

MONAGHAN: L. Martin; G. McNally, S. Courtney, C. Reilly; A. McAnespie, N. Fahy, L. Connolly; A. Casey, C. Courtney; T. McNally, E. McCarron, C. McConnell; C. McAnespie, N. Kindlon, C. Mohan.

Subs: I. Kierans for C. Courtney (25), L. McEnaney for N. Kindlon (42), C. Courtney for E. McCarron (42), E. McElroy for I. Kierans (50).

Referee: J. Niland (Sligo).

Player of the Match: Angela Walsh (Cork).

2012

Cork 0–16, Kerry 0–7, Croke Park

Scorers for Cork: V. Mulcahy 0–7 (0–6 f), D. O'Sullivan 0–4, G. O'Flynn 0–2, B. Corkery, O. Farmer, N. Cleary 0–1 each.

Scorers for Kerry: S. Houlihan 0–3 (0–2 f), L. Scanlon 0–2, L. Ní Mhuircheartaigh 0–1 (f), P. Dennehy 0–1.

CORK: E. Harte; A. M. Walsh, B. Stack, D. O'Reilly; B. Corkery, R. Buckley, G. O'Flynn; J. Murphy, N. Kelly; O. Farmer, D. O'Sullivan, C. O'Sullivan; N. Cleary, V. Mulcahy, R. Ní Bhuachalla.

Subs: Angela Walsh for A. M. Walsh (38), O. Finn for R. Ní Bhuachalla (38), L. McMahon for O. Farmer (46), A. Hutchings for N. Kelly (53), Annie Walsh for C. O'Sullivan (57).

KERRY: E. Murphy; C. Lynch, A. Leonard, A. Lyons; J. Brosnan, A. Desmond, C. Kelly; L. Scanlon, B. Breen; S. Houlihan, E. Sherwood, L. Galvin; M. O'Connell, D. Corridan, L. Ní Mhuircheartaigh.

Subs: P. Dennehy for D. Corridan, S. J. Joy for E. Sherwood, M. Fitzgerald for L. Galvin, D. Corridan for M. O'Connell.

Referee: G. Corrigan (Down).

Player of the Match: Geraldine O'Flynn (Cork).

2013

Cork 1–10, Monaghan 1–9, Croke Park

Scorers for Cork: V. Mulcahy 1–4 (0–4 f), J. Murphy, N. Cleary 0–2 each, G. O'Flynn, Annie Walsh 0–1 each.

Scorers for Monaghan: C. McConnell 0–4 (f), L. Martin 1–0 (pen), C. Mohan 0–2, L. McEnaney, T. McNally, C. McAnespie 0–1 each.

CORK: E. Harte; A. M. Walsh, Angela Walsh, B. Stack; B. Corkery, R. Buckley, G. O'Flynn; D. O'Reilly, J. Murphy; N. Cleary, Annie Walsh, D. O'Sullivan; C. O'Sullivan, V. Mulcahy, R. Ní Bhuachalla.

Subs: O. Farmer for R. Ní Bhuachalla (h-t), O. Finn for Annie Walsh (49), R. Ní Bhuachalla for O. Farmer (52), A. Barrett for A. M. Walsh (60).

MONAGHAN: L. Martin; G. McNally, S. Courtney, C. Reilly; L. McEnaney, E. McCarron, A. McAnespie; A. Casey, Y. Connell; T. McNally, C. Mohan, C. Courtney; C. McConnell, E. McKenna, C. McAnespie.

Subs: E. McElroy for A. McAnespie (h-t), N. Kindlon for C. Mohan (56).

Referee: J. Niland (Sligo).

Player of the Match: Bríd Stack (Cork).

2014

Cork 2–13, Dublin 2–12, Croke Park

Scorers for Cork: V. Mulcahy 0–6 (0–1 f), R. Ní Bhuachalla 1–1, G. O'Flynn 0–3, E. Scally 1–0, O. Finn 0–2, C. O'Sullivan 0–1.

Scorers for Dublin: L. Peat 2–0, S. Aherne 0–4 (0–1 f), L. Davey, N. Healy, C. Rowe 0–2 each, S. Woods, S. Goldrick 0–1 each.

CORK: M. O'Brien; R. Phelan, Angela Walsh, B. Stack; V. Foley, D. O'Reilly, G. O'Flynn; R. Buckley, B. Corkery;

Annie Walsh, O. Farmer, C. O'Sullivan; G. Kearney, V. Mulcahy, O. Finn.

Subs: N. Cleary for Annie Walsh (h-t), R. Ní Bhuachalla for G. Kearney (42), D. O'Sullivan for O. Farmer (44), E. Scally for O. Finn (50).

DUBLIN: C. O'Connor; S. Furlong, R. Ruddy, L. Caffrey; S. Finnegan, S. Goldrick, S. McGrath; D. Masterson, M. Lamb; N. Healy, L. Davey, C. Rowe; L. Peat, N. Hyland, S. Aherne.

Subs: S. Woods for N. Hyland (44), S. McCaffrey for M. Lamb (53), L. Collins for S. Furlong (54), N. McEvoy for N. Healy (57).

Referee: M. Farrelly (Cavan).

Player of the Match: Valerie Mulcahy (Cork).

2015

Cork 0–12, Dublin 0–10, Croke Park

Scorers for Cork: V. Mulcahy 0–7 (0–6 f), D. O'Sullivan 0–2, R. Buckley, C. O'Sullivan and E. Scally 0–1 each.

Scorers for Dublin: C. Rowe 0–6 (0–5 f), N. McEvoy, L. Davey, A. Connolly and S. McCaffrey 0–1 each.

CORK: M. O'Brien; M. Ambrose, B. Stack, A. Barrett; V. Foley, D. O'Reilly, G. O'Flynn; R. Buckley, B. Corkery; C. O'Sullivan, A. Hutchings, Annie Walsh; V. Mulcahy, Á. O'Sullivan, D. O'Sullivan.

Subs: R. Phelan for G. O'Flynn (15), E. Scally for Á. O'Sullivan (39), O. Finn for A. Hutchings (42), R. Ní Bhuachalla for Annie Walsh (49).

DUBLIN: C. Trant; O. Carey, M. Uí Scanaill, F. Hudson;

S. Furlong, S. Finnegan, C. Barrett; M. Lamb, S. Goldrick; N. Healy, A. Connolly, C. Rowe; N. McEvoy, L. Davey, H. Noonan.

Subs: K. Flood for H. Noonan (h-t), N. Owens for C. Barrett (39), N. Collins for F. Hudson (47), S. McCaffrey for A. Connolly (51), N. Rickard for S. Goldrick (56).

Referee: J. Niland (Sligo).

Player of the Match: Briege Corkery (Cork).

2016

Cork 1–7, Dublin 1–6, Croke Park

Scorers for Cork: R. Ní Bhuachalla 1–0, O. Finn 0–3 (0–2 f), D. Sullivan 0–3 (0–1 f), O. Farmer 0–1.

Scorers for Dublin: S. Aherne 1–3 (1–0 pen, 0–1 f), N. Healy, L. Davey, N. McEvoy (0–1 each).

CORK: M. O'Brien; R. Phelan, B. Stack, M. Ambrose; S. Kelly, D. O'Reilly, V. Foley; A. Walsh, B. Corkery; R. Buckley, A. O'Sullivan, O. Farmer; C. O'Sullivan, D. O'Sullivan, O. Finn.

Subs: R. Ní Bhuachalla for A. O'Sullivan (h-t), E. Scally for A. Walsh (44).

DUBLIN: C. Trant; O. Carey, D. Murphy, L. Caffrey; S. Goldrick, S. Finnegan, N. Collins; L. Magee, M. Lamb; N. Healy, N. Owens, C. Rowe; N. McEvoy, S. Aherne, L. Davey.

Subs: S. Woods for N. Owens, M. Ní Scanaill for L. Caffrey (both 44), S. Furlong for M. Lamb (50), L. Collins for D. Murphy (53).

Referee: B. Rice (Down).

Player of the Match: Rena Buckley (Cork).

2018
Dublin 3–11, Cork 1–12, Croke Park

Scorers for Dublin: S. Aherne 1–7 (1–0 pen, 0–4 f), C. Rowe 2–0, N. Owens 0–2, N. McEvoy, S. Goldrick 0–1 each.

Scorers for Cork: O. Finn 0–8 (f), A. O'Sullivan 1–2, C. O'Sullivan 0–1, D. O'Sullivan 0–1 (f).

DUBLIN: C. Trant; N. Collins, L. Caffrey, M. Byrne; S. Goldrick, L. Magee, S. Finnegan; O. Carey, N. McEvoy; L. Davey, S. McGrath, C. Rowe; S. Aherne, N. Healy, N. Owens.

Subs: J. Dunne for N. Owens (52), H. O'Neill for N. McEvoy (53), A. Connolly for N. Healy (59).

CORK: M. O'Brien; R. Phelan, M. Duggan, E. Spillane; M. O'Callaghan, E. Meaney, S. Kelly; A. O'Sullivan, H. Looney; D. O'Sullivan, A. Hutchings, C. O'Sullivan; L. Coppinger, E. Scally, O. Finn.

Subs: S. Noonan for Coppinger (h-t), O. Farmer for H. Looney (54), C. Collins for E. Spillane (54).

Ref: G. McMahon (Mayo).

Player of the Match: Carla Rowe (Dublin).

CORK'S ALL-STAR RECORD (2004–2018)

2004

Nominations (5): Juliet Murphy, Angela Walsh, Valerie Mulcahy, Geraldine O'Flynn and Rena Buckley.

Winners (2): Rena Buckley and Valerie Mulcahy.

2005

Nominations (10): Elaine Harte, Angela and Ciara Walsh, Rena Buckley, Briege Corkery, Juliet Murphy, Norita Kelly, Amanda Murphy, Valerie Mulcahy and Deirdre O'Reilly.

Winners (5): Angela Walsh, Briege Corkery, Juliet Murphy, Deirdre O'Reilly and Valerie Mulcahy.

2006

Nominations (8): Angela Walsh, Rena Buckley, Bríd Stack, Juliet Murphy, Norita Kelly, Nollaig Cleary, Valerie Mulcahy and Mary O'Connor.

Winners (4): Angela Walsh, Rena Buckley, Nollaig Cleary and Mary O'Connor.

2007

Nominations (10): Elaine Harte, Rena Buckley, Angela Walsh, Briege Corkery, Bríd Stack, Juliet Murphy, Norita Kelly, Nollaig Cleary, Valerie Mulcahy and Deirdre O'Reilly.

Winners (7): Rena Buckley, Angela Walsh, Juliet Murphy, Briege Corkery, Bríd Stack, Valerie Mulcahy and

Deirdre O'Reilly.

2008

Nominations (10): Elaine Harte, Angela Walsh, Linda Barrett, Bríd Stack, Briege Corkery, Geraldine O'Flynn, Juliet Murphy, Nollaig Cleary, Mary O'Connor and Amanda Murphy.

Winners (7): Angela Walsh, Elaine Harte, Linda Barrett, Briege Corkery, Bríd Stack, Juliet Murphy and Nollaig Cleary.

2009

Nominations (12): Amy O'Shea, Ciara O'Sullivan, Juliet Murphy, Angela Walsh, Elaine Harte, Rena Buckley, Geraldine O'Flynn, Briege Corkery, Bríd Stack, Norita Kelly, Valerie Mulcahy and Nollaig Cleary.

Winners (6): Geraldine O'Flynn, Briege Corkery, Norita Kelly, Juliet Murphy, Nollaig Cleary and Angela Walsh.

2010

Nominations (6): Rena Buckley, Geraldine O'Flynn, Bríd Stack, Juliet Murphy, Nollaig Cleary and Valerie Mulcahy.

Winners (1): Bríd Stack.

2011

Nominations (8): Angela Walsh, Briege Corkery, Bríd Stack, Geraldine O'Flynn, Deirdre O'Reilly, Juliet Murphy, Rhona Ní Bhuachalla and Amy O'Shea.

Winners (6): Deirdre O'Reilly, Briege Corkery, Bríd Stack, Geraldine O'Flynn, Juliet Murphy and Rhona Ní Bhuachalla.

LGFA Players' Player of the Year: Juliet Murphy, Cork.

2012

Nominations (12): Elaine Harte, Deirdre O'Reilly, Anne-Marie Walsh, Bríd Stack, Briege Corkery, Geraldine O'Flynn, Rena Buckley, Juliet Murphy, Ciara O'Sullivan, Doireann O'Sullivan, Valerie Mulcahy and Nollaig Cleary.

Winners (7): Briege Corkery, Elaine Harte, Bríd Stack, Geraldine O'Flynn, Rena Buckley, Ciara O'Sullivan and Valerie Mulcahy.

LGFA Players' Player of the Year: Briege Corkery, Cork.

2013

Nominations (11): Rena Buckley, Briege Corkery, Deirdre O'Reilly, Geraldine O'Flynn, Juliet Murphy, Valerie Mulcahy, Bríd Stack, Anne-Marie Walsh, Angela Walsh, Doireann O'Sullivan and Nollaig Cleary.

Winners (5): Deirdre O'Reilly, Briege Corkery, Juliet Murphy, Valerie Mulcahy and Geraldine O'Flynn.

LGFA Players' Player of the Year: Geraldine O'Flynn, Cork.

2014

Nominations (10): Róisín Phelan, Vera Foley, Annie Walsh, Briege Corkery, Angela Walsh, Bríd Stack, Deirdre

O'Reilly, Geraldine O'Flynn, Ciara O'Sullivan and Valerie Mulcahy.

Winners (6): Angela Walsh, Bríd Stack, Geraldine O'Flynn, Ciara O'Sullivan, Briege Corkery and Vera Foley.

2015

Nominations (11): Martina O'Brien, Marie Ambrose, Vera Foley, Geraldine O'Flynn, Bríd Stack, Deirdre O'Reilly, Rena Buckley, Briege Corkery, Valerie Mulcahy, Ciara O'Sullivan and Annie Walsh.

Winners (6): Marie Ambrose, Geraldine O'Flynn, Vera Foley, Rena Buckley, Briege Corkery and Valerie Mulcahy.

LGFA Players' Player of the Year: Briege Corkery, Cork.

2016

Nominations (11): Vera Foley, Róisín Phelan, Deirdre O'Reilly, Ciara O'Sullivan, Annie Walsh, Briege Corkery, Rena Buckley, Marie Ambrose, Bríd Stack, Martina O'Brien and Orla Finn.

Winners (6): Ciara O'Sullivan, Bríd Stack, Deirdre O'Reilly, Briege Corkery, Marie Ambrose and Orla Finn.

LGFA Players' Player of the Year: Bríd Stack, Cork.

2017

Nominations (9): Ciara O'Sullivan, Doireann O'Sullivan, Orla Finn, Martina O'Brien, Emma Spillane, Róisín Phelan, Melissa Duggan, Shauna Kelly and Eimear Scally.

Winners (1): Emma Spillane.

2018

Nominations (12): Emma Spillane, Martina O'Brien, Eimear Meaney, Róisín Phelan, Melissa Duggan, Máire O'Callaghan, Ashling Hutchings, Eimear Scally, Áine O'Sullivan, Orla Finn, Ciara O'Sullivan and Doireann O'Sullivan.

Winners (4): Doireann O'Sullivan, Emma Spillane, Róisín Phelan and Ciara O'Sullivan.

ACKNOWLEDGEMENTS

To Clodagh for your unwavering patience and support. To my parents, Michael and Jo, sister Sue, brother Mike, and John Dineen, thank you so much for your honesty and encouragement.

To Eamonn Ryan for all your wise words, time and numerous chats. To Mary Collins, Frankie Honohan, Charlie McLaughlin, Liz Ahern, Juliet Murphy, Elaine Harte, Valerie Mulcahy, Bríd Stack, Deirdre O'Reilly, Mary O'Connor, Angela Walsh, Rena Buckley, Geraldine O'Flynn, Nollaig Cleary, Norita Kelly, Mairéad Kelly, Amy O'Shea, Cora Staunton and Gemma Begley, thank you for allowing me on your journey.

To Patrick O'Donoghue of Mercier Press for coming to me with the idea. From our first meeting on Christmas Eve 2014, I knew you believed wholeheartedly in the project, and your positivity made it all so much smoother. To Noel, Wendy and all the staff at Mercier, a huge thank you.

To Pat O'Leary, Áine Geaney, Ann Murphy, Robert O'Shea, John Roycroft, Jim Ryan, Tommy Seward, Sharon O'Keeffe, Mary Power, John Kelleher, Tom Russell of AnoisPhotography.com, the Cork ladies football county board, the *Evening Echo* and *Irish Examiner* sports and picture desks, Sportsfile, and Inpho Photography, another big thank you for all your help.

A special mention, too, must go to the players' parents and families with whom I've shared sidelines and stands for over a decade – Tom and Mary Harte, Tom and Marie

Mulcahy, Michael, Mary and Maggie Murphy, Mick, Liz and Muireann Stack, Donie and Kathleen Walsh, Michael and Kitty Corkery, Charlie and Ann O'Reilly, Liam and Nan O'Flynn, Eamon and Siobhán Kelly, Ned and Kathleen Cleary, Tim and Helen Buckley, Ina and Gerry O'Sullivan and everyone else along the way.

Finally, to all the players over the years, the biggest thank you of all. I hope these pages do you justice.

L255,432   ANF Ld

LEABHARLANN CHONTAE LONGFOIRT
Longford County Library & Arts Services

796.33082094A

This book should be returned on or before the latest
date shown below. Fines on overdue books will
accrue on a weekly basis or part thereof.

RP17723